ENVIRONMENTAL ASSESSMENT

Approaching Maturity

ENVIRONMENTAL ASSESSMENT
Approaching Maturity

Selina Bendix

Environmental Review Officer
City and County of San Francisco
San Francisco, California

Herbert R. Graham

Task Manager
TRW Energy Systems
McLean, Virginia

ANN ARBOR SCIENCE
PUBLISHERS INC
P.O. BOX 1425 • ANN ARBOR, MICH. 48106

FOREWORD

The National Environmental Policy Act of 1969 (NEPA) directs that a systematic, interdisciplinary approach be used to prepare detailed environmental impact statements for major federal actions significantly affecting the quality of the human environment. Since its passage, this law has spawned allied laws, orders, regulations and guidelines which now constitute the NEPA process.

After six years of experience, the environmental professional community decided that the time had come to take a look at just how well the NEPA process was serving our nation. In February 1977, the National Association of Environmental Professionals (NAEP) sponsored a three-day seminar in Washington, D. C., during which all aspects of the process were explored by environmental professionals representing government, industry, law, consultants and academe. This book, the proceedings of the seminar, sets forth the problems and successes of the present process and then straightforwardly explores ways and means for improvement. The one theme that runs throughout is that, despite the problems in the current state-of-the-art, significant environmental benefits have been and continue to be derived from the NEPA process.

C. F. Zirzow
President, NAEP

PREFACE

Norman W. Arnold

The program for this seminar was based on the conviction that enough time and experience had been accumulated to make it profitable to evaluate the environmental impact assessment process. The participants were not dilettantes. They were not outside observers. They were people who work every day in the process, or who had spent several months in examining the process from different viewpoints. Consequently, any satisfaction or dissatisfaction expressed came from people who are trying to make it work—and work well—in the real world. These papers deal with concrete experience, not abstract concepts.

The seminar was divided into five sessions, generally grouped by similar topics. The topics addressed were:

How Much is Enough? How much information is sufficient to assess an environmental impact adequately and make a decision? There was universal agreement with the Council on Environmental Quality's stricture against lengthy documents. There was also recognition and detailing of the reasons why documents are so long. Among these are the accumulation of case law which is taken to be universally applicable, and hence adds requirements, and the necessity of responding to comments which assert that inadequate attention has been paid to a particular area.

State-Federal Requirements: Are they complementary or competing? The papers reviewed the situation in seven different states, and we found that the approaches are various among these states. Further, by no means can one assume that if federal requirements have been met, state requirements will also be fulfilled. There is commonality, but no congruency.

Public Responsibilities: Public participation in the process of environmental evaluation has brought a group of new problems. There is no disagreement with the objective. Assuring that it works effectively is another problem. In esoteric subjects, there is difficulty in translating to common language. False issues are sometimes raised to cover other motives. Evaluators may misinterpret the public's view of the importance of a given issue. These kinds of questions, and the ethical problems they raise, were examined from several points of view.

The Review Process: The objective of this session was to explore how the review process might be made more effective, and it ranged from such issues as improvement in prediction of public response to details of experiences in going through the review process.

Why Did it Fail? or Succeed? In this session, lessons were drawn from specific experience, from four perspectives: administrative, technical, private decision-making, and public decision-making. Several problems raised in previous sessions were discussed, and proposals advanced for alleviating them.

This volume is the result of the experience of the seminar participants. It was made possible by the efforts of the various speakers and session chairpeople who are named in the body of the material. The ideas expressed are theirs, and not necessarily those of the National Association of Environmental Professionals. The book is also a result of the effort of the seminar committee, without whose dedication and enthusiasm the seminar would not have taken place. They are:

General Chairperson	Norman W. Arnold
Co-Chairperson	Lynne P. Sparks
Program Chairperson	Herbert R. Graham
Program Co-Chairperson	Lindsay M. Tipton
Finance	Charles F. Zirzow
Local Arrangements	Andrew E. Kauders
Publicity	Susan C. Watkins
General Arrangements	Penny L. Harrison

Selina Bendix is the Environmental Review Officer of the City and County of San Francisco. Dr. Bendix advises California legislators and their staffs in the drafting of environmental legislation. Her office produces approximately 500 environmental legal documents annually.

Dr. Bendix holds a BS in Chemistry from UCLA and received her PhD in Zoology from the University of California-Berkeley. Past activities include basic research in molecular biology, college teaching and consulting.

She is active in the National Association of Environmental Professionals and serves on numerous advisory committees at the state and national level.

Herbert R. Graham is Task Manager for TRW Energy Systems, McLean, Virginia. His current responsibilities include Project Engineering Support for the Division of Magnetohydrodynamics for ERDA. He also participated in environmental assessments in air, transit, rail and highway transportation modes.

He received BS and MS degrees in aeronautics from the Massachusetts Institute of Technology and the California Institute of Technology, respectively. He also attended the Harvard Graduate School of Business Administration.

Mr. Graham is a member of several professional societies, and has been a guest lecturer at universities. He has written or had direct responsibility for over 35 technical publications. He was the recipient of an award for outstanding contribution to the environmental profession by the National Association of Environmental Professionals in 1977.

CONTENTS

SECTION III: PUBLIC RESPONSIBILITIES—PUBLIC ETHICS

Introduction: *Carol Ford Benson*

SECTION IV: THE REVIEW PROCESS—FERTILE OR FUTILE?

Introduction: *Robert P. Thurber and Rebecca W. Hanmer*

SECTION V: WHY DID IT FAIL? OR SUCCEED?

Introduction: *Ned J. Cronin and Gerald P. Mylroie*

SECTION I

HOW MUCH IS ENOUGH?
BOON OR BOONDOGGLE?

Ernest P. Evans

Assistant Director for Advocacy
Commission on Federal Paperwork
Washington, D.C.

The questions "How Much is Enough? Boon or Boondoggle?" are being heard today not just in the arena of the National Environmental Policy Act environmental impact statements, but in all facets of American life. The Paperwork Commission was established by Congress as a result of a cry from all over the country, from persons in all walks of life, small businesses, educators and public officials, to try to bring some rhyme and reason to the main contact citizens have with their government; and that is through paperwork. The Paperwork Commission is charged not just with reducing paperwork, but with improving the quality of information that reaches the federal government.

We have three basic types of paperwork. The first is administrative paper. You could say that an environmental impact statement (EIS) is administrative paper. When someone wants something, whether it's a student loan or public works project, one applies to the federal government, supplying all the necessary data to effect the granting of that benefit.

The second type of paper is regulatory paper, which presumes that you are going to tell the federal, state and local governments that you are obeying the laws. That paper is your method of proving it. Some believe that an EIS is regulatory in nature.

1

The third type of information is statistical, the foundation for making major decisions. EIS's also contain statistical information.

When we have bad information, it's as the computer scientists say: "garbage in, garbage out." Bad information leads to bad decisions. The development of the three different types of information has resulted in major overlap, duplication and redundant effort.

It is clear that the objective of environmental assessment is to provide sufficient information for a decision. On one hand, the Council on Environmental Quality admonishes us to summarize. On the other hand, each discipline is likely to find that its particular interests have been slighted, and legal decisions result in new requirements. Chapters 1 through 5 explore the problem of deciding the overall content, volume, detail and depth of studies required to assess impact adequately.

CHAPTER 1

THE DEVELOPING ART OF DECISION-MAKING
IN A PEOPLE-ORIENTED SOCIETY

James K. Thompson
President, Thompson Enterprises
Arlington, Virginia

We begin the review of environmental assessment by considering How Much is Enough? Boon or Boondoggle? These themes are ideal topics for this first section, as they reflect the diverse evaluations of the environmental process. Some people think of the process in terms of mountains of paper and endless review, while others think of it as their only alternative to more noise, air and water pollution. Both groups may be right.

What is the environmental process? Our topic will be easier to discuss if we define the environmental process. Is it anything more than the environmental assessment and review system we associate with environmental impact statements? I think so.

It all begins with Section 102 of The National Environmental Policy Act (NEPA) of 1969 (Public Law 91-190). The purpose of Section 102 is two-fold. First, it authorizes and directs public officials to give appropriate consideration to environmental amenities and values when they interpret and administer the policies, regulations and public laws of the United States. Second, through Section 102 (2) (C), it directs use of a consultation, coordination and public record system when the complexity and significance of environmental factors are of such consequence that they should be a matter of national concern. With respect to the consideration requirement, responsible officials are directed to give appropriate weight to environmental amenities and values even though such decision factors are not presently quantifiable.

This requirement affects the judgment aspect of decision-making and is applicable to actions that do and do not produce significant impacts on the human environment.

The decision, as well as the environmental assessment and review system, must be part of the environmental process because the principal purpose of Section 102 is to define requirements for interpreting and administering the policies, regulations and public laws of the United States.

We must consider environmental assessment, review, decision-making and the decisions we make to interpret and implement NEPA to gain a perspective of the environmental assessment process and determine how much is enough and whether it might be a boon or boondoggle.

What is a boondoggle? It is the term originally used to describe an ornamental leather strap-on harness. It is now used to describe valueless work. Boondoggle is much too extreme a term to describe the environmental process, for it cannot be accurately called valueless.

What is a boon? This term was originally used to connote kind, pleasant, merry and generous. It is now used to describe a benefit or advantage freely bestowed. None of these terms is an appropriate description except, perhaps, generous. Some of you may argue that the term generous describes the amount of paper and time we associate with environmental activities and the term, boon, might be relevant in this respect to some actions.

The environmental process cannot be precisely described as either a boon or a boondoggle. Nevertheless, both terms have at least some merit, for a great deal of waste is involved in the way people tend to implement a very good policy.

ENFORCEMENT CONTROLS

Two key controls for enforcing environmental policy are incentives and judicial actions. Everyone will benefit to some extent from environmental excellence in decision-making. Unfortunately, someone else may receive the immediate benefit, and the incentive aspect of control does not provide a strong motivation for all people to meet environmental objectives.

The second control for environmental policy enforcement is the stop and go penalty that can be imposed through judicial action. This control combines with uncertainty to greatly increase the content of environmental reports and the time required to process a controversial action. I recently examined reports prepared by several agencies. Redundancy within each increased content by 10-15%. I also found large amounts of information that served no essential purpose except that they might be pertinent if the action were litigated. These factors often increased the content of controversial reports by 50-60%.

I know of two instances when a headquarters staff completely rewrote an entire final environmental report, and even though it was necessary to include additional information, the revised final reports were reduced so much in size that their contents were no more than 25% of the content of the proposed final statements.

It would be wise for someone to study environmental documentation for a few controversial actions to evaluate the effect of controversy on report content.

How does the stop and go penalty combine with uncertainty to increase report content? Think about some very important and sensitive letter you may have composed for the chief of your organization. You probably revised your own draft at least once. Then your supervisor and the staff assistants for the chief made revisions. Finally, you made changes to satisfy the chief. The difficulty resulted because no one knew precisely what the chief would want to say in the letter. Letters of this type are more or less difficult depending upon the number of people involved in the review and the complexity of the subject discussed.

The environmental process is something like the letter problem except that the subject is more complex. Also, greater numbers of people are involved in the review. There is one other important difference. Your chief was the final authority with respect to the content of the letter: the courts are the final authority in the instance of a highly controversial environmental statement.

Your report-writing problem is an exhausting struggle. It might be something like climbing the mountain illustrated in Figure 1-1.

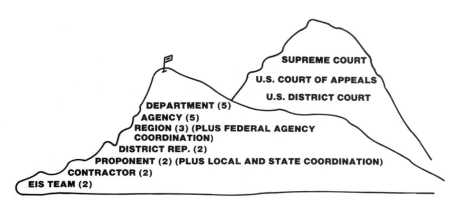

Figure 1-1. Environmental review mountain.

Imagine yourself as a member of the environmental team shown at the foot of the mountain. You work for a firm hired by the contracting firm employed by the proponent of a controversial action. You may have to climb through 20-25 management levels, not including the courts. You must satisfy your team chief who may need to satisfy one or two levels of supervision in the contracting firm. There will be additional review by the proponent, and changes will be made to accommodate the viewpoints of persons and organizations involved in the local and state review process. Then you begin the federal review. The mountain gets a little steeper when the federal review begins, because this review is more difficult. Finally, you obtain federal approval and you plant your flag of success on top of the mountain. But are you through? Maybe not. The proposal is highly controversial and the stop and go penalty may be invoked. Your letter-writing problem has been multiplied many times in complexity.

How do you react to the problem? If the action is litigated, you are stuck with the content of the statement. Nothing more can be added to support your case. You know that there is no penalty for including too much information and that there is real trouble if something is missing. You respond to the situation by including anything remotely relevant to the proposal. That is why so much is added to a report and why so little is removed. The result is usually a mess. I find very few statements that approach the quality of the average scientific or engineering report.

Should we revise the penalty control aspect of the environmental process? I think not. It would be better to attempt to solve the problem by improving the expertise and confidence of persons involved in the preparation and review of environmental assessment reports and by using a more rational and scientific approach to the environmental report-writing problem.

CONTROVERSY

Does uncertainty combine with the litigation control aspect of the process to expand agency definition of processing requirements? The effect of controversy on agency requirements for Section 102 (2) (C) coordination is considered in Table 1-1, which shows that NEPA PL 91-190. The Council on Environmental Quality (CEQ) and the various agencies all require the coordination pursuant to Section 102 (2) (C) when there is a significant impact on the human environment. Nothing in the NEPA act indicates that processing is also required to cover any other situation. However, CEQ expanded the requirement to include potentially significant impacts and those likely to be controversial with respect to environmental impact. Some agencies make an additional expansion to include situations for which the actions are controversial and situations for which the number of opponents might be significant. The agency expansions are made even though the magnitudes of the environmental impacts are not really debatable.

Table 1-1. Effect of Controversy on
Agency Requirements for Section 102 (2) (C) Coordination[a]

Environmental Impact	NEPA	CEQ	Agency
Definitely significant	X	X	X
Potentially significant		X	X
Impacts are likely to be highly controversial		X	X
Action is highly controversial			X
Number of opponents might be significant			X

[a]Appropriate consideration must be given to environmental amenities and values even though NEPA Section 102 (2) (C) coordination is not required.

Each organization has expanded the basic requirement, but this particular expansion may have merit if the process is being knowingly used as a good way to handle controversial issues. In this respect, it is wise to recall that appropriate consideration of environmental amenities and values is required even though NEPA Section 102 (2) (C) coordination is not required. Additional work resulting from this use of the environmental process may therefore be limited to that associated with coordination because appropriate consideration is required in any event.

A great deal of boondoggle results because too many decisions are made at the federal level when the federal issue should be associated with the cumulative impact of many similar decisions. Controversy over purely local issues is not sufficient to require decision-making at the federal level. On the other hand, much waste effort results when national issues are debated again and again in terms of proposed actions at each locality. Under existing guidelines, action-oriented proponents of a project attempt to cope with national as well as local issues and are overwhelmed by the scope of the problems they encounter. This type of failure to use the environmental process at the correct level is a major source of boondoggle that could be minimized by improved guidance for managing controversy.

Controversy is the central theme of the environment struggle, but what guidance has been given to help cope with the controversy? Something more substantial is needed than procedural steps and the CEQ public hearing criteria. How would you cope with controversy if you were preparing, reviewing or approving a proposal?

MOTIVATION

Motivation can be used for evaluating the significance of controversy. as shown in Table 1- 2. For this purpose, I divide people into three groups. I examine motivation to determine the scope of perceived issues and to consider practical steps that might be used to ameliorate opposition to an otherwise desirable proposal.

Table 1 -2. Motivation as a Factor for Evaluating the Significance of Controversy

Proponents: Those who:
1. Have something to gain
2. Believe the community has something to gain

Opponents: Those who:
1. Oppose an action for good and sufficient reasons
2. Believe other needs are more important
3. Oppose change
4. Fear ominous environmental threats
5. Will suffer adverse consequences including inadequate compensation for loss
6. Feel their compensation for loss will not be adequate
7. Desire public attention
8. Oppose the establishment

Neutral: Those who:
1. Do not know that they will be affected
2. Think they do not know enough to have an opinion
3. Believe the community has little to gain or lose
4. Are too concerned with other personal matters
5. Believe their action could not affect the course of events

Project Proponents

Those who are proponents of a proposal either have something to gain or believe that the community has something to gain. There is nothing wrong with either motive, except that motivation may have affected their judgment. This is particularly true when considering arguments made by proponents who may experience a large gain or loss. Their distorted perspective can produce self-serving bits of propaganda I call soap commercials. These commercials may aggravate opponents and be difficult to defend if litigation develops. Also, arguments for a proposal may be overstated and can then contradict other arguments concerning lack of significant impact.

Project Opponents

Considerable attention is generally given by the approving authority to arguments made by those who oppose a proposal, but the response to these arguments may address only the stated issues. Much waste results in these circumstances because the real issue is not identified and solved. Public officials involved in decision-making actions also represent opponents and their just needs, and it is necessary to consider how lack of expertise as well as motivation may have affected definition of basic issues. This consideration is difficult to accomplish and is contrary to our tendency to organize into teams with team members adopting strategies to win the contest.

I associate opponents with the eight motivating forces shown in Table 1-2. The first motivation is opposition to an action for good and sufficient reasons such as real personal loss or adverse environmental impacts. How would you respond to individuals who believe some other need is more important? Opposition because of a competing need may indicate failure of the proponents to consider a reasonable alternative. Look for this possibility when the opposing need relates to the proposed action. A bit of "log rolling" to accomplish both needs may be appropriate if the opposing need does not conflict with the proposal. A few people will oppose a proposal because they tend to oppose any change. The number of people who respond to this motivation is small, and opposition for this reason generally does not require significant effort.

Many individuals oppose proposals because they fear ominous environmental threats. Motivation is real and may be difficult to resolve. A good public information system may be effective but is complicated by the media perspective that information is newsworthy only if it is ominous, tragic or anti-establishment. Solving the fear problem is also complicated by debate or the appearance of debate within the scientific community. Many individuals take a neutral or opposition viewpoint when experts appear to disagree. Effort to get experts to jointly define areas of agreement and uncertainty may be helpful.

Much opposition results because individuals expect to suffer adverse consequences if a proposal is implemented. In these instances it is important to consider compensation for loss. Opposition can often be minimized to the extent that people can be convinced their compensation is adequate. However, adequate compensation may not be feasible and a new search for feasible and prudent alternatives may be warranted. If none are available, the responsible official will probably demand demonstration of compelling need if he is to approve the proposal. Few people understand the difference between an ordinary and a compelling need.

An ordinary need occurs when consequences associated with disapproving a proposed action are much worse for the proponent than consequences associated with approval. A compelling need occurs when adverse consequences associated with disapproval are much worse for the society than those associated with approval. A much stronger justification for approval of an action is provided if a compelling need can be demonstrated.

The last two forces are important because individuals who respond to these motivations are often leaders and mainly concerned with ways to enhance opposition. The merit of the proposal is a matter of secondary concern. These individuals lead others who might otherwise have taken a neutral or favorable position. One can sometimes surmount problems caused by these opponents if the people-oriented problems associated with the proposal can be solved. However, the solution is of no practical value if it is not recognized as a solution. The objective is to remove the issues they use to support arguments against the proposal.

Neutrality and Public Information

One can learn a great deal about a proposal by considering the views of those who are neutral. The relative number of neutral individuals may also be important. However, this information is not apt to be available because those who are neutral tend to be silent. The public information system is not effective in most instances when a large number of affected people are neutral. I am alarmed when I find numbers of adversely affected people who simply do not know about a proposed action. Notices published on or during major holiday periods, such as the fourth of July, are a form of boondoggle because they suggest devious motives on the part of proponents. I like to ask my taxi driver what he thinks about some proposals. He should at least know that an action is being considered if it affects his area of operations.

A good public information program is generally effective in developing support for a worthy proposal. Lack of concern by relatively large numbers of affected individuals is a good sign when they are aware that an action is being considered. However, it may also indicate that the public impact is not understood.

Some individuals are too concerned with other matters of a personal nature to be aware of an action that would adversely affect them if it is approved.

Some people say they are neutral because their actions would not affect the course of events. They justify their attitude by asserting that the establishment does what it pleases in any event, and that opposition is useless. These individuals may be telling you only that they are neutral because they do not perceive a significant adverse impact on themselves. However, the attitude may result from a history of dictatorial action by an establishment that was not previously concerned with the effects of its actions on people. Motivation for these attitudes should be examined by the approving authority to determine its significance and an appropriate response.

THE DECISION PROCESS

Decisions to develop major facilities evolve slowly in most instances. Although there may have been proper consideration of environmental factors, formal effort to prepare and process environmental documentation may not be initiated until after the decision is made to adopt a particular plan for a proposal. This delayed approach to environmental consideration produces much waste effort through duplication of information. Waste may also result because of a need to make revisions in the proposal to accommodate environmental considerations.

We pay too much attention to the organization of a final environmental statement that meets requirements for legal sufficiency and not enough attention to a logical, time-oriented consideration of the various factors upon which the decision is to be based. Some organizations prepare decision papers as a final step in the environmental process. These papers and the reports could be used to satisfy the environmental impact statement requirement if they were to be based upon a meaningful assessment of the various factors affecting the decision. They might also satisfy another problem that results when environmental consideration is a separate and delayed part of the decision process. It is not sufficient to merely define the various adverse and beneficial impacts and effects. It is necessary to show the rationale used to make multidisciplinary judgments involved in the decision. Decision papers are the appropriate tool for accomplishing this objective.

For example, consider a fully coordinated series of timely reports that progressively considered the following subjects:

1. Description of the existing facility
2. Need for expansion
3. Alternatives to satisfy established need
4. Selection of feasible alternatives
5. Impacts of feasible alternatives (engineering, economic, environmental, social, etc).
6. Actions to avoid and ameliorate adverse effects
7. Special considerations
8. Coordination and review, including public meetings and hearings

9. Proposed plans and specifications
10. Steps to ensure compliance with environmental assurances

The decision paper prepared for the proposal by the staff of the responsible official could then incorporate the various studies by reference. It would not be highly technical and would fully explain decision considerations including rationale pertinent to multidisciplinary judgments made with respect to the selection and rejection of feasible alternatives. The decision paper might be organized as follows:

1. Proposed action
2. Principal issues
3. Rationale for multidisciplinary judgments
4. Positions of organizations with pertinent expertise, interest and responsibility
5. Sufficiency of review process
6. Options available to responsible official
7. Sufficiency of steps to be taken to ensure environmental compliance
8. Findings and conclusions
9. Recommendations with concurrences and approval signatures

The final environmental statement for the Concorde decision provides an interesting opportunity to compare such a statement with the resulting decision paper. The statement includes a basic text of about 300 pages including a large stack of figures as Volume I. Three additional volumes were used for additional information such as comments and transcripts. Secretary Coleman chose to hold his own public hearing and to prepare a small, very readable decision paper. It contained 100 pages including figures. The final statement considered four alternatives: yes, no, do nothing and a yes with special restrictions. Secretary Coleman chose a different alternative. He decided to permit operations for no more than 16 months to collect data based upon actual real world experience. His decision was controversial, but did it produce a significant impact on the human environment? Was an environmental statement even needed for his decision? What is required if a decision is made to extend the permit? How much is enough?

Decision papers present an interesting opportunity to reduce the content of documentation needed to explain controversial decisions. However, the environmental statement prepared for the Concorde action cannot be compared to the report series needed to support such papers.

The entire environmental review process is a boondoggle if there is no compliance. Some noncompliance actions might be easily observed by affected people. Selecting a route that is not the same as the one approved for a highway is an example. Affected people would observe and report such a noncompliance action to public officials. What about the less apparent items such as catch basins for water runoff control? If an environmental assurance or control is essential to approval of an action, then there must be a compliance control. How much boondoggle do you suppose we could associate with a lack of controls?

My reaction to the section subject is to conclude that the primary factor in the generation of boondoggle is reflected in the related question, "How much is enough?" *Those who prepare, review and approve documentation for proposed actions are not confident and therefore make decisions to include in reports information that is not really needed.* They process actions unnecessarily to avoid making judgments. They simply do not know how much is enough. Their confidence is adversely affected by the lack of standards for making judgments and by the critical impact of a potential court decision against the sufficiency of their judgment.

I believe that it should not be necessary to tear down and reconstruct the existing environmental process to eliminate most of the waste we call boondoggle. Much can be done within the established system. However, CEQ and agency guidelines should be reviewed to determine if successive expansions of basic policy by the various agencies are necessary. It would also be prudent to explore modifications of the environmental process to make use of the decision paper approach with supporting reports. Decision papers would insure appropriate integration of environmental consideration into the decision process while division of considerations into reports covering smaller units should enable improved comprehension of pertinent problems and solutions. Substantial reduction of extraneous material should be possible, thereby reducing boondoggle.

Finally, I associate the environmental movement with an administrative revolution in the scope of authority and responsibility delegated to officials in people-oriented societies. I view the change as a major step in the evolution of government of the people, by the people, and for the people. Failure to understand the significance of this change in government and refusal to accept the change cause much difficulty.

Officials must now represent people who are adversely affected by proposed actions as well as the special groups they have historically represented because of mutual interest. This change is a major milestone in the art of decision-making in people-oriented societies and signifies an administrative revolution. I attribute much of the waste we call boondoggle to a failure of many people to comprehend this aspect of environmental consideration requirements and objectives.

THE REVOLUTIONARY ANALOGY

An analogy between revolution and the environmental movement is sometimes useful to illustrate an important point. The list of characters who play various roles in the revolutionary analogy is particularly helpful.

1. *Patriots:* Patriots are the loyal supporters of the environmental movement. They are the front-line soldiers. Some do not fully understand policy and purpose of the movement and may destroy good along with the bad, all in the name of the revolution. Like soldiers, they need leaders.

2. *Extremists:* Extremists are those zealots who give disproportionate importance to environmental factors and to our ability to solve problems through technical analysis. They prevent rational implementation of NEPA.

3. *Guerillas:* These individuals represent the pre-NEPA, action-oriented proponents of special interests. They continue to wage a very bitter struggle to overthrow environmental policy and procedure as it applies to their area of interest.

4. *Carpetbaggers:* Carpetbaggers take advantage of uncertainty in the environmental movement. They use environmental requirements or regulations as weapons to achieve personal objectives unrelated to environmental purpose.

5. *Environmental Professionals:* This group includes all the enlightened patriots who provide leadership to the environmental movement: those government, industry, university and community scientists, engineers, managers and citizens who act individually and collectively to reduce waste and boondoggle in the environmental process and to ensure rational and efficient interpretation and implementation of environmental policy.

I included the analogy to revolution because of the need to more fully develop the concept of the role of environmental professionals in environmental matters. Are you a patriot, an extremist, or are you one of the environmental professionals? Environmental professionals should affirm their interest in activity to ensure rational consideration of environmental amenities and values. An environmental professional will oppose the irrational environmental extremist as well as the guerilla. The National Association of Environmental Professionals and its members will serve a useful role in the revolution if the organization and its members act to ensure appropriate consideration of environmental amenities and values.

CHAPTER 2

DECISION-MAKING WITHIN THE ENVIRONMENTAL IMPACT ANALYSIS PROCESS— THE NEW YORK CITY EXPERIENCE

Gerald J. Franz*
> Partner, Environmental Policy and
>   Planning Consulting
> McKeown & Franz
> New York, New York

New York City (NYC) currently has in effect two governmental layers of environmental assessment procedural requirements—the Federal National Environmental Policy Act (NEPA) and the City Environmental Protection Order (CEPO). A third, the New York State Environmental Quality Review Act (SEQRA), came into full effect September 1, 1977. Further, the Housing and Community Development Act of 1974 requires that the applicant for the Community Development Block Grants (CDBG) be responsible for NEPA compliance. (The Community Development Block Grant refers to the part of the 1974 Federal Housing and Community Development Act which combined federal funding for several previously separate programs (*e.g.,* sewers, parks, etc.) into one comprehensive block grant.) All this, plus the addition of the more day-to-day environmental planning analyses, forms the sum total of the city's environmental impact analysis process.

I estimate that since 1970, twenty NYC projects or city-related projects have received full NEPA environmental impact statement (EIS) analysis. Several hundred project reviews, several hundred environmental planning analyses, and

---

*Formerly Director of Environmental Planning, Department of City Planning, New York, New York.

almost one hundred CDBG-NEPA Environmental Reviews have also been completed. The body of hard-won knowledge from these documents and their related procedures is currently being applied to the soon-to-be instituted SEQRA procedures. Accordingly, an evaluation of the city's overall EIA procedure, especially with regard to an optimum level of effort and thus an answer to the "how much is enough" question, is most timely. By reviewing the major decision points within the process and reflecting on the criteria used in each and the experience with these criteria, we may be able to approach an answer. What is clear is that we must apply our experience to breaking an all-too-common self-sustaining vicious cycle. Frequently, a negative attitude toward the EIS has become a self-fulfilling prophecy. This cycle can be characterized as follows: the EIA procedure delays the project and is considered unnecessary but it must be done; thus, it is poorly done, leads to delay, the EIS document must be improved which delays the project, etc. This cycle could and should be changed to a more harmonious cycle such as: only do an EIS when really necessary—improved document, less delay, improved project, improved document, less delay, etc. The more harmonious cycle would require closer cooperation between the project sponsors, planners and reviewers.

DECISION POINTS

The judgments made at several key stages of the impact analysis process will determine the nature and efficiency of the assessment procedure established. These decision points within the process include:

1. the definition of "project" and "major project" that may require EIS analysis;
2. determination of significance—definition and procedural identification of significance;
3. work load distribution by function among participating agencies—division of labor for the preparation of the project description, physical impact analysis, socioeconomic analysis and other sections of the document and processing;
4. notification procedures for both agencies and the public;
5. choice of specific EIS methodology;
6. outline development;
7. level of detail;
8. public participation procedures and distribution of draft environment impact statement (DEIS);
9. nature of re-draft from DEIS to final environmental impact statement (FEIS);
10. utilization of consultants; and
11. method of incorporation of mitigation measures during project implementation and possible alternative development strategies.

Each of these, individually and in combination, determines the success of the EIS effort. Each is really a "how much is enough" decision and will directly affect the number, size, quality and time allocation for the NEPA procedure or NEPA-related procedures. For example, the working definition of project in terms of size and/or significance will determine the number of assessments, reviews, draft statements and final statements produced and thus contribute to the determination of the time expended, and the quality (*i.e.,* required depth) and size of each document. The chosen level of detail and methodology also help determine the document length, readability and quality. The scope and intensity of participation will clearly reflect the level of detail and notification procedures. The success at each decision point significantly affects the likely success at future decision points. In turn, these factors additively determine the real and perceived value of the entire process.

FUNDAMENTALS

Taking a step back, the effort given to initially making the necessary judgments throughout the process and at each decision point reflects the answers to a set of much more fundamental questions, such as: (1) what is the prevailing relative concern for environmental quality management? (2) what is the relative concern for planning? and (3) how is the validity of the EIS procedure generally viewed within the larger decision-making process? The answers to these questions frame the nature of the operative cycle, vicious or harmonious. The "how much is enough" question and its companion, "boon or boondoggle," have the beginnings of their answer within these fundamentals. If the answer to these basics is a one-sided negative, the answer to the more refined questions almost never will be positive.

THE COMMUNITY DEVELOPMENT BLOCK GRANT— NEPA EXPERIENCE IN NYC

This case study may help answer the less fundamental decision point questions, and thus the "how much is enough" and "boon or boondoggle" questions.

For the most part, the fundamentals for this program were in place. High-profile planning and environmental impact concerns were definitely required by the overseeing federal agency, the Department of Housing and Urban Development (HUD). The object of the CDBG funding of about $150 million a year for several years in NYC is that it be spent in a broad-based geographic and programmatic (*e.g.,* sewers, parks, roads, etc.) manner with built-in planing and environmental considerations. Adequate resources for planning and

NEPA requirements in a financially stricken city were provided by the grant itself.

With the selection of the Department of City Planning as the lead agency, the complex interpretation of HUD's regulations for Environmental Review Procedures for CDBG (*Federal Register,* January 7, 1975) began in earnest. The NEPA Coordinating Unit (NCU) was created within the Department, and I became NEPA Coordinator for the City. The unit carried out the extensive, multiagency education and coordination function necessary to produce and process the onslaught of required documents. Starting in September 1974, the NEPA Coordinating Unit designed, developed and supervised the institution of the HUD-NEPA mandates on CDBG actions. This initially led to the procedure diagrammed in Figure 2-1, and the Environmental Review contents, as briefly outlined in Table 2-1. Thus, NEPA responsibility slowly became internalized within the city government over the 12-month period, September 1974 to September 1975. To date, almost 100 Environmental Reviews have been prepared and processed through the resulting procedure.

During the early stages of development, each decision point enumerated earlier, had to be analyzed, discussed and cleared before an operational procedure could be managed effectively. A brief look at criteria for each decision point (keyed to the previous listing) should be beneficial.

1. A project was defined by its line budget status; that is, if it had a discrete funding allocation in the CD budget, it was considered a "project" in terms of NEPA.

2. All nonexempt projects that were questionable in any way underwent Environmental Review (ER) analysis. Significant determinations, *i.e.,* whether a full EIS is required, is based on an all-inclusive definition of the term "significant." For our purposes, this includes actions that: are precedent-setting, may incrementally lead to important adverse impacts, initiate important cumulative impacts, adversely effect unique or critical resources or may be highly controversial. At present we do not employ numerical indices, or strict quantitative threshold levels for automatic trigger or clearance purposes.

3. The division of labor across the city agencies involved, was based on available resources, perceived function and need. Thus, a central coordination unit, at the Department of City Planning (NCU), technical input from city EPA (including sanitation and sewers), DCP and the Transportation Administration (TAD), and project and setting description input from the action-initiating agencies became the natural work load distribution.

4. The dissemination of notices and draft reviews focused in the NCU. The structure and content of the notices and mailing lists was determined by the Unit with the aid of counsel and community participation experts.

5. The original choice of methodology was made with simplicity and reliability in mind. The sacrifice of some short-term time loss (*i.e.,* to prepare proper explanations) for longer term gain (*i.e.,* for ease

in understanding) was the method of choice. More recently we have evolved into more of a format approach that employs fill-in tables and yes or no responses. It is a hybrid between the narrative and matrix approaches and appears to be succeeding.

6. The basic content (Table 2-1) of the ER and the EIS was formulated in the NCU. Aside from the obvious major headings, the inclusion of a considerable amount of specific socioeconomic concerns should be of interest. By their objective and subjective incorporation into the entire process the ER becomes, as intended, a planning document to be used for decision-making.

7. The overall and the specific level of detail applied to each subcategory of the ER is determined by its relative importance to the whole and the nature of the specific project.

8. The degree and timing of any public participation was decided by the basic procedural requirements and the controversial nature of the specific project under review.

9. The redrafting of the draft ER or EIS is done by the NCU in conjunction with the appropriate individuals and agencies. The time constraints are likewise determined on a case by case basis.

10. Although consultants have not been employed, an in-depth review of possible firms has been conducted.

11. Where and when possible, the mitigation measures are incorporated into the project contract specifications. When this is impossible, a tracking by NCU of the mitigation measures is used to enforce their requirement throughout the project's implementation.

In each case, the one overriding determinant must be plain common sense applied within the constraints of available resources, time and legal requirements. The law of diminishing returns should rule supreme.

The lessons learned from the CDBG-NEPA experience are numerous and valuable. Some of the more obvious can be specified in the following statements:

1. Actions, *i.e.,* projects, plans or policies must be defined so that they can be isolated into manageable units for analysis.

2. The determination of significance procedure, in this case the Environmental Review, must be as inclusive as possible while at the same time streamlined and self-explanatory. The more the action-initiating agency (direct applicant) can contribute to the completion of the procedure, the better.

3. The division of labor and resources to accomplish the determination of significance stage and the potential EIS phase in a timely manner is critical. Smooth integration of physical impact analysis (air, noise, water, etc.) is most often the weak link that must be focused on and controlled.

4. Direct, appropriate education and necessary re-education of the procedure participants is essential to a smooth process. Mid-course corrections save valuable time. An ounce of prevention saves days!

5. A uniform approach to a level of detail philosophy is highly beneficial.

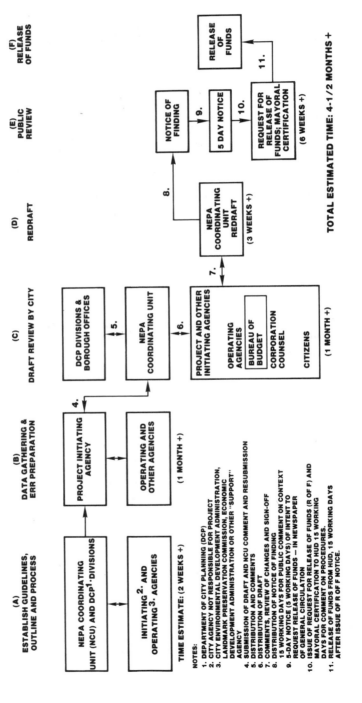

Figure 2-1. Community Development Block Grant Environmental Review Record Process.

6. Strong legal advice throughout is mandatory. However, this must be balanced with basic environmental planning fundamentals and hands-on logic.

7. In the preparation of NEPA documents, the space given to the project's history and other less important areas should be kept to a minimum.

8. The importance of historic preservation, indirect impacts, growth and energy considerations must not be underestimated—often they become high-profile areas of concern and controversy. When required, historic preservation procedures are long and difficult and take on a life of their own.

9. The existence of a strong central coordination for the entire process is essential.

10. There must be clear mitigation measure follow-through if the process is to have credibility and planning worth.

11. Small, adequate, centralized staffing is more effective than large, diversely organized staffing. A generalist or two is essential to proper coordination.

12. One must constantly be aware of attempts to abuse the ER procedure by using it simply to delay unwanted projects for nonenvironmental impact reasons. A good, honest document is the best defense against these attempts.

To date, the total effect of these lessons has been distinctly positive. Considering the work load, the complexity of analysis, some of the limited resources available and the broad scope of public involvement (our mailing list equals almost 1000), there have been only minimal problems.

The single major delay came in regard to the nature and degree of analysis given to the extensive residential demolition program funded through the CDBG. The concerned public groups demanded that more intensive analysis be given to the social and economic consequences of demolition, that implementation of proposed mitigation measures be monitored effectively and that the administration of the entire program be upgraded. The Environmental Review was used both as an information piece and the leverage for program improvement. Extensive discussion and negotiation, with the imminent possibility of a full EIS, characterized the impasse. Most of the specific public comments were accommodated, and the ER was refined and expanded, the administration of the program was broadened to include more citizen and interagency participation and the mitigation measures were more carefully tracked and applied. The delay proved mutually beneficial to all.

While this process within a process occurred several times, no project delay was insurmountable or wasted. The first two years of the CDBG-NEPA procedure in NYC has been a productive learning period for almost all of those involved.

Table 2-1. A Brief Outline of a CDBG Environmental Review

I. Overview of the Action
   General description of project activities. Reasons for the project, local need for the project and whether it will answer local need, general location.

II. Specific Project and Site Description
   A. Site location
   B. Maps and photographs
   C. Activities to be undertaken
   D. Right-of-way characteristics
   E. Surrounding land
   F. Budget

III. Physical Environmental Setting and Impact Analysis (existing conditions, impacts, and mitigation measures are included)
   A. Land and climate
      1. site topography
      2. foundation conditions
      3. man-made hazards
      4. climate
   B. Vegetation, wildlife, natural areas
   C. Infrastructure
      1. water supply
      2. solid waste
      3. sewage
      4. transportation
      5. energy
   D. Air pollution
   E. Noise pollution
   F. Water pollution
   G. Aesthetics

IV. Socioeconomic Environmental Setting and Impact Analysis—(existing conditions, impacts and mitigation measures are included)
   A. Community facilities and services
      1. schools
      2. parks and playgrounds
      3. cultural facilities
      4. police, fire, telephone
      5. social services
      6. health facilities
      7. employment centers and commerical facilities
      8. character of the community
      9. population/housing
   B. Historical considerations—analysis of the impact of the proposed project on those properties which are listed, nominated, or could be potentially nominated to the National Register of Historic Places.
   C. Growth inducing impact—consideration of the impact of the project on the already established, nonproject, population and economic trends in areas affected

Table 2-1, Continued.

V. Proposed Mitigation Measures—Actions Being Taken or Contemplated to Reduce the Identified Adverse Environmental Impacts

VI. Cumulative and Incremental Impact—Discussion of the Additive Effects of the Individual Impacts Analyzed in Early Sections of the Review; and Discussion of the Additive Effects of the Projects with those of other Juxtaposed Projects.

VII. Alternatives to the Proposed Project—Full Discussion of any and all Alternatives to the Project under Review that may Minimize or Eliminate any Identified Adverse Environmental Impacts.

VIII. Government and Community Participation—Description of the Joint Participation of Community Elements and Government Agencies in the Planning and Design of the Proposed Project.

IX. Environmental Review Finding.

THE ANSWER

What does all this tell us about "how much is enough" within the NEPA process or whether it is a "boon or a boondoggle?"

It tells us that the answer to "how much is enough" begins with a thorough knowledge of the letter and intent of NEPA's 102.(2)(C), and that the application of NEPA's letter and intent must be done on a case-by-case basis where the specifics mold the degree of investment in resources, quality control, citizen participation and decision-making relevance. Thus, liberal servings of compliance with legal requirements, project management objectives and common sense are all prerequisites to a valid answer to the "enough" question.

The "boon or boondoggle" answer is likewise elusive, but we do have the beginnings of the answer. In turn, this beginning must be found in the answers to several other questions: (1) have NEPA-reviewed projects been inordinately delayed by NEPA? (2) have the delays that have occurred been useful from a project evaluation and improvement viewpoint? and (3) has decision-making for these projects been improved? My answers to these questions, in order would be, no, sometimes and somewhat.

The answer to another basic question: are the elements in place to improve the process and increase the boon and decrease the doggle?—must be yes! NEPA has been in existence seven short years. In that time it has been asked to fill a vacuum that has been in existence since the American Revolution. The more than 600 court cases involving NEPA have finally begun to fully define the law and give it functional status. This, combined with its rapidly increasing public familiarity, is shaping NEPA into a vital environmental planning-land use tool. As these and other trends, such as the increasing use of programmatic EIS's, continue, we should see NEPA truly come of age.

RECOMMENDED READING

Council on Environmental Quality. *Environmental Impact Statements—An Analysis of Six Years' Experience by Seventy Federal Agencies,* Washington, D. C. (March 1976).

Comptroller General of the United States. "Improvements Needed in Federal Efforts to Implement the National Environmental Policy Act of 1969," Report to the Subcommittee on Fisheries and Wildlife Conservation Committee on Merchant Marine and Fisheries House of Representatives, Washington, D. C. (May 1972).

Ditton, R. and T. Goodale, Eds. "Environmental Impact Analysis: Philosophy and Methods," *Proceedings of the Conference on Environmental Impact Analysis, Green Bay, Wisconsin.* National Oceanic and Atmospheric Administration, Washington, D. C. (January 1972).

"Compilation of the Housing and Community Development Act of 1974," Public Law 93-383, Subcommittee on Housing of the Committee on Banking and Currency, House of Representatives, 93rd Congress, Second Session, Washington, D. C. (October 1974).

Department of City Planning, New York. "Community Development Program and Application First Program Year—City of New York," NYC DCP 75-05 (April 1975).

CHAPTER 3

AN APPROACH TO THE DETERMINATION OF
SIGNIFICANCE IN THE PREPARATION OF
ENVIRONMENTAL ASSESSMENTS

George F. Ames
Section Head
Environmental Matters Section
Washington Suburban Sanitary Commission
Hyattsville, Maryland

The National Environmental Policy Act (NEPA) requires the assessment of major federal actions, basically through an evaluation of their effects' significance. It is, in the final analysis, the collective/cumulative significance of effects that plays the crucial role in determining the worthiness of a project. Adverse effects must be explored in depth and remedial or mitigative measures outlined to deal with them. If the offsetting benefits of a project fail to demonstrate conclusively that the public interest is served by implementation, or if mitigation measures are inadequate to bring adverse effects within acceptable limits, then presumably a negative environmental finding would result.

While NEPA and subsequent Environmental Protection Agency (EPA) administrative regulations frequently refer to the significance of effects, neither makes an adequate effort to define an approach applicable to determination of significance. A major area of confusion can occur when significance is evaluated relative solely to other effects instead of defining it in absolutist (or unconditional) terms. The statement that the "most significant adverse effect of a project is on water quality" does not actually make any conclusive finding as to whether this effect is or is not significant. It merely says that of the entire array of adverse effects, the effect on water quality is the most important.

25

It is clear, however, that EPA requires a nonrelativistic evaluation, *i.e.,* an effect is either significant or insignificant. Once it is determined that an effect is consequential, then degrees of importance can be assigned or comparative rankings made. Without clear procedural guidelines or valid evaluative criteria, the determination of significance may be erroneous or biased.

The Environmental Matters Section of the Washington Suburban Sanitary Commission (WSSC), a public corporation providing water and sewer services to several suburban Maryland counties, is responsible for the preparation of environmental assessments on WSSC projects in compliance with EPA regulations and the Maryland Environmental Policy Act (MEPA). The Maryland law essentially requires the preparation of Environmental Assessment Forms (EAF) on the projects of state agencies involving legislative action. An EAF (see Appendix I at the conclusion of this chapter) is a series of questons on land, water and air use, biological, socioeconomic and historical considerations. An EAF should provide enough data on the project so that the preparing agency can make a decision on the significance of both adverse and beneficial effects. If the agency decides that the effects are significant, either adverse or beneficial, then an Environmental Effects Report (EER) must be prepared, covering in detail the major areas of concern and the measures that will be taken to "minimize adverse environmental effects and maximize beneficial environmental effects" as required in the Commission guidelines.

The EAF checklist is definitely helpful as it lends a certain structure to the analysis of a project and identifies the natural and socioeconomic resources that must be considered and some of the evaluative criteria that should be used. The checklist, however, provides little guidance in the form of procedures to follow in developing the information that will be used to answer the questions and judge significance. In an effort to clarify the meaning of significance and, concomitantly, to reinforce the objectivity and justification of its findings, the Environmental Matters Section (EMS) developed a procedural guideline that has potential application to a wide variety of projects requiring environmental assessments.

The EMS approach involves first- and second-order determinations of significance that lead directly to an unconditional finding, individually vis-a-vis a specific resource, or collectively on environmental quality.

FIRST-ORDER SIGNIFICANCE DETERMINATION

The procedure involves two steps. First, an assessment should be made of an effect's significance in its immediate context, *i.e.,* the site. This is the first-order determination. The effect is initially identified, described and evaluated in the setting in which it occurs and in no other. An analysis is made (as applicable) of the nature, scope, magnitude, intensity and duration of an effect on a site-specific basis. The essence of the first-order determination is the avoidance of comparisons with or without references to other factors beyond those which directly pertain to the site setting and/or situation.

Examples of site-specific significant effects related to the design and construction of wastewater treatment facilities include:

1. the removal of a large number of mature hardwoods;
2. the blockage or major disturbance of a spawning run;
3. the permanent change of a channel cross section;
4. the installation of a point source of pollution;
5. the disturbance of a known archeological or historical site;
6. the temporary closing of a major highway;
7. a permanent degradation in the water quality of a stream making it uninhabitable to important fish species;* and
8. the installation of a noise source which raises ambient levels in a residential community above regulatory standards.

The so-called first-order determination is a necessary step but incomplete by itself. It does not account for the potential significance of an effect beyond the impact site or setting of the project. (Note: The difference between the first and second steps should not be confused with the distinction between primary and secondary effects which refers to the relationship of effect to cause, *i.e.,* direct for primary and indirect for secondary; both primary and secondary effects could occur onsite as well as off). Second, relative comparisons with other projects, sites and situations are not involved in the first-order determination, nor are the cumulative effects of related projects, such as a set of contracts for a lengthy sewer line. Third, local and regional implications of an effect are not considered. Lastly, some effects are not considered in the first-order determination; they are primarily, but not necessarily, limited to secondary effects. But all effects have some degree of second-order influence.

SECOND-ORDER SIGNIFICANCE DETERMINATION

The second step concerns the determination of significance in a broader context. Beginning with whatever first-order information is available, it takes into consideration nonsite-specific factors uninvolved in the first step. It provides a vital perspective (and balance) to the analysis. As such, second-order findings on significance either confirm or override first-order findings.

---

*For example, important from a utilitarian or endangered species perspective.

Example I: If a project has first-order significant effect on a known archeological site (*e.g.,* would destroy it), this by itself does not make the effect of the project on archeological resources significant. Such a finding depends on the importance of the site in the region. If the site had some unique characteristics or qualities, then the effect should be judged significant. If, on the other hand, there are many similar sites in the region and nothing has surfaced to suggest the uniqueness of the one in question, the effect should be judged insignificant.

Example II: In a first-order determination, the temporary disruption of recreational use of an area for a given outdoor activity would generally be considered insignificant. During the second step, however, if the investigation of the use and availability of facilities for this activity in the county reveals that (1) few are available, (2) the one affected is heavily used, and (3) diversion of users to other facilities would cause serious overcrowding, then the effect on recreational resources would be significant.

Example III: If a project required the removal of a large number of mature trees, the site-specific effect (first-order) on vegetation would probably be significant. However, unless the trees had a special value (*e.g.,* designated Bicentennial Tree—Maryland Forest Service designation in 1976 for selected trees over 200 years old; high commercial value; rare, endangered or threatened species), a second-order (and conclusive) finding would hold the effect insignificant. In this case, cumulative effects may be important. If the project is one of a series of sewer lines to be installed in a stream valley, the second-order determination should also make note of the overall effect on vegetation.

The criteria used to assess significance are largely a function of the nature of an effect. Criteria include federal, state and local standards and regulations, natural resource inventories, lists of rare, endangered and threatened species, and planning goals. Specific examples are the state's water quality standards, fish and wildlife population surveys, noise and air pollution standards, state lists of archeological and historical sites, and master plans. The Maryland Environmental Assessment Form also contains a useful list of criteria-oriented questions, which relate the effects of an action to important environmental concerns.

At the conclusion of the second step, the findings made regarding significance remain unavoidably judgmental for the great majority of effects. *Numbers, checklists and matrices cannot replace sound, analytical judgment, particularly in the realm of intangible or immeasurable resources and uses.* A valid analytical approach to the determination of significance, once accepted, understood and applied by any group involved in the preparation of assessments, can reduce to an acceptable level the dual risks of error and bias.

RECOMMENDED READING

1. Environmental Protection Agency. "Preparation of Environmental Impact Statements—Final Regulations," *Federal Register* 40(79):16814-16827 (1975).
2. "Maryland Environmental Policy Act," Chapter 702 of the Laws of Maryland, S.B. 689 (1973).
3. "National Environmental Policy Act," Public Law 91-190, 91st Congress (1969).
4. Washington Suburban Sanitary Commission. "Guidelines of the Washington Suburban Sanitary Commission for the Implementation of the Maryland Environmental Policy Act" (1975).

Appendix. Environmental Assessment Form (EAF)

This form is to assist the reviewers in determining whether a proposed action could cause significant natural, socioeconomic and historic environmental effects and thus require an Environmental Effects Report.

Department_____ Division_____

Other_____

Project Title_____

Predicted Dates: Commencement_____ Completion_____

Projected Cost_____

I. Background Information

1. Give a brief description of the proposed action/project(s).

2. Describe the geographical area(s) which will be affected by the action/project(s). Specifically locate the project by using the Maryland Coordinate Grid System, include distinguishing natural and man-made features and a brief description of the present use of the area(s). Include a suitable location map (sketch map or copy of the U.S. Geological Survey map, etc.).

The following questions should be answered by placing a check in the appropriate column(s). If desirable, the "comments attached" column can be checked by itself or in combination with an answer of "yes" or "no" to provide additional information or to overcome an affirmative presumption.

In answering the questions, the significant beneficial and adverse, short- and long-term effects of the proposed action, on-site and off-site during construction and operation should be considered.

All questions should be answered as if the agency is subject to the same requirements as a private person requesting a license or permit from the state or federal
government.

	Yes	No	Comments Attached

A. Land Use Consideration
1. Will the action be within the 100-
    year floodplain?
2. Will the action require a permit for
    construction or alteration within the
    50-year floodplain?
3. Will the action require a permit for
    dredging, filling, draining or altera-
    tion of a wetland?
4. Will the action require a permit for
    the construction or operation of
    facilities for solid waste disposal in-
    cluding dredge and excavation soil?
5. Will the action occur on slopes ex-
    ceeding 15%?
6. Will the action require a grading
    plan or a sediment control permit?
7. Will the action require a mining per-
    mit for deep or surface mining?
8. Will the action require a permit for
    drilling a gas or oil well?
9. Will the action require a permit for
    airport construction?
10. Will the action require a permit for
    the crossing of the Potomac River
    by conduits, cables or other like
    devices?
11. Will the action affect the use of a
    public recreation area, park, forest,
    wildlife management area, scenic
    river or wildland?
12. Will the action affect the use of
    any natural or man-made features
    that are unique to the county, state
    or nation?
13. Will the action affect the use of an
    archaeological or historical site or
    structure?

B. Water Use Considerations
14. Will the action require a permit for
    the change of the course, current,
    or cross section of a stream or other
    body of water?

Appendix, Continued

		Yes	No	Comments Attached
15.	Will the action require the construction, alteration or removal of a dam, reservoir or waterway obstruction?	___	___	___
16.	Will the action change the overland flow of storm water or reduce the absorption capacity of the ground?	___	___	___
17.	Will the action require a permit for the drilling of a water well?	___	___	___
18.	Will the action require a permit for water appropriation?	___	___	___
19.	Will the action require a permit for the construction and operation of facilities for treatment or distribution of water?	___	___	___
20.	Will the project require a permit for the construction and operation of facilities for sewage treatment and/or land disposal of liquid waste derivatives?	___	___	___
21.	Will the action result in any discharge into surface or subsurface water?	___	___	___
22.	If so, will the discharge affect ambient water quality parameters and/or require a discharge permit?	___	___	___

C. Air Use Considerations

23.	Will the action result in any discharge into the air?	___	___	___
24.	If so, will the discharge affect ambient air quality parameters or produce a disagreeable odor?	___	___	___
25.	Will the action generate additional noise which differs in character or level from present conditions?	___	___	___
26.	Will the action preclude future use of related air space?	___	___	___
27.	Will the action generate any radiological, electrical, magnetic, or light influences?	___	___	___

D. Plants and Animals

28.	Will the action cause the disturbance, reduction or loss of any rare, unique or valuable plant or animal?	___	___	___
29.	Will the action result in the significant reduction or loss of any fish or wildlife habitats?	___	___	___

Appendix, Continued

	Yes	No	Comments Attached

E. Socioeconomic

31. Will the action result in a preemption or division of properties or impair their economic use? _____ _____ _____

32. Will the action cause relocation of activities, structures or result in a change in the population density or distribution? _____ _____ _____

33. Will the action alter land values? _____ _____ _____

34. Will the action affect traffic flow and volume? _____ _____ _____

35. Will the action affect the production, extraction, harvest or potential use of a scarce or economically important resource? _____ _____ _____

36. Will the action require a license to construct a sawmill or other plant for the manufacture of forest products? _____ _____ _____

37. Is the action in accord with federal, state, regional and local comprehensive or functional plans—including zoning? _____ _____ _____

38. Will the action affect the employment opportunities for persons in the area? _____ _____ _____

39. Will the action affect the ability of the area to attract new sources of tax revenue? _____ _____ _____

40. Will the action discourage present sources of tax revenue from remaining in the area, or affirmatively encourage them to relocate elsewhere? _____ _____ _____

41. Will the action affect the ability of the area to attract tourism? _____ _____ _____

F. Historical Considerations

42. Will the action affect an area which is an important historic site? _____ _____ _____

43. Will the action affect a resource included in the Maryland Inventory of Historic Sites? _____ _____ _____

G. Other Considerations

44. Could the action endanger the public health, safety or welfare? _____ _____ _____

Appendix, Continued

	Yes	No	Comments Attached
45. Could the action be eliminated without deleterious effects to the public health, safety, welfare or the natural environment?	___	___	___
46. Will the action be of statewide significance?	___	___	___
47. Are there any other plans or actions (federal, state, county or private) that, in conjunction with the subject action, could result in a cumulative or synergistic impact on the public health?	___	___	___
48. Will the action require additional power generation or transmission capacity?	___	___	___

G. Conclusion

49. This agency will develop a complete environmental effects report on the proposed action.	___	___	___

CHAPTER 4

BOON OR BOONDOGGLE?
A CRISIS IN OUR ADOLESCENCE

Robert S. De Santo
Chief Ecologist
DeLeuw, Cather & Company
New Haven, Connecticut

Adolescence is the process of growing up, certainly that is what we are doing as members of a new profession seeking an identity, and it seems that we are in the very midst of that crisis. Although the initiation of this country's commitment to formal requirements for environmental sensitivity and sound environmental management is generally associated with the National Environmental Policy Act (NEPA) of 1969, the practical implementation of that board policy is a dynamic procedure. It is expressed at all levels of government, education and industry.

The success of the philosophy behind that policy is essentially dependent upon ethics, our social values and our conscious or subconscious commitments to the cost versus the benefits of environmental values. We are growing up in this profession to weigh and decide these values. They are not easy nor are they clear. The dilemma with which we must deal is suggested by the language of NEPA, which says that the purpose of the act is " . . . To declare a National Policy that will encourage productive and enjoyable harmony between man and his environment; to promote efforts that will prevent or eliminate damage to the environment and biosphere and stimulate the health and welfare of man; to enrich the understanding of the ecological systems and natural resources important to the Nation . . ." (42 United States Code 4321). That new, or renewed, philosophy is the "Boon" attributed to NEPA. The "Boondoggle" frustration grows out of the unfortunate, although necessary, period of gaining experience in the field. The complex and confusing path that we follow should ultimately be aimed at not only answering the spirit and letter of NEPA, but it should also be directed at the creation of a tutorial program for the next generation of Environmental Professionals that supports the good goals of NEPA.

At best, the Environmental Impact Statement (EIS), represents a philosophy which deals thoughtfully and dispassionately with the short- and long-term uses of natural and human resources. At worst, the EIS is thought of as a cookbook—a matrix which, when followed, tells whether a project is good or bad. Our best service to NEPA will ultimately grow out of the so-called "Boondoogle." We will mature in our academic and technical perception of the growing need for environmental stewardship.

Perhaps surprisingly, it seems that the published beginnings of environmental assessments in the United States appeared with the somewhat isolated studies of the U.S. Army Corps of Engineers in the 1870s,[1,2] where field methods were specifically employed to unravel environmental interactions created as a result of man-made manipulations. Countless reams of good and bad materials have been generated on the subject over the intervening 100 years, with a gathering momentum that now tends to boggle the logical mind. Yet, knowing more and more, we seem continually less able to deal with our environment and to live our lives with some sense of controlling strategy for achieving environmental well-being. We do not have that sense any longer, and a good statement of our dilemma is made in the carefully chosen language of NEPA. It calls out a charge that has been a cornerstone for many at the same time as it has become a millstone to others, who see it taking away some personal freedoms.

A recent book by Joseph Lee Rodgers, Jr.,[1] of the University of Oklahoma, begins, "Evidence of an environmental crisis is world wide." Certainly it is an undisputed knell calling us all to save ourselves. Do we remain calm and careful or do we revolt violently? Well-trained horses sink out of sight in the quicksand before they realize they must act violently and early to save themselves; panic causes a swimmer to thrash and drown. Which model of behavior should we follow? Perhaps these are the basic questions we ask when seeking to understand what is meant by the boon or the boondoggle confronting Environmental Professionals.

THE BOON OF ENVIRONMENTAL SENSITIVITY

Our modern temper is being tested by the knowledge that we, as a species, are ultimately responsible for the overall state of the environment. Many of us are trying on a sense of stewardship which leads us, perhaps too proudly, to call ourselves "Environmental Professionals," who see man as a part of nature. One boon brought to us by our state of nervousness is our recognition of man as a part of nature, but that ethic is not an inheritance of our society. It is newly learned, for the past evolution of man's common ethic has really not seen it at all. Our past history has embraced man as somehow apart from nature. Perhaps it will be concluded that we, self-esteeming and unique creatures in this universe, will never win a chance to live in harmony with the biosphere. That frustration is not a modern one, nor have we made much real progress toward protecting its realization. "Look on my works, ye Mighty, and despair!" Ozymandias, in Percy Bysshe Shelley's 1817 sonnet, spoke eloquently on behalf of man the conqueror, and the wisdom of Walt Kelly's Pogo is no less disquieting than Shelley's: "We have met the enemy and he is us!" Can we moderns effectively use our past and present knowledge to leave our biosphere in good and productive shape for posterity? It is healthy for us to face and address that question.

It would be too simple were we able to point to Rachel Carson's *Silent Spring*[2] as the start of our uprising, just as it was too simple for us to quaintly point to Harriet Beacher Stow's *Uncle Tom's Cabin*[3] as the starting tinder of the Civil War. Many, such as Commoner,[4] Dubos[5] and McHarg,[6,7] as well as Carson, have focused our attention and public interest on the diffuse and complex issues of environmental management not yet answerable but nevertheless for which the public, a great and faceless force, believes an answer does exist in our endless technological dexterity. But those who serve as specialists, the Environmental Professionals, do not always seem so hopeful and expectant. Most are exceedingly sober and somewhat unsettled. That sobriety is a boon helping to muster our good sense to carry us successfully through the environmental crisis which continues to loom upon the horizon.

Charles A. S. Hall[8] has recently commented on just one, albeit multi-faceted, aspect of our potentially dim future, which he sees dominated by the depletion of cheap and flexible energy supplies (Figure 4-1). Based on his evaluation of our state of affairs, Hall calls for five management strategies aimed at a redirection of our perception of the environment:

1. Resources must be viewed as scarce and must not be marketed as if they were not.
2. Coal will again become an important energy source.
3. Industry will have to adjust radically to the lack of resources.
4. Natural systems for water and waste purification will invite increased reliance from man in an energy-scarce society.
5. There will be increasing moral and political pressure directed toward the United States by the Third World, seeking access to energy resources such as coal.

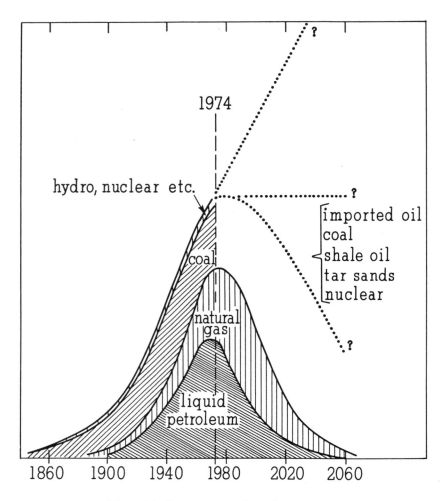

Figure 4-1. Energy source mix vs time.

Taken together, it appears that the environmental crisis has evolved rapidly since the 1930s, during a period of unprecedented affluence in the western countries. The enveloping shock of resource scarcities in the 1970s has clearly created a sense of conservation and caution which is the fundamental boon we can associate with these sensitivities—an awakening to recognition of the multifaceted problems and prospects of environmental management as an issue that is both visible and threatening to the public.

A boon of public, nervous perception, calls us to address these issues. As Environmental Professionals, we are handicapped by the public's adolescent and still somewhat premature expectations. First, we must learn all the unknown skills of environmental management, and this process is eliciting hefty frustration and fury.

One of the best examples of this frustration, as tendered by academia, is represented in the brief editorial which was recently prepared for *Science* by D. W. Schindler.[9] His frustration saw environmental impact statements forming a "grey literature" unchecked by the scientific community at large and seldom receiving " . . . the hard scrutiny that follows the publication of scientific findings in a reputable scientific journal." Schindler, an experienced and respected scientist, fears that the advancement of the "scientific method" is in jeopardy. He sees other specters as well, including " . . . a declining credibility for environmental science and scientists" and " . . . a reduction in the overall quality of scientific personnel." He sees such consequences coming from the environmental professional who chooses to apply " . . . the same old bag of tricks . . . " practiced by " . . . a traveling circus of 'scientists' . . ." and from " . . . studies often done by scientists who cannot successfully compete for funding from traditional scientific sources." Yet, others involved in environmental issues and the management of these issues, have very different views, which question whether we can justly brand as a boldfaced boondoggle our present system of trying to resolve these issues, by an admittedly imperfect method.

Harkins[10] has provided a rather clear perception of this problem of frustration and namecalling, which I believe he sees from his vantage point of both naturalist and philosopher. As such, he defines the goal of environmental management as a discipline, but recognizes that the systematic solution of environmental problems still has some way to go before we can reach that goal. And he cites Skinner, Commoner and Hardin, as well as Schindler, to piece together a logical view of our fundamental problem of deciding who has the right answer to environmental problems. He concludes that the solution lies in the recognition that our decisions must involve a dynamic balance of scientific, economic, social and ethical facts and values, and furthermore, that we must confess that no " . . . single body of experts possesses all the requisite knowledge and wisdom" needed to resolve environmental problems.

Even more fundamentally, I believe Harkins is saying that successful and correct environmental management does not rest solely on the laurels of the "scientific method." More fabric is needed in this sort of intricate management, including such elusive ingredients as an ethic that transcends science. Indeed, good environmental management does seem to transcend science, politics and ethics alone since it requires these in combination. If this is so, it is easy to understand that, not yet being adequately prepared for so transdisciplinary a confrontation, some environmental management spokespersons are frustrated by the difficulty of full communication across the traditional boundaries of individual and somewhat insulated education and experience.

Aside from the growing number of projects requiring some environmental evaluation, each project carries a daily growing list of environmental facets promulgated by those agencies responsible for legislating ecology. Some such direction seeks to justify the contention that good environmental management and conservation cannot rely solely on an evaluation of economic and ecological factors. That direction also calls for the conservation of "nonresources," just as we are called to conserve energy, water and land.

Ehrenfeld[11] defines nine values that he assigns to nonresources, including:

1. recreational and aesthetic values, such as scenic views, hiking, the visible diurnal Australian mammals, etc;

2. undiscovered or undeveloped values, such as were found in the oil of the Jojoba bean substituting for sperm whale oil;

3. ecosystem stabilization values, such as are proposed to exist when many different organisms produce a "diversity-stability;"

4. examples of survival, such as the good design of extensive natural ecosystems from which man may better learn how to survive;

5. environmental baseline and monitoring values provided by natural systems, such as the use of honeybees as monitors of heavy metal pollution;

6. scientific research values, such as the use of certain organisms with unique experimental properties as laboratory materials;

7. teaching values, such as may be associated with outdoor laboratory areas and nature study sites;

8. habitat reconstruction values, such as may be gained by using a site as a working model and a source of living components to reconstruct and repopulate one elsewhere that had been damaged or destroyed; and

9. conservative value and the avoidance of change as might otherwise be caused were we to inadvertently cause irreversible change in some natural order, which would cause a hidden, unknown risk to a much wider sphere of influence.

Ehrenfeld has expounded on the direction and the misdirection of conservation strategies, and a number of the points he makes are indeed being implemented,[12] but an even more interesting aspect of his thesis suggests that the ethical facet of environmental management is the crucial keystone for us to recognize. Some have defined this facet as "natural art value."[4] C. S. Elton[13] emphasized that the central motive for environmental protection is religion; this kind of geopiety is well dissected by

L. H. Graber in her fascinating treatise entitled "Wilderness as Sacred Space."[14] In that sense, preservation is a religious experience that needs no justification.

How does this all relate to our work as Environmental Professionals? For me, it supports the belief that we must not expect there to be a singularly endowed sect of ecologists who have all the requisite knowledge to solve our mutual environmental problems. Also, it provides me with some understanding that environmental studies must recognize man's insistence to mix ethics with science. There is a need for the Environmental Professional to appreciate these circumstances and to address them objectively and as thoroughly as he judges appropriate.

The self-education of the Environmental Professional helped along by such hickory sticks as NEPA, have caused us much frustration because we often do not really know enough to answer all the complex scientific and ethical questions, which someone insists be answered based on the evolving NEPA charge. Yet out of that frustration has come a persistent curiosity and a continuing technical development in the many diverse disciplines that define environmental studies.

If we assume that Ehrenfeld is correct when he states that "not all problems have acceptable solutions," and if Harkins is correct when he states that we should be opposed to priesthoods, no matter how well intentioned, than the success of our course toward good environmental management decisions rests with the adult perception of the need for meaningful, open and honest teamwork by professionals joined by a willingness to accept our individual limits. If the early course of environmental management is called a "boondoggle," it is an unfair label that will fall away in time. Perhaps a fairer label, if one is necessary, would be "persistence."

REFERENCES

1. Rodgers, J. L., Jr. *Environmental Impact Assessment, Growth, Management and the Comprehensive Plan* (Cambridge, Massachusetts: Ballinger Publishing Co., 1976), p. 185.
2. Carson, R. *The Silent Spring* (Greenwich, Connecticut: Faucett Publishing .Co., 1962).
3. Stowe, H. B. *Uncle Tom's Cabin* (Garden City, New York: International Collector's Library), p. 475. (A reprint of the original published in 1852 by Houghton Mifflin Co.).
4. Commoner, B. *The Closing Circle* (New York: Alfred Knopf, 1972).
5. Dubos, R. *So Human an Animal* (New York: Charles Scribner and Sons, 1969).
6. McHarg, I. "A Comprehensive Highway Route-Selection Method," *Highway Res. Rec.* (246):1-15 (1968).

7. McHarg, I. *Design With Nature* (Garden City, New York: Natural History Press, 1969), p. 198.
8. Hall, C. A. S. "The Implications of Future Energy Supplies for Environmental Management," *Environ. Managemt.* 1(1):5-6 (1976).
9. Schindler, D. W. "The Impact Statement Boondoggle," *Science* 191(4239):509 (1976).
10. Harkins, J. P. "Thou Canst Not Stir a Flower," *Environ. Managemt.* 1(1):4-5 (1976).
11. Ehrenfeld, D. W. "The Conservation of Non-Resources," *Am. Scientist* 64(6):648-656 (1976).
12. Franklin, J. F. "The Biosphere Reserve Program in the United States," *Science* 195(4275):262-267 (1977).
13. Elton, C. S. *The Ecology of Invasions by Animals and Plants* (London, England: Methuen, 1958), p. 143-145.
14. Graber, L. H. *Wilderness as Sacred Space* (Washington, D.C.: Association of American Geographers, 1976), Monograph 8, p. 124.

CHAPTER 5

ENVIRONMENTAL CONSIDERATION FOR U.S. ASSISTANCE PROGRAMS IN DEVELOPING COUNTRIES

Albert C. Printz, Jr.
Environmental Coordinator
Agency for International Development
Washington, D.C.

I am not sure what the meaning is of How Much is Enough? Boon or Boondoggle? as it applies to the issue of Third World development. It could relate to the question so often posed by the Council on Environmental Quality (CEQ) and others of agencies such as the Agency for International Development (AID), Export-Import Bank and the World Bank, as to what and how much analysis should be carried out on environmental issues in countries other than the U.S.

THE AGENCY FOR INTERNATIONAL DEVELOPMENT

First, let me describe the AID and how it evolved. The Foreign Assistance Program started some 30 years ago, after World War II, with the Marshall Plan. A major element at that time was a program of loans to countries in Europe to permit reconstruction of their economies. This successful initial effort established the pattern of foreign assistance that has persisted until this day, even though the needs and skills of recipients of our help have radically changed. Instead of helping people already having highly sophisticated technical skills, as the European countries did 30 years ago, we are now helping the poorest of the poor, the least educated people in the poorest countries of the world.

After the Marshall Plan concept, AID underwent a number of changes. The programs were usually designed to provide capital to governments, more or less like the Marshall Plan, in the hope that the benefits would "trickle down" to everyone along the way. That approach fell into disrepute because the benefits did not seem to trickle down.

U.S. development assistance is now targeted at a world in which:

1. more than one-fourth of the world's population lives on an income of less than $150 per year;
2. life expectancy is 52 years, compared with 71 in the U.S.;
3. there are 220,000 new mouths to feed every day;
4. millions are malnourished and food must be imported for human survival;
5. 40% of the children die before the age of 5; and
6. more than half the children do not attend school.

Foreign economic assistance provided by AID fits broadly into two categories:

1. *Development assistance,* which is aimed at the lives of the poorest people in underdeveloped countries (the so-called Third and Fourth Worlds, which cover two-thirds of the earth's land area and contain 74% of the world's population). 1.2 billion dollars was appropriated for such assistance in Fiscal Year 1976; and
2. *Security-supporting assistance,* which seeks to promote economic stability in selected countries, whose well-being is important to U.S. security. An example is the Middle East, where we are attempting to encourage the peaceful development of an area embracing Israel, Jordan, Syria and Egypt to thereby reduce the incentives to violence and conflict. 1.7 billion dollars was appropriated in Fiscal Year 1976 for such assistance.

Prior to 1973, when the Foreign Assistance Act was modified, many AID activities were of the large capital development type, such as dams, highways, industrial plants, power generating facilities, ports and harbors. Today, the AID program, as directed through the Foreign Assistance Act, concentrates on specific programs of population planning, increased food production, health and nutrition, education and human resources development.

ATTITUDES TOWARD DEVELOPMENT

For thousands of years, human beings have been engaged in creative transformations of the wilderness and have humanized environments, but the process has been greatly accelerated and intensified since the 19th Century. As René Dubos[1] has recently pointed out, one of the psychological effects of the industrial revolution was to encourage the belief that any kind of change was justified if it was economically profitable—

even if it caused a degradation of human life and environmental quality. During recent decades, there have been signs of a reversal in this psychological attitude. As recently as 1933, when Chicago held a World's Fair, one central theme was entitled "Science discovers, Industry applies, Man conforms." The prevailing belief was that the real measure of progress is industrial development, regardless of consequences. Today we acknowledge that the concern for the environment is in essence a concern for humanity. Others, however, still harbor the 1933 beliefs, especially countries of the Third World.

Dr. Mostafa Tolba, Executive Director of the United Nations Environmental Program (UNEP) pointed out that one of the greatest challenges facing humanity today is to design development that satisfies basic human needs, and is, at the same time, environmentally realistic and appropriate. Development is a dynamic and complex process in which all nations strive to improve the well-being of their people. Developing nations strive to reach levels of economic well-being already attained by the more advanced countries. The more technologically advanced countries seek to sustain and improve their current standards of living. The issues of resources, population, environment and development are before all of us and in recent years have come to dominate the world's agenda. Examples include the United Nations Conferences on the human environment, population, food, trade and development and human settlements, and the general deliberations of the General Assembly. These problems are all interrelated and present decision-makers with a complex and challenging situation for all concerned with the human environment.

TYPES OF ENVIRONMENTAL PROBLEMS

The environmental problems of the developing countries can generally be divided into two categories: effects of poverty and effects of economic development. The former are the most difficult to handle because of the complex interrelationships that exist when poverty, disease, malnutrition and illiteracy are prevalent. In most instances, not merely the quality of life but rather life itself is endangered. Poverty breeds an exploitation of both natural and human resources. Under the conditions of poverty, the biophysical environment often exhibits the ravages of long years of mismanagement. Examples include the wasting of once fertile agricultural lands, denuding of forests, erosion, water pollution from lack of sanitary facilities, air and water pollution from marginal industries, and the loss of human productivity through disease and malnutrition; these individually and collectively place increasing pressure on ecosystems. These problems of poverty in developing countries are just as significant environmentally as the direct pollution of air, water and soil in our country. Both lead to the rapid depletion of natural resources and degradation of our environment.

The second problem—the environmental effects of economic development—is easier to grasp because of our recent experiences with comparable problems. It is therefore the focus of more attention today by those concerned with the environment. What we often fail to accept is that development will and must go on regardless of the presence of the U.S. Across the world today we hear a central theme being repeated over and over again by the developing world: "We want the ability to make our own choices. That is what we want in addition to, and as urgently as, assistance in getting more food and better health." The ability to make their own choices is important both to them and to us.

ATTITUDE CHANGE

At the time of the 1972 Stockholm Conference, the developing countries generally felt that concern over the environment was something for only the more developed countries; a means by which we intended to keep them from developing. Gradually this outlook has changed. More and more countries today recognize the need to take the environment into account as development goes forward. Some countries are more advanced in this recognition than others; but all have in common the desire to make their own decisions, whether right or wrong.

Just as the level of receptivity varies on the part of the developing countries toward the utility of environmental evaluations, the desire to incorporate environmental assessments into the projects supported by the developed world also vary. Some welcome it, others tolerate it to a degree, and others don't want to hear about it. In the U.S. we have had NEPA since 1969 and are familiar with its advantages and its requirements, but in other parts of the developed world, the idea is just beginning to catch on. At a recent meeting of the Common Market countries of Europe, they identified consideration of the environmental aspects of projects they support in the developing world as a future goal.

ENVIRONMENTAL ANALYSIS

The techniques of environmental review need to be tailored to fit the type of development under review. The questions we ask may often be the same as those that would be asked in this country for similar type activities; but the final decisions we make may often be vastly different, because the benefits derived for the risk are so different. Nevertheless, environmental assessment is necessary to ensure that those decision-makers going forward with the development understand any likely consequences, consider alternative approaches, and make conscientious decisions based on such recognition.

In 1975, AID enunciated its policy with regard to environmental aspects of development assistance programs. Two principal goals were set forth:

1. to ensure that environmental consequences of AID-financed activities are identified and considered in collaboration with the host country prior to final decisions to proceed and that environmental safeguards are built into the project design; and

2. to assist developing countries in strengthening their appreciation and ability to evaluate potential environmental effects of their development strategies and projects.

The latter is more difficult than ensuring that we identify environmental aspects of our projects, principally because host countries are at different levels of understanding and appreciating environmental consequences. Programs must be tailored to their receptivity.

With respect to looking at host country projects to be considered for AID financing, we do have environmental regulations that outline the procedures the Agency follows in identifying impacts on the human environment and specific means by which these will be examined in depth. As near as I am able to tell, AID is the only donor country agency to have specific procedural requirements for environmental review and decision-making. Because these procedures apply to all the Agency's activities, not just capital improvement activities as in years past, we must seek ways in which environmental analyses can be structured both to fit the types of programs AID administers and meet the basic intent of NEPA—analysis before decision. Project-by-project analyses as well as generic or programmatic analyses are being carried out within AID.

The regulations are complex, even for those of us who begin to understand the process by which projects are considered, reviewed, analyzed and eventually approved. In preparing the regulations, we sought a means of integrating environmental analysis into the normal processing scheme, much as the Corps of Engineers does with their projects. We require an early screening analysis as soon as the project has been sufficiently formulated to determine whether it fits in with the overall Agency mandate, and then more detailed analysis based upon the results of the early investigation. I personally view this approach with mixed emotions. On one hand, it has been very helpful for ensuring that our Missions in developing countries realize that environmental analysis must be fully taken into account just like social and economic implications. On the other hand, requiring every action of an Agency to be subjected to a case-by-case

review has the potential for creating an atmosphere in which this requirement is seen only as a paper exercise, and an attitude of indifference is
developed on the part of Mission personnel.

We expect to reform this process by taking a more comprehensive look
at entire program actions, following these with more specific statements
on individual actions with significant impacts not addressed by the broader
analysis. This tiered approach is followed domestically by the U.S. Forest
Service. As soon as possible, we would like to look at many of our programs and evaluate where there is the potential for significant effects on
the human environment and how these effects can be eliminated or minimized. Such a review should identify components of the program that
will always need to be subjected to a more thorough individual environmental assessment.

We expect a programmatic or generic look would result in a document
that would be discussed with other governmental agencies and the public
before officially advising the CEQ of the conclusions we have reached
relative to a program. It would be a forerunner of Agency policy with
regard to the program studied. CEQ has suggested we call our generic
analysis a survey or review document. Prime examples of programs that
would fit this approach are activities of the Office of Food for Peace, integrated health care services, family planning programs, small-scale irriga-
tion projects, rural electrification, village-sized potable water systems, loans
to intermediate credit institutions, educational programs, and others which
seem to cross all regional bureaus.

The goal of stengthening the indigenous capabilities in the developing
countries is the more difficult and certainly the longer range goal. Its
approach must be varied and often utilize imaginative techniques. For
example, AID is utilizing and reimbursing local people in the Philippines
as part of their staff for development. Because we are not alone in supporting the development of the Third World and recognize that our principles of environmental concern may be different from those of other
donor countries, AID expects to put greater emphasis in the years ahead
on strengthening the institutional capabilities of countries to manage their
environment, regardless of who might be providing financial support to
development activities. If the Third World wants to make its own decisions, we should emphasize helping them to do that in a systematic and
responsible way, taking the environment into account.

It will mean helping them build or improve upon environmental training and management institutions that will educate their future policy-
makers, preparing and offering seminars and other instructional programs
that can help today's leaders realize the virtues and techniques of environmental analysis, and enlisting the assistance and advice of private voluntary

and international environmental organizations. It will also require communication of our actions and beliefs to those other donor countries and international bodies supporting development. We should take the leadership in working with these other groups to ensure that the environmental aspects of development are fully considered regardless of the origin of financing. The techniques may be different, but our objective of analysis as a prerequisite to decision-making should be universal.

The question "How much is enough?" is difficult to answer and is often dependent upon the type and location of the activity under consideration. We hope in AID that an environmental analysis will always be a timely benefit (boon) and not a trivial or wasteful activity (boondoggle).

REFERENCES

1. Dubos, Rene. "Symbiosis Between Earth and Humankind," *Science* 193:459-462 (1976).

SECTION II

STATE-FEDERAL REQUIREMENTS
COMPETING OR COMPLEMENTARY?

Paul E. Zigman

President
Environmental Science Associates
Foster City, California

Allan Milledge

Milledge and Hermelee
Miami, Florida

Almost from the time the United States was founded, different individuals and groups have expressed concern for the state and condition of America's environment. However, it wasn't until the 1950s and 1960s, that the progressively degrading condition of the environment we live in really received recognition. Public concern resulted in major legislation dealing with the control of water and air pollution, and in 1969 the enactment of a highly significant federal statute, the National Environmental Policy Act (NEPA). This Act has already resulted in major changes in the ways we approach and carry out land and resource use.

Following acceptance of NEPA—a broad-scale affirmative statement of national policy concerning the environment in which we live—a large number of states (and some of the nation's cities) enacted "mini-NEPA's"; that is, state statutes that were patterned after NEPA. These state laws vary both in scope and the manner in which they are applied. Although different in many respects, almost all state environmental laws start at a common point, *viz* that certain contemplated, significant state-funded land use projects must be preceded by

51

an analysis of their environmental consequences. Proceeding from this point of common departure, the individual state environmental statutes differ from each other in important ways.

This section includes chapters that discuss the environmental processes practiced in six states and in one large, metropolitan city. Chapters comment on the environmental legislation that exists in each state, and on the environmental ordinance that applies in the City and County of San Francisco. Individual experience is discussed, as well as the relationship of the separate state laws to the National Environmental Policy Act.

CHAPTER 6

THE CALIFORNIA ENVIRONMENTAL QUALITY ACT AND ITS IMPLEMENTATION

Paul E. Zigman

President
Environmental Science Associates
Foster, City, California

BASIC ENVIRONMENTAL QUALITY LEGISLATION

Within recent years, the United States has enacted environmental quality legislation which reflects new and striking changes in national and state policies and interests. If these new, emerging expressions of environmental concern do not diminish, we can expect that they will strongly influence future land and resource use. It is essential that all levels of government and all concerned organizations and citizens examine and understand the implications of this new legislation.

Because it expresses a *national* policy which deals with the *total* environment, the National Environmental Policy Act[1] is perhaps the single most important federal environmental quality statute. NEPA, directed primarily although not exclusively at public projects, contains the requirement for a written analysis—the Environmental Impact Statement—describing the possible environmental consequences of a proposed land use or other action. This requirement, in fact, "forces" compliance with the spirit and environmental protection policies of the Act. Of equal significance, NEPA has served as a foundation for similar legislation adopted by many states [for example, the California Environmental Quality Act (CEQA)[2]]. In some instances, the state-level legislation also specifies the need for some sort of environmental impact document.

It is difficult to overestimate the present and potential value of the environmental impact document. These reports have already exerted tremendous influence on decisions concerning the use of land and other natural resources. They have altered public administration practices. The latter is true not only in respect to the procedures followed, but also in the degree of public involvement in decisions reached.

In most states, the operating impact document has been the Federal EIS. As noted, some states require documents similar to the EIS. One of these is the California Environmental Impact Report (EIR). The EIR assumes special meaning because it results from a *state* environmental policy. Additionally, the California EIR is inclusive; it applies to both public *and* private projects. Finally, the California environmental statute and its concomitant impact report may well provide the model for similar legislation, containing similar impact report specifications, which will be enacted in other states.

Consequently, it is desirable to comprehend the primary features of CEQA and to recognize the nature and content of the mandated EIR. Such understanding can best be achieved by first examining the origins of the Act and, then, by reviewing its past and present administration. Moreover, because CEQA is patterned after NEPA, it is valuable to compare the two statutes and their implementing guidelines, and to define their differences and similarities.

THE CALIFORNIA ENVIRONMENTAL QUALITY ACT

As with the National Environmental Policy Act, the real importance of the California Environmental Quality Act is contained in its policy statements. The policy declaration in CEQA recognizes that the capacity of the environment is limited and states that the preservation of environmental quality is a statewide concern. Moreover, the Act asserts that every citizen has a responsibility to preserve and enhance the environment. The declared policy (21000)* also requires that the "State shall develop and maintain a high-quality environment..." and instructs that the "...long-term protection of the environment shall be *the* guiding criterion in public decisions" (emphasis added).

The significance and implications of the CEQA policy declarations are far-reaching and obvious. The quoted statements appeared in the statute as enacted in 1970. It is probably equally significant that when the Act was revised by the legislature in December 1972, and again in late 1976, after periods of extensive review, discussion and controversy, the policy statements remained as originally enunciated.

---

*CEQA citations are to sections contained in the Act.[2]

The California Environmental Quality Act was approved by the Governor in September 1970. It contained three elements of special importance, namely: an exposition of state environmental policy; a section that dealt with the requirement that all state agencies, boards and commissions shall prepare a detailed statement (21000) on "any project they propose to carry out which could have a significant effect on the environment;" and the requirement that the State Office of Planning and Research (OPR), which is in the Executive Office of the Governor, coordinate development of criteria and procedures for preparation and evaluation of the required detailed environmental statement (*i.e.,* the environmental impact report). In 1972 this responsibility was made more direct; OPR was instructed to "develop" not "coordinate development".

It is fair to say that for about two years after its passage, the Act was accorded only passing attention; response throughout the state was not very impressive, partly because of the statewide interpretation that the EIR requirement applied only to projects conducted or at least financially supported by state agencies. This nonresponsive attitude changed abruptly and decisively in late September 1972 as a result of what is referred to as "The Friends of Mammoth Decision."[3] The situation which occurred was as follows. One of the more attractive recreational ski areas in California is located near Mammoth Lake in the Sierra Nevada in Mono County. During the late 1960s, this recreational land use led to extensive residential development, and when the County Board of Supervisors issued a use permit for a large condominium project, a citizens organization, the Friends of Mammoth, brought suit to stop the development. The plaintiffs held that CEQA with its EIR requirements applied to any private project for which a permit or similar entitlement was needed. The California Supreme Court upheld this view and on September 21, 1972 delivered a judgment to the effect that it had been the intention of the California Legislature in enacting CEQA that it be applied to private developments as well as public projects.

The immediate results of this judicial ruling were dramatic. In some California cities construction literally stopped. However, many cities and counties moved rapidly to implement the EIR preparation and review process; in these, the only delay was that imposed by the process itself. No one was really sure of legal implications. In some instances, planning commissions refused to authorize permits. Much of the confusion rested in definition of "significant effect." In early November, in an obvious attempt to provide immediate guidance, the California Supreme Court issued a Modification of Opinion which addressed the significant-effect issue. This helped to some extent, but the uncertainty remained as to the exact intent and position of the legislature.

Immediately following the September court ruling, the Legislature began to reconsider CEQA with some urgency. During early December 1972, Assembly Bill 889[4] —which had been introduced in March of the year as a proposed amendment of CEQA—was enacted and amended the original 1970 Act. This amendment did a number of things, including affirming that CEQA indeed applies to private projects. This was done by defining "project" to include "activities involving the issuance to a person of a lease, permit license, certificate or other entitlement for use by one or more public agencies."

The new legislation contained two other important dictates. First, the State Office of Planning and Research was again instructed to prepare (and transmit to the State Secretary of Resources) Guidelines implementing CEQA. Within 60 days after enactment of the statute, the Secretary was to issue these guidelines. In the following, citations are made to specific California Guidelines sections. Unless otherwise noted the citation refers to California Guidelines revisions effective through September 30, 1975.[5] Second, the legislation declared, in effect, that a 121-day moratorium (ending in early April 1973) on EIR preparation was adopted. However, cities and counties that had established an EIR process were permitted to continue it during the moratorium; many did so.

During the period December 1972 to late 1975, some minor amendments were made in CEQA. Legislative attempts during the same period to modify CEQA in major ways were unsuccessful. The proposed major changes included such items as altering policy to declare that "long-term protection of the environment shall be a principal, rather than a guiding criterion in public decisions," and expanding the nature of the impact report to "include an economic impact statement," and regulating the report preparation process so that "no person shall be eligible to prepare an environmental impact report upon a project in which such a person has an economic interest." This proposed modification was originally introduced as AB938 (73/74 Legislative Session). The modification was reintroduced during the 74/75 session as AB 629, which would also have changed the policy statement of CEQA to include "decisions by governmental agencies at all levels shall be based and made upon a balanced consideration of all relevant environmental and economic factors." One change of lesser consequence than those cited was adopted during the 1972-75 period. This change deals with Notices of Determination (agency summary statements describing environmental consequences and project approval) and with legal recourse under the Act.

In late 1976, after months of deliberation and a number of hearings, the California legislature enacted AB 2679,[6] a bill amending CEQA. In the discussions leading to final formulation of AB 2679, a number of attempts were made to weaken the strong environmental policy statements of the original Act. None of these attempts was successful, and the State policy relative to environmental quality and environmental protection remains as expressed in the 1970 statute. However, other changes were made. These changes became effective on January 1, 1977; the more important are discussed in the following.

SIMILARITIES OF AND DIFFERENCES BETWEEN THE FEDERAL AND CALIFORNIA ENVIRONMENTAL ACTS

In many of its features, the California Environmental Quality Act is essentially the same as the National Environmental Policy Act. The nature and thrust of the policy pronouncements are the same (although CEQA is a much stronger and more directive environmental law.) Both statutes call for detailed impact statements on projects (actions) that might have significant environmental effects. Interagency review is specified in CEQA; this is also true in NEPA. Both laws encourage public participation in review and decision-making. Both instruments are supported by a set of implementing guidelines.[2,7] Other similarities can be cited. California seems to be somewhat more definitive in specifying *classes* of projects that require environmental impact reports; however, in a broad overall sense, the two Acts categorize projects with potential impact in not dissimilar terms.

NEPA states [102(2)(C)]:* "...include (an EIS) in every recommendation or report on proposals for legislation and other major federal actions, *significantly affecting the quality of the human environment...*" (emphasis added), and further explains significant effect on the quality of the human environment as originating "...by directly affecting human beings or by indirectly affecting human beings through adverse effects on the environment." In CEQA (21100), the parallel statement is "...shall prepare, or cause to be prepared by contract...an environmental impact report on any project...which may have a significant effect on the environment...."

In the 1976 CEQA amendments, significance is defined as meaning "...a substantial, or potentially substantial, adverse change in the environment." A somewhat expanded definition of significance is contained in the CEQA implementing Guidelines (15040), which address the definition in the following manner: "Significant effect on the environment means a substantial, or potentially substantial, adverse change in any of the physical conditions within the area affected by the activity including land, air, water, minerals, flora, fauna, ambient noise, and objects of historic or aesthetic interest."

---

*NEPA citations are to sections contained in the Act.[1]

Admittedly, the preceding only assists in understanding the differences and apparent similarities between the federal and California requirements for an environmental impact document. The differences reside primarily in interpretations of the words "action" (in the federal case) and "project" (in the California case). In this regard, further elaboration of significance occurs in both statutes.

In spite of its positive general statement concerning actions requiring detailed environmental statements, NEPA really provides minimum guidance concerning the "classes" of actions covered by the EIS requirement. Some clarification can be found in the NEPA Guidelines promulgated by the (federal) Council on Environmental Quality (CEQ), which states that the requirement includes project or program activities which use federal money or need a federal entitlement; actions which are likely to be highly controversial; a project whose impacts in combination (with each other) are considerable; projects which can curtail beneficial uses of the environment; projects which serve short-term objectives to the disadvantage of long-term aims (in the Act itself); and projects where several government agencies make decisions about partial aspects and it is reasonable to presume a cumulative significant impact. The NEPA Guidelines [1500.8(a) (3) (ii)] do comment on a few major classes of actions, such as highway, airport, sewer-system and water-resource projects.

CEQA Guidelines (15037) provide further clarification of the California EIR requirement by relating "Project means the whole of an action, which has the potential for resulting in a physical change in the environment, directly or indirectly" to (1) activities directly undertaken by any public agency, including but not limited to public-works construction; (2) activities undertaken by a person which are wholly or partly supported by public (financial) assistance; and (3) activities involving issuance by a public agency of a use entitlement.

Additional direction on the classes of projects that fall under the impact-document requirement is provided by both sets of guidelines in their appraisals of what constitutes "significant effect." NEPA Guidelines (1500.6) note that significant effects to be considered include secondary effects and both beneficial and detrimental effects. The NEPA Guidelines include an appendix which illustrates categories of environmental concern of impact which must be considered in arriving at a decision of significance or nonsignificance; those categories include water and air quality (energy and mobile source emissions), wastes, noise, radiation, land use changes and management, energy supply and natural resource development (petroleum, natural gas, coal, etc.), use in coastal areas, etc.

In addition to the definitions of "significant effect" reproduced above, CEQA Guidelines also speak to primary and secondary effects and contain

(Appendix G) examples of environmental consequences that must be considered in evaluation of significant effect and determination of need for the impact document. These examples include: possible conflicts with community environmental plans and goals; substantial negative aesthetic impact; effects on endangered species; impacts that breach official standards relating to solid waste; effects concerned with air and water quality and with ambient noise; effects leading to wasteful use of fuel, water or energy; and effects that may lead to adverse impacts on ground water, flooding, erosion, siltation, or could expose people or structures to geologic hazards.

The CEQA Guidelines (15082) contain four categories of conditions that *must* result in a finding of significance. Of these, the first (which is reasonably inclusive), states that significance obtains when "the project has the potential to degrade the quality of the environment, substantially reduce the habitat of a fish or wildlife species, cause a fish or wildlife population to drop below self-sustaining levels, threaten to eliminate a plant or animal community, reduce the number or restrict the range of a rare or endangered plant or animal or eliminate important examples of California history or prehistory." The remaining categories of mandatory significance are similar to the general assertions of significant impact found in the NEPA Guidelines. That is, they speak to short-term versus long-term impacts, cumulative impacts, and substantial adverse effects (both direct and indirect) on human beings.

Section 102(2)C in NEPA and Section 21100 in CEQA stipulate certain subjects that must be addressed in preparing a Federal EIS or California EIR, respectively. CEQA contains all the subjects specified in NEPA, and in addition, two others. However, a CEQA change made by the legislature in 1976[6] removes the mandatory consideration of all the listed topics in all EIRs. This change states that (1) relationships between short-term uses of the environment and the maintenance and enhancement of long-term productivity, and (2) significant irreversible environmental changes which would be involved in project implementation, need only be considered when the EIR deals with a plan, policy, or ordinance of a public agency, or the adoption by certain commissions of a resolution making a determination, or when the project in question will be subject to the Federal EIS requirement.

The two CEQA mandated subjects are induction of growth and measures for mitigation of impacts. The inclusion in CEQA of these topics is frequently cited as an indication of a significant difference between the state and federal acts. This is true only to an extent. Although NEPA wording does not dictate explicitly the exploration of growth-inducing impacts, the guidelines to this legislation encompass the concept in that they specify (1500.8) that ". . . population and growth impacts should be estimated if expected to be significant...and an assessment made of the effect of any possible change in population patterns or growth upon the resource base...," and also that "Agencies should also take care...to determine secondary population and growth impacts resulting from the proposed action and its alternatives." Thus, it would seem that the intent of both federal and California legislation concerning growth-inducing considerations in the impact analysis is much the same. NEPA may not require growth-inducing impacts but CEQA Guidelines do, see 1500.8(a)(1) (a)(3)(ii).

The second substantial distinction between the federal and the California Acts, consideration of mitigation measures, was further amplified as the original 1970 CEQA underwent revision. NEPA does not direct that impact mitigation be considered in preparing an impact statement, although its guidelines, in a single sentence, do instruct that when mitigation of adverse effects appears possible, the EIS should discuss how mitigation can be accomplished. In contrast, mitigation *must* receive direct attention in the California impact report. Not only does CEQA mandate this, but its implementing guidelines [15143(c)] direct that the EIR "describe significant, avoidable, adverse impacts, including inefficient and unnecessary consumption of energy, and measures to minimize these impacts." Proposed changes, dated November 12, 1976,[8] to these guidelines would insert "and water" after "energy." The discussion of mitigation measures "shall distinguish between the measures which are proposed by project proponents to be included in the project and other measures that are not included but could reasonably be expected to reduce adverse impacts. This discussion shall include an identification of the acceptable levels to which such impacts will be reduced, and the basis upon which such levels are identified. Where several measures are available to mitigate the impact, each should be discussed and the basis for selecting a particular measure should be identified. Energy conservation measures, as well as other appropriate mitigation measures, shall be discussed when relevant."

The issue of mitigation measures assumed even greater importance on January 1, 1977, when certain changes were made in CEQA. Prior to these changes, although mitigation had to be discussed in the EIR, the suggested measures could be ignored out-of-hand. Now the actual implementation of mitigation measures, although not mandatory, *is strongly encouraged*. Two changes (21002.1)[6] in the prior law have brought this about. The first of these changes states that one of the expressed purposes of the EIR is to "indicate the manner in which...significant effects can be avoided." The second reads, *"Each public agency shall mitigate or avoid significant effects on the environment of projects it approves or carries out whenever it is feasible to do so"* (emphasis added). Although the last directive is not absolute (because a subsequent section of the law indicates that mitigation is not required if its imposition is not feasible because of economic, social or other conditions), the state's desire to encourage use of mitigation is obvious.

To ensure that suggested mitigation is not disregarded because of arbitrary or capricious reasons, a companion change in CEQA (21081)[6] to the preceding insists that the public agency reviewing the mitigation section make a finding that the mitigation has been adopted or that adoption of the suggested mitigations are within the responsibility or jurisdiction of another public agency, or that certain conditions make adoption of the mitigation infeasible. This "finding" stipulation was reinforced by simultaneous change in the California guidelines [15088(b)][9] which repeats the Act's wording concerning use of mitigation and then states that such findings "...*shall be supported by substantial evidence in the record*" (emphasis added). There is no question that the record available of how and why a jurisdiction arrived at a particular decision on a proposed land use action will be valuable. Making such a record mandatory certainly responds to a court decision[10] that "The EIR process will enable the public to determine the environmental and economic values of their elected and appointed officials thus allowing for appropriate action come election day should a majority of the voters disagree."

A substantial difference between NEPA and CEQA came into being January 1, 1977. This difference deals with the time now permitted for preparation of the California EIR. Because much dissatisfaction has been expressed concerning the time it takes to prepare EIRs, the California statute, in Section 21151.5, has been revised to state that it is necessary for local agencies to establish time limits, *not to exceed one year,* for completing environmental impact reports. The initial one-year time point is the date on which the local agency receives the request for approval of the project. [Note: The one year stipulation applies to *all* (*i.e.,* private *and* public proposed projects subject to CEQA requirements. One can anticipate some difficulty here–how is the date requesting project approval, fixed for public projects?] A reasonable extension of the one-year period is permitted in the event of unforeseen circumstances *and* project applicant consent to the extension.

Many expect that, in some circumstances, it will be enormously difficult, *if not impossible,* to comply with the one-year time limit. If such circumstances do obtain, the local jurisdiction could be placed in an impossible position–it could extend the permitted time (presuming the applicant agrees) even though no unforeseen circumstances exist (and this would violate the statute provisions), or the jurisdiction could be forced to accept (and certify as complete) an incomplete EIR–again at variance with the provisions of the Act!

The recent CEQA amendments have led to another major apparent difference between the California Environmental Quality Act and the National Environmental Policy Act. In effect, the revised California Act (21100) now permits the EIR to limit its range of consideration to major environmental impacts. When this is done, it is necessary that the EIR briefly state the reasons for concluding that other project consequences, not dealt with in a detailed manner, are not significant.

Differences also appear on those parts of the federal and California guideline instructions dealing with preparation of the Final Impact Statement. (The Final Impact Statement (report) is the official document, certified as complete and adequate by the appropriate agency, which shall be considered by every public agency prior to its approval or disapproval of the project subject to the EIR requirement.) NEPA Guidelines stipulate, "where opposing professional views and responsible opinion...are brought to the agency's attention..., the agency should review the environmental effects of the action in light of those views and should make meaningful reference in the Final Statement to the existence of any responsible opposing view, indicating the agency's response to the issues raised." This may be compared to the California Guidelines instructions (15146) on preparation of the Final report, whose instructions include "Response (to comments received) shall describe the disposition of significant environmental issues raised...in particular, the major issues raised when the Lead Agency's position is at variance with recommendations, and objections raised in the comments must be addressed in detail giving reasons why specific comments and suggestions were not accepted." (The Lead Agency is the public agency which has the principal responsibility for conducting or approving a project and for preparing the environmental documents concerning the project.) The California instructions obviously are more demanding, not only in the choice of "shall" and "must" instead of "should," but also in the phrase, "addressed in detail."

Finally, another important difference between NEPA and CEQA deserves mention. This difference rests not in the consideration of projects, environmental effect or report preparation, but in the responsibilities given to the two organizations directed to prepare implementing guidelines. The California law states that the Office of Planning and Research shall prepare the appropriate guidelines for implementation of the Act. The directions to OPR are detailed and speak to objectives and criteria, procedures for determining significant impact, and specification of classes of projects that will not have a significant impact. Also, OPR is told that it must periodically review guidelines and that it must arbitrate disputes concerning Lead Agency status. By contrast, NEPA does not actually empower or direct the Council on Environmental Quality to prepare guidelines, although the Act does state that federal agencies are to identify and develop methods and procedures in consultation with CEQ to assure that unquantified environmental values are given appropriate consideration in decision-making. Guideline development instructions to CEQ are contained in Executive Order 11514[11] (which was promulgated "in furtherance of the purpose and policy of the National Environmental Policy Act") in the single statement [Section 3(h)]: "Issue guidelines to Federal agencies for the preparation of detailed statements on proposals for legislation and other Federal actions affecting the environment, as required in Section 102(2)(C) of the Act."

In regard to implementing guidelines, there is no doubt that instructions to the California Office of Planning and Research are more detailed than those received by the Federal Council on Environmental Quality. However, NEPA assigns other duties to CEQ which are not reflected in CEQA's directives to OPR. These additional responsibilities, given in Section 204 of the Act, and which are extended in Executive Order 11514[11] are important in that they include the conduct of research and development, collection and analysis of environmental information, review of agency environmental programs, preparation and recommendation of national environmental procedures, etc. In the long term, exercise of these functions can be more significant than specifications of impact report content.

IMPLEMENTATION AND IMPACT OF THE CALIFORNIA ENVIRONMENTAL QUALITY ACT

It has been about four years since the "Friends of Mammoth" decision, the California Legislature's acceptance of AB 889, and the consequent adoption of an amended California Environmental Quality Act. This is a substantial period of time, and it is appropriate to inquire how effective the legislation has been. Although a clear-cut and definitive answer is not yet possible, certain conclusions are possible.

It appears that statewide reaction to CEQA has varied quite a bit and, of course, this has resulted in a variety of local applications of the Act. In general, local strategies for administration of the Act have depended upon a number of factors, including the depth of environmental concern within a particular region and agency; the prevailing attitudes of a locale concerning growth and growth control (or resource use); the nature of the project under consideration; and, importantly, the degree of citizen interest and participation.

There is no doubt that many of the results of CEQA have been desirable. One very important beneficial aspect concerns the planning processes of individual jurisdictions. Two recent studies [12,13] concluded that

CEQA has brought more order and structure to the administrative procedures used to review and process proposed land developments. This has
taken place because of the formalized steps outlined in CEQA which
must be followed in conducting the initial environmental review and the
impact document preparation-review process. Because of this, in many
instances better decision systems to examine and judge planned developments have evolved, especially at the local level. This trend is encouraged
by a suggested Guideline revision (15013.5)[8] under review at present,
which admonishes "Public agencies should integrate the requirements of
CEQA with planning and environmental review procedures required by
law or administrative practice, so that all such procedures, to the maximum feasible extent, run concurrently, rather than consecutively." One
study[12] states emphatically, "Many local and State agencies have initiated
changes which have produced more effective *and accountable* decision-
making" (emphasis added). One presumes that accountability will become
even greater as individual jurisdictions start to comply with the recently
adopted (CEQA, 21081 and Guidelines, 15088) provisions concerning
"findings" and "substantial evidence in the record" (as related to use of
mitigation measures for adverse impacts).

There is much greater interagency examination of proposed projects
than previously. In a sense, CEQA has forced this to occur. As a case
in point, in 1974 an environmental impact report was prepared[14] dealing
with water importation to a California county. The Lead Agency was
the countywide water district. The report projected county growth as
a function of time, which differed from growth computations made by
county staff. Because the actual (true) growth which will be experienced
will be so important to jurisdictions in this county, valid prognostications
are obviously basic to future planning. As a result of the EIR, then,
planners from the different intracounty jurisdictions, particularly the incorporated cities, have met with the EIR preparers and with county representatives in attempts to understand and resolve the differences. In the
long run, this "forced" coordination must have a beneficial impact on
planning within the county. It is proper to note that sometimes this amplified coordination leads to delays in processing of the project. However,
in an overall sense, the intentions of this cooperative behavior are laud-
able; its value has been proven.

The CEQA Guidelines state (15013), "An EIR is a useful tool to enable environmental constraints and opportunities to be considered before
project plans are finalized. EIRs should be prepared as early as possible
in the planning process to enable environmental consideration to influence
project program or design." Although one recent investigation[12] notes
and deplores the fact that environmental assessments frequently are

provided late in the project design process, the sense and objectives of the Section 15013 directive are beginning to be realized. There is beginning to be a greater consideration of potential environmental consequences during initial project formulation and planning. Both in the private and public sectors, appreciation of the downstream requirement for an EIR has made the planner more sensitive to possible adverse environmental impacts of his project. Moreover, there is increasing recognition that preliminary generalized environmental assessment can, in fact, improve planning and design.

Not only do positive environmental protection or enhancement benefits accrue with early use of environmental data, but early environmental assessment is proving to be cost-effective. For example, a few years ago in conducting an environmental reconnaissance[15] of a proposed nature instruction facility in the Santa Cruz mountains, the environmental consultants provided useful data (e.g., geologic, hydrologic and ecological) shortly after the inception of the project. The remainder of the project design team (architect, engineer, geologist, etc.), using this information, could focus their efforts and avoid unnecessary work. It is expected that the value of early environmental assessment/reconnaissance will become increasingly apparent with time. One can expect that, at least for certain classes of proposed projects, development of precise project plans will be preceded more and more by a preliminary environmental reconnaissance.

In conforming to CEQA, state and local agencies have adopted different report-preparation and processing procedures. Sometimes the EIRs are prepared by in-house staff; on other occasions the reports are prepared by the applicant or his consultants or by consultants hired by the Lead Agency. Regardless of the manner of initial preparation, by law the ultimate responsibility for the EIR and its content resides in the Lead Agency.

As might be expected, the procedures used to arrange for preparation of the report can influence the end product. In general, it appears that reports prepared by consultants under contract to the agency are more dispassionate and evidence less bias. EIRs prepared by agency staff on their own public projects or reports prepared on private projects by, or directly for, the applicant have on occasion been out-and-out proponent advocacy documents. Of course, this is not always, or even frequently, the case. However, it is unrealistic to expect a project designer to be totally objective about the potential adverse environmental consequences of his own project. It is reasonable to expect—and demand—such objectivity when a "disinterested" third party prepares the environmental impact report.

The state, realizing that advocacy EIRs have been prepared, has taken a step that will assist in solution of this problem. This was done through a 1976 CEQA change[6] describing who prepares the EIR. The original Act's instructions (21151) to local government on this subject were "All local agencies shall prepare, or cause to be prepared by contract, and certify the completion of an environmental impact report. . . ." The 1976 change (21082.1) states "Any environmental impact report...shall be prepared *directly by, or under contract to,* a public agency" (emphasis added). Unfortunately, the 1976 amendment continues by saying that this doesn't prohibit public agency receipt of EIR information in any format. This is unfortunate because presumably "any format" would include an applicant-prepared, candidate Draft EIR. In any event, the thrust of the amendment is clear—public agencies should control preparation of the EIR.

It is mandatory that Draft EIRs be available for inspection by the public. This part of the environmental process is followed uniformly throughout the state. However, with this exception, there is no single, common set of overall procedures employed by separate state and local agencies to process Draft and Final Environmental Impact Reports. Although the Guidelines stipulate 30-90-day review periods (except in unusual circumstances), some jurisdictions established very short time spans for public review of Draft EIRs—as brief as 10 days. Other agencies have used very long periods.

The implementing Guidelines instruct that EIRs must be reviewed by public agencies having jurisdiction by law over the project and be made available to the public. The guidelines do not demand that public hearings on the EIRs be held. This is almost always done, however. Usually, the public hearings are convened at the end of the Draft EIR review period and before the Final EIR is prepared. This is not always so; at least one city holds the public hearing after preparation and publication of the Final EIR.

One undeniably adverse aspect of CEQA and environmental impact reports is that on some occasions the process has resulted in delay in project processing. When such delay is caused by the information contained in the EIR, such delay is understandable, and probably wholly justified. In such situations, planning commissions and city councils or their staffs first learn from the report of adverse impacts of the proposed project. Thus, more time is occasionally required to consider the project interactions, or perhaps to acquire additional explanatory information. Delays because of such circumstances seem reasonable. In other situations, delays are occasioned by overlong public agency review of the environmental document. Again, such delays are understandable (if not acceptable) if they result from high agency work loads or insufficient agency staff. Regrettably, sometimes agency delays result from agency procedures that are inadequate for reviewing and processing the environmental report. As discussed above, the upper limit on delay that has been imposed recently now requires that an environmental impact report be completed within a year following the time an application requesting approval of the project is received by the local agency.

The subject of delay is closely related to another aspect of the environmental report process—namely, the cost. The different components that contribute to the costs of California environmental impact reports have been discussed, and some studies have been completed.[12,13,16-19] However, these studies have dealt with different contributions to the total cost, have used different estimation methodologies, and have been of differing depths and complexities. As of this time, detailed, definitive information concerning total cost and the elements of total cost simply is not available.

Recognizing that the investigations carried out to date are inconclusive—that a really comprehensive study is sorely needed—it still remains of interest to note some of the results. One study[18] conducted during 1975, concluded that the total annual statewide costs associated with CEQA were in the range of $50-75 million and that CEQA costs (including processing delays) were on the order of 0.5% of total project costs. As an indication of the uncertainty in such figures, it is instructive to review the estimate made by another investigator. This study[19] involved roughly the same calendar time and concluded (based on extrapolation of data for one major California city), that statewide CEQA costs were somewhere in the range of $15-30 million per year. A third 1975-76 study[12] examined CEQA costs of state projects. This investigation provides the following: costs of environmental document preparation for state administration service facilities varied between 0.001% and 0.18% of project costs; for major state capital outlay projects, CEQA costs ranged from 0.01% to 2.6% of project costs; and, third, environmental document costs for state regulatory projects are typically less than 1% of projects being regulated.

CEQA implementation has certainly stimulated public participation in project evaluation. Some environmental consulting firms solicit public involvement and input during the time that the impact report is in preparation. This process not only reveals environmental concerns, but often will discover nonpublished sources of applicable environmental information and data. Regrettably, to date most public input (into the overall process) has occurred during the EIR review process and at the time when the Draft EIR is under formal consideration by the Lead Agency. Regardless of the time and method of citizen input, it is undoubtedly true that both public and private proposed projects now receive much more citizen attention than was the case prior to CEQA.

CEQA has had another real, beneficial consequence. Some planned projects, which appeared to have substantial adverse environmental impacts not counterbalanced by other positive attributes, have been deemed inappropriate and were not permitted to proceed as proposed. In some cases, the projects simply were not allowed, regardless of applicant-proposed modification or redesign. In other situations, the project was approved only after redesign or alteration to remove or mitigate the potential adverse environmental consequences.

In those California jurisdictions which really take CEQA seriously and attempt to conform to the spirit as well as the letter of the law, the mitigation measures and alternatives advanced in the impact report have been of substantial value. Either the project applicant voluntarily and independently altered his plans to remove or diminish undesirable impacts, or jurisdictions have imposed reasonable mitigations as a condition for acceptance of the project and issuance of the necessary entitlements to proceed. In one California city, the preparer of environmental impacts reports must actually relate possible mitigation measures to applicable city enforcing codes and ordinances. This permits the city planning commission and city council to perceive immediately those situations where the suggested mitigation is legally enforceable. One investigation[18] concluded that in 31% of the cases analyzed (23 California cities and 185 EIRs), project applicants mitigated at least one adverse impact identified in the environmental process. A companion result: in approximately 30% of the projects analyzed in the study, project approval was conditioned by inclusion of at least one special condition to mitigate an adverse impact. This report summarizes by stating "a total of 56% of the adverse environmental impacts for which mitigation was proposed in Draft EIRs are being mitigated as a result of combined decision-maker and applicant action." As noted previously, the issue of mitigation assumed increased importance on Jan. 1, 1977 when certain changes were incorporated into CEQA. The probable results of these changes are discussed elsewhere.[20]

The California Environmental Quality Act enunciates far-reaching and ambitious objectives for the preservation and enhancement of the total environment of the state. During the Act's relatively brief existence, it has proved to be a worthwhile, valuable statute and one that is slowly attaining its expressed goals and policies. Although much remains to be done to improve the overall effectiveness of the environmental process mandated by the Act, CEQA has resulted in better land and resource use decisions. Because of CEQA and its stipulated environmental impact report, more knowledgeable, informed judgments concerning land and resource development are possible. The exercise of these judgments has contributed to the preservation and improvement of environmental quality.

REFERENCES

1. PL 91-190, National Environmental Policy Act, January 1, 1970 (42 U.S.C. 4321 *et seq.*).
2. California Environmental Quality Act of 1970, September 18, 1970 (California Public Resources Code, Division 13, Section 21000 *et seq.*).
3. Friends of Mammoth v. Mono County Board of Supervisors, 8 Cal. 3d.
4. Knox, J. State of California Assembly Bill No. 889 (Chapter 1154), December 5, 1972.
5. Guidelines for Implementation of the California Environmental Quality Act of 1970 Incorporating all Amendments through September 30, 1976. (California Administrative Code, Title 14, Division 6).
6. Knox, J. State of California, Assembly Bill No. 2579 (Chapter 1312) September 28, 1976.
7. Council on Environmental Quality, Preparation of Environmental Impact Statements—Guidelines, August 1, 1973 (38 FR 147) and Amendment, September 27, 1974 (39 FR 189).
8. The Resources Agency of California. "Notice of Proposed Changes in the Regulations of the Resources Agency" (November 12, 1976).
9. The Resources Agency of California. "Order Adopting and Amending Regulations of the California Resources Agency" (December 23, 1976).
10. People v. County of Kern, 39 Cal. App. 3d 830.
11. Executive Order 11514, Protection and Enhancement of Environmental Quality, March 5, 1970 (35 FR 4247).
12. Office of Planning and Research, State of California. "The California Environmental Quality Act: A Review" (March 1976).
13. Public Policy Research Organization, University of California (Irvine). "The California Environmental Quality Act: Local Government Response" (December 1975).
14. Environmental Science Associates (Foster City, CA). "Environmental Impact Report—San Felipe Water Distribution System," EIR-ESA-3874 (December 1974).
15. Environmental Science Associates (Foster City, CA). "Environmental Reconnaissance and Impact Assessment—Outdoor Education Facility," ESA-EIR-1874 (June 1, 1974).
16. Zigman, P.E. "Costs of Environmental Impact Reports," Environmental Science Associates (Foster City, CA), remarks prepared for presentation at San Jose State University, San Jose, California, (October 31, 1975).
17. Construction Industry Research Board. "Cost of Delay Prior to Construction" (April 1975).
18. State of California Assembly Committee on Local Government. "California Environmental Quality Act: an Evaluation" (November 1975).

19.   Jokela, A.W. "Self-Regulation of Environmental Quality: Impact Analysis in California Local Government," EPA-600/3-76-040 (April 1976).
20.   Zigman, P.E. "Implications of the January 1977 Amendments to the California Environmental Quality Act," Environmental Science Associates (Foster City, CA), remarks prepared for presentation at the League of California Cities 1977 Planning Commissioners' Institute, Los Angeles, California, February 2, 1977.

CHAPTER 7

ENVIRONMENTAL ASSESSMENT:
THE FLORIDA PERSPECTIVE

Allan Milledge
Earl G. Gallop
> Milledge & Hermelee
> Miami, Florida

The National Environmental Policy Act and the Florida experience are both the progeny of the humanistic ethic of the turn of this decade. That ethic asserts that government has a responsibility to encourage "productive and enjoyable harmony between man and his environment."[1] While NEPA and the Florida experience derive from the same community genetic pool, NEPA and Florida have different characteristics and perspectives.[2]

NEPA was an attempt to create a new frame of reference for considering major activities undertaken by the federal government: a frame of reference that would include consideration of the effects of federal action upon the environment.[3] To achieve this, NEPA created a scheme for generating environmentally related information, and required the decision-making or action-taking agency to ingest, weigh and balance this environmental information with other factors in the agency decision-making process.

NEPA is revolutionary because it deals with environmental problems on a preventive and anticipatory basis. Rather than attempting to reclaim resources from past excesses and abuse, the Act enhances the basis for rational and cost-effective decision-making. Sections 2 and 101 provide a statement of purpose and a declaration of national environmental policy, respectively. The statement of purpose is worth repeating:

> "To declare a national policy which will encourage productive
> and enjoyable harmony between man and his environment; to

> promote efforts which will prevent or eliminate damage to the environment and biosphere and stimulate the health and welfare of man; to enrich the understanding of the ecological systems and natural resources important to the Nation. . . ."

Senator Henry Jackson summarized the philosophy of the Act in the following remark:

> "What is involved is a congressional declaration that we do not intend, as a government or as a people, to initiate actions which endanger the continued existence or the health of mankind. That we will not intentionally initiate actions which will do irreparable damage to the air, land, and water which support life on earth."[4]

SECTION 102 STATEMENTS

While the statement of purpose and declaration of national environmental policy form the heart of the Act, Section 102 is the muscle which provides "action-forcing" procedures. Federal agencies are required to determine the environmental impact of their action in decision-making. Section 102 requires agencies, which propose legislation or major federal actions significantly affecting the quality of the human environment, to prepare an EIS. The Act provides for circulation and input in the preparation of the statement. However, it is court decisions that suggest that substantive consideration of that input is required in the decision-making.[5]

In 1969, NEPA was radical and trendy. It attracted tremendous attention and became famous overnight. Even before experience under NEPA was substantial and its implications appreciated, environmentalists at the state level rushed to file bills and enact NEPA-like legislation. Puerto Rico was first, in 1970, followed by California. In 1971, Montana, New Mexico, Washington, Nevada, Delaware, Hawaii and North Carolina joined the ranks. The 1972 vintage crop brought in Indiana, Wisconsin, Massachusetts and Connecticut.[6]

THE ENVIRONMENTAL LAND AND WATER MANAGEMENT ACT (ELMS)

Florida did not take the EIS approach. Modeled after the American Land Institute (ALI) Model Land Development Code, Florida took a broader approach and enacted the Environmental Land and Water Management Act of 1972,[7] which is derived from an awareness that sound land use and growth guidance measures are needed to facilitate orderly development that is environmentally and economically sound. The Act provides for involvement of state, regional and local officials in *two* significant categories of land use.

Areas of Critical State Concern

The first involves Areas of Critical State Concern (ACSC).[8] The ACSC process focuses upon:

1. areas containing, or having a significant impact upon environmental, historical or archeological resources of regional or statewide importance;
2. areas significantly affected or having significant impact upon existing or proposed major public facilities or other areas of major public investment; and
3. proposed areas of major development potential, such as new communities.

The intent is to identify areas where uncontrolled or inadequately planned development would be unadvisable and to ensure, by designation as Areas of Critical State Concern, that general development principles are established for these areas. (See Florida Statutes, Chapter 380.05.)

Developments of Regional Impact

The second category involves Developments of Regional Impact.[9] A Development of Regional Impact (DRI) is broadly defined as "any development which, because of its character, magnitude, or location would have substantial effect upon the health, safety or welfare of citizens of more than one county."

The DRI concept is a new approach to land use management. It is a decision-making tool which ensures the inclusion of state, regional and local concerns in significant decisions relating to a number of large-scale land uses. As specified in administrative guidelines,[10] there are 12 types of projects that qualify as Developments of Regional Impact. However, not all projects in these categories are required to be reviewed. State guidelines provide threshold and location criteria which further define projects that are presumed to be of regional impact. Development types reviewed pursuant to Chapter 380 include:

- Airports
- Attractions and Recreation Facilities
- Electrical Generating Facilities and Transmission Lines
- Hospitals
- Industrial Plants and Industrial Parks
- Mining Operations
- Office Parks
- Petroleum Storage Facilities
- Port Facilities
- Residential Developments
- Schools
- Shopping Centers

A notable omission is major or interstate highways and interchanges.

If a project qualifies as a DRI, the appropriate Regional Planning Council analyzes the material provided by the applicant in the "Application for Development Approval" (ADA) and determines whether or to what extent the development:

1. will impact upon the environment or natural resources of the region;
2. will impact the economy of the region;
3. will affect the efficiency of public facilities in the area;
4. will affect the existing housing market;
5. will affect the efficiency of public transportation facilities;
6. will or will not comply with other criteria deemed appropriate by the Regional Planning Agency for determining regional impact.

The Council analyses and recommendations, the "Development of Regional Impact Assessment," are forwarded to the appropriate local government for consideration. After a DRI public hearing, local government issues a Development Order, approving, conditionally approving or denying the project. This Development Order is then reviewed by the Regional Planning Council and is subject to administrative appeal. The Regional Planning Council, the Division of State Planning, the owner or the developer have the right to appeal the Development Order to the Land and Water Adjudicatory Commission (the Governor and Cabinet).

FLORIDA GROWTH POLICY

In Florida, the Land Use Ethic means growth management within the context of a state growth policy, a policy which is lacking in the federal experience. Florida's state growth policy, enacted in 1974, was the first of its kind ever to be approved by any state legislature.[11] In its resolution, the Florida Legislature declared that:

> "It is the Policy of the State of Florida that the foremost function of its government shall be to help its citizens maintain and enrich the quality of life in Florida. . .
>
> This shall be done through Laws and Programs designed primarily to influence the kind, rate and extent of growth and ways of adjusting to that growth in any area in Florida. . .
>
> It shall not be the State's policy to stimulate further growth generally but to plan for and distribute such growth as may develop."[12]

In the context of Florida's State Growth Policy, one of the most important tools available to local government is the DRI review of large-scale developments, which has established a balancing process to assess such developments in terms of economic and environmental costs and benefits, the potential stress on public facilities and transportation systems, and the contribution of new development to housing needs of Florida citizens.[13]

NEPA AND THE FLORIDA ACT

In comparing NEPA and the Florida Environmental Land and Water Management Act, it is significant to note that both are brought infrequently to bear on the same development activity. It is a rare occasion that an entire development proposal requires both a DRI statement and an EIS. For example, the proposed development of an airport would require both. In the more usual case, where the proposed development requires a DRI statement, only certain aspects require an EIS. For example, a major residential development would require a DRI review, while the only connection of canals to navigable waters might require an EIS. Interestingly, the most frequent user in Florida of the EIS, the Department of Transportation, is essentially exempt from the state DRI requirements. Airports, ports, and some federally funded housing projects are subject to both requirements. An EIS prepared for an Army Corps of Engineers dredge and fill permit or for a complex source permit for a shopping center may be related to a development subject to DRI. The defunct New Communities program, of which there is no Florida experience, would be subject to both requirements. Finally, FHA or Veterans Administration loan assurances may relate to a development subject to DRI review.

THE APPLICATION FOR DEVELOPMENT APPROVAL

In moving from interface to philosophy and process, we see an identity of purpose: to encourage the productive and enjoyable harmony between man and his environment, and an intent to internalize in the government decision-making process, environmental impact considerations. From this point on, the Florida perspective becomes broader. Regional Planning Agencies are given a strong role and a statutory responsibility in preparing a report and recommendation upon the application for development approval (ADA), which is then utilized by local government in making their land use decision. What the role of the federal courts has been to the EIS in requiring a substantive and detailed statement, the Florida Regional Planning Councils are to the DRI process. The Councils have considerable statutory authority to determine the information sufficiency of the ADA. Upon acceptance of the ADA, the Council then has a statutory responsibility to determine the proposed development's impact upon the environment and natural resources of the region: upon the economy; upon the water, sewer, solid waste disposal and other necessary public facilities; upon the public transportation facilities; and upon the ability of people to find adequate housing within the region.

Under the federal system, action-taking, decision-making agencies evaluate their own proposals. Under the state system, the Regional Planning Council, having a strong geographic identity and a commitment to improving both the economy and the environment of the area, prepares the statement for use in the decision-making function of local governments. The Regional Planning Council and the Division of State Planning are given a statutory role, through an administrative appeal process, to assure substantial compliance by the local governments with the stated goals and intents of the ELMS Act. A final significant distinguishing feature is that the Florida ELMS Act is closely tied in with state, regional and local comprehensive planning functions which have recently received new statutory impetus. The DRI review process, then, can be viewed as a tool to implement growth policies incorporated into coordinated land development plans.

In conclusion, it is the Florida perspective and the developing Florida experience that the true benefits of the Land Use Ethic can be realized only by incorporating an impact statement into a larger, more comprehensive scheme of information generation and dissemination, regulation and growth management.

REFERENCES

1. NEPA of 1969, 42 USC Section 4321.
2. Finnell, G. L. "Emerging Issues Under the DRI Process of Section 380.06, F.S.," report and recommendations prepared for the Division of State Planning, Department of Administration, State of Florida, January 6, 1975.
3. Reitze, A. W., Jr. *Environ. Law,* 1(1): (1972).
4. 115 *Congressional Record* 4416 (1969); id at 1(2).
5. Environmental Defense Fund v. Corps of Engineers, 470 F.2d 289 (8th Cir. 1972); Minnesota Pub. Interest Research Group v. Butz, 498 F.2d 1314 (8th Cir. 1974).
6. Trzyna, T. C. *Survey of State Environmental Policy Acts,* Center for California Public Affairs, Claremont, 1973, cited in Donald G. Hagman, *NEPA-Like State Laws,* UCLA Law School, Los Angeles, 1973.
7. Chapter 380, *Florida Statutes.*
8. §380.05, *Florida Statutes.* This section was declared unconstitutional in *Cross-Key Waterways, Inc. v. Askew,* Case No. Y-362, Fla. 1st, D.C.A., decided 10 August 1977. The authors, with the firms Paul & Thomson and Flemming & Neuman, represent the Florida Audubon Society and The League of Women Voters as Amici on the appeal to the State Supreme Court.
9. §380.06, *Florida Statutes.*
10. Chapter 22 F-2, *Florida Administrative Codes.*
11. Rhodes, R. M. "DRI's and Florida's Land Development Policies," *Florida Environmental and Urban Issues,* II(3) (1975).
12. House Resolution 1033, Florida Legislature, 1974.
13. Rhodes, R. M. "DRI's and Florida's Land Development Policies," *Florida Environmental and Urban Issues,* II(3):16(1975).

CHAPTER 8

ENVIRONMENTAL ASSESSMENT IN MICHIGAN: THE MAN/ENVIRONMENT RELATIONSHIP IN THE HUMAN ECOSYSTEM

Terry L. Yonker

Executive Secretary
Michigan Environmental Review Board
Lansing, Michigan

MICHIGAN ENVIRONMENTAL REVIEW BOARD

Governor William G. Milliken established the Michigan Environmental Review Board on July 26, 1973, by issuing Executive Order 1973-9.[1] The Board was given responsibility to advise the Governor on major environmental issues and policy matters and to coordinate a state environmental impact review process.

In his written charge to the Board on December 7, 1973, the Governor carefully set forth the approach he desired the Board to take in formulating environmental policy recommendations and environmental impact review procedures:

> I am particularly concerned that the Board carry out its duties and responsibilities utilizing a broad human ecological approach. By this I mean that policy recommendations and environmental impact review procedures should give due consideration to people, the relationships among people, their collective relationship to the environment as a whole. Key factors that should be considered are:
>
> 1. The health, safety and welfare of the people.
> 2. Technology available to solve economic, social and environmental problems and the limitation technology imposes.

3. The role of organizations in dealing with economic, social and environmental problems, including state and local governments, industries, agriculture, transportation, commerce, and public and private institutions.
4. The maintenance and enhancement of the total environment, including not only the vitality of flora and fauna, but also the quality of our basic physical resources of air, water, land, minerals and energy.[2]

After several months it was determined that the legal limits to the Board's authority as an advisory body required modification to be consistent with the Governor's authority as Chief Executive under the Michigan Constitution. Executive Order 1973-9 was extensively rewritten to more clearly define the scope of the Board duties and responsibilities. The revised Order, Executive Order 1974-4, was issued by Governor Milliken on May 3, 1974.[3] Less apparent, but equally significant, were language changes in Executive Order 1974-4 which clearly mandated a different approach to the formulation of environmental policy recommendations and environmental impact review procedures. These language changes were consistent with the Governor's original charge to the Board. Emphasis was placed on the need to consider the impact that proposed State policies and actions may have, not only on the environment, but also on human life. Environmental decisions were not to be made in a vacuum while disregarding the impact that such decisions may have on health, safety and welfare of Michigan citizens.

Human ecological definitions of the terms "environment" and "human life" were written into the concluding paragraph of Executive Order 1974-4 to provide additional guidance to the Board on the extent to which consideration was to be given to human as well as environmental factors in fulfilling the Board's advisory duties and responsibilities:

> For the purpose of this Order, environmental shall be defined as the natural resources of the State, including air, water, land, mineral and energy resources, and the flora and fauna (not including human beings). Human life shall be defined as the citizenry, possessing unique demographic, socioeconomic and cultural characteristics, socially organized, and possessing a repertoire of techniques (technology) to obtain sustenance from the environment.[3]

The remainder of this chapter discusses the human ecological approach and its application in the formulation of environmental policy recommendations and procedures for the review of state and federal environmental impact statements.

CLASSICAL ECOLOGY

Ecology as a science is historically related to the biological sciences. Ecologists have traditionally studied the pattern or relations between organisms and their physical environment.

An ecosystem is defined by Odum in *Fundamentals of Ecology* as "a unit that includes all of the living organisms (*i.e.,* the 'community') within a given area interacting with the physical environment so that a flow of energy leads to clearly defined trophic structure, biotic diversity and material cycles (*i.e.,* exchange of materials between living and nonliving parts) within the system."[4] Ecologists may define an ecosystem as being a forest, pond, meadow or other complete unit in a giver area. Figure 8-1 illustrates an idealized concept of a classical ecosystem.

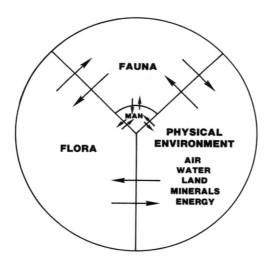

Figure 8-1. The idealized classical ecosystem.

Until recently, little attention has been focused by ecologists on the specter of human dominance in the biological scheme of things. Human beings occupy but a niche in the classical ecosystem, yet have the capacity to virtually destroy it in a single devastating blast. Modern industrial man has managed to delay the operation of negative feedback mechanisms that would normally reduce human overpopulation and stabilize the ecosystem. He has forestalled ecological Armageddon.

HUMAN ECOLOGY

It is generally recognized that if humans were still inventing the wheel, marvelling at fire and picking and gathering, they could not exist in such large numbers as they do today. People, by virtue of their technology and social organization, have attempted to shape an ecosystem favorable to their own continued domination over natural systems. They utilize virtually the entire classical ecosystem of the ecologists as their "environment" and functionally separate themselves from it wherever possible. For example, they build houses to insulate themselves from the cold; they develop an agricultural industry to sustain themsleves and to lessen dependence on natural food chains; they form public utilities to purify water; and they develop independent sources of energy to supplement their daily dole from the sun. Although humans are beginning to realize they are totally dependent on the environment for their very existence, they continue to extract physical resources from the environment at a record pace and return their wastes to the environment without much concern about its long-term productivity and regenerative capacity.

The science of human ecology was not developed out of human arrogance, but because scientists had to take a closer, more realistic look at the beast that dominates all others on the face of the earth. It is an eclectic science, that borrows heavily from both the biological and social sciences. Generally, human ecology deals with the relations between human groups and their physical or geographical environment.

Otis Dudley Duncan, in *From Social System to Ecosystem,* suggests that an interdisciplinary approach be taken in the study of human ecology, including input from physical as well as social scientists, economists as well as biologists, and capable scholars from other disciplines. Duncan proposes a simple framework for study, which he calls the human ecological complex. The complex is composed of four elements: population, organization, environment and technology (POET).[5]

Duncan defines population as an aggregate of human beings having unit characteristics, living in a given area. His organization includes the sociofunctional relationships that exist among humans which facilitate sustenance-producing activities and satisfy institutional and other social needs. (Organization would include such entities as government, industrial, agricultural, commercial and transportation organizations as well as public, private and religious institutions.) He defines technology as the repertoire of techniques employed by humans to assist in the organization of sustenance-producing activities. Duncan's environment includes the physical environment (air, water, land, minerals and energy) and the flora and fauna found in the biologist's ecosystem.[5] Figure 8-2 illustrates the human ecological complex.

The Duncan complex serves a useful purpose in that it forces consideration of socioeconomic, cultural and technological factors in studying the man/environment relationship. An impact on any one complex element will stimulate a response in another. For example, an uncontrolled increase in the population of a given area, creating food shortages, will likely stimulate an organizational response for the development of new technology for improved

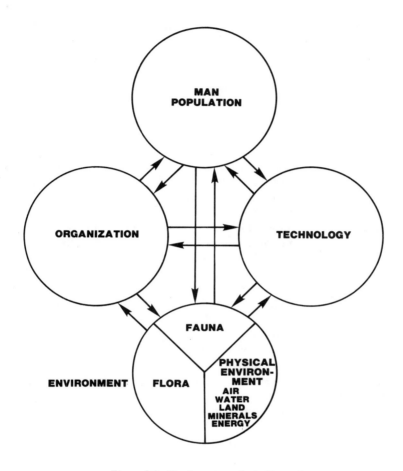

Figure 8-2. The human ecological complex.

birth control methods, increased food production or both. In either case, there is a measurable impact on the environment: reduced stress due to controlled population growth or increased stress due to the expansion of agriculture.

THE HUMAN ECOSYSTEM

Professor Duncan did not take the final step in the synthesis—that of actually defining the human ecological complex and the interacting complex elements as a human ecosystem.[6] The elements of population, organization and technology do interact as a unit of human life with the environment in

a given area. Flow of resources and wastes within and between the units of
the system constitutes a material cycle which lends further credance to the
definition. As intended, the definition of human life as comprising the complex elements of population, organization and technology is consistent with
the definition of human life in Executive Order 1974-4. Duncan's definition
of environment is also consistent with its definition in the Order. Again, for
the purposes of this chapter, human ecosystem shall be defined as a unit of
human life interacting with the environment in a given area.

How the human life unit interacts with the environment within the human
ecosystem should be explored in greater depth. Many humans attempt to
avoid direct contact with their environment, preferring instead to control
man/environment interaction in a way to maintain human dominance in the
ecosystem. Human beings, through their organization and technology, have
designed an ecosystem filter which they utilize to control the flow of resources and wastes in an effort to forestall the operation of negative feedback
mechanisms that would diminish this position of dominance.

The ecosystem filter concept is useful in that it serves as a focal point for
decisions within the human ecosystem. It serves as the primary point where
resource flows from the environment and waste flows to the environment
can be monitored. By testing the vitality of the human life unit and the
environment and by monitoring resource and waste flows, measures can be
taken to balance resource and waste flows to minimize adverse impacts to
either the human life unit or the environment. If toxic waste flows threaten
the vitality of the environment, as determined by monitoring indicator species
of flora and fauna, the toxic wastes can be treated within the human life
unit before being discharged to the environment, providing the organization
and technology are available to do it. Wastes can also be recycled within the
human life unit so that harmful discharges to the environment can be reduced. If a resource flowing to the human life unit is of poor quality and it
threatens the vitality of that unit, as indicated by increased human morbidity
or increased treatment costs, lower productivity and adjustments in lifestyle
may result. Figure 8-3 illustrates the human ecosystem and the ecosystem
filter.

THE STATE AS A HUMAN ECOSYSTEM

Biological ecologists tend to see an ecosystem as a unit containing all
living organisms interacting with the physical environment within a given
area. The boundaries of the ecosystem tend to be natural, such as a lake,
bog or meadow.

Human ecologists view the ecosystem as a unit of human life interacting
with the total environment (air, water, land, minerals, energy, flora and other

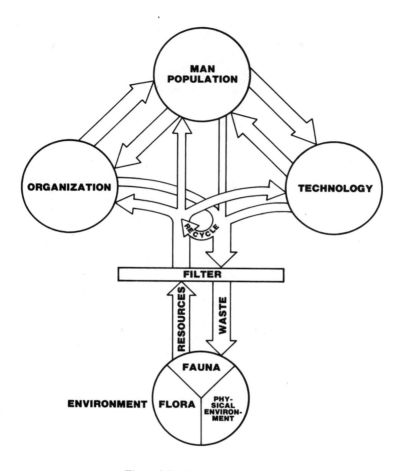

Figure 8-3. The human ecosystem.

fauna) in a given geographical area that has politically determined boundaries. A state can be defined as a human ecosystem without seriously compromising the definition. The citizens of the state are a population of human beings that is organized and in possession of a repertoire of techniques (technology) to obtain sustenance from the environment.

APPLICATION–THE FORMULATION OF ENVIRONMENTAL POLICY

One of the most valuable features of the human ecological approach is the thought-ordering process it evokes–a systematic view of the

man/environment relationship. The flow of resources and wastes through
the ecosystem filter represents the focal point for major decision-making.
Monitoring resource and waste flows and vitality indicators of both the environment and human life provide essential information on the condition of
the human ecosystem. An ability to determine the condition of the human
ecosystem leads logically to a decision as to whether the condition of the
ecosystem is acceptable in the eyes of the population. A decision by the population through an organizational entity such as state government to improve
the condition or health of one of the units of the human ecosystem would
constitute public policy. Webster defines policy as: "a definite course or
method of action selected from among alternatives, and in light of given
conditions, to guide and determine present and future decisions."

A policy to improve the quality of the environment must consider ecological realities: the relationship between man and his environment, the
organization that has evolved enabling man to cope with his environment
and the technology man has developed to facilitate his existence. Utilizing
the human ecological approach, alternative policies can be evaluated sys-
tematically to determine which course of action will produce the desired
improvements in environmental quality, *i.e.*, balancing resource and waste
flows, improving the stability of the ecosystem, altering existing organizational responses to environmental problems and applying new technology.

Although a comprehensive environmental policy has yet to be formulated
for Michigan, the task represents less of a chore when the man/environment
relationship in the human ecosystem is well understood. Further monitoring
and data gathering will be necessary to better inform the public of the available alternatives before decisions are made.

MICHIGAN ENVIRONMENTAL IMPACT REVIEW PROCESS

The primary purpose of environmental impact review processes is to enable
decision-makers to assess the impact of proposed actions on the environment
before proceeding with the action. In Michigan, under Executive Order
1974-4, decision-makers are obligated to consider not only the impacts of
proposed actions on the environment but also impacts of such actions on
human life.

Crucial questions regarding vitality of the human life and environmental
units and the flows of resources and wastes between these units follow
naturally. For example, what impact will a proposed action have on waste
and resource flows across the ecosystem filter? Will wastes be recycled within
the human life unit or is treatment of the wastes the only alternative? Does
technology exist to mitigate adverse impacts or must new technology be
developed? Will special organizational and institutional responses be required

to mitigate adverse impacts? Will mitigation require additional resources? Will ecosystem stability be impaired permanently? The human ecological approach serves as a fairly sophisticated, thought-ordering process for determining the impacts that can be anticipated should an action proceed.

Although Michigan has had an environmental impact review process since 1971, the review of state environmental impact statements was conducted by a rather specialized group of individuals from a selected number of state departments most directly involved with the actions proposed. The review was not broad enough to satisfy the major concerns of a majority of state departments which deal broadly with issues affecting the vitality of the state ecosystem as a whole.

Interdepartmental Environmental Review Committee

To broaden the review, Governor Milliken provided for the establishment of the Interdepartmental Environmental Review Committee in Executive Order 1974-4.[3] The Committee, or INTERCOM as it is called, is composed of members in high-level positions from each of the 19 state departments. INTERCOM has the essential interdisciplinary breadth and depth of experience to provide a thorough review of proposed state actions from a human ecological perspective.

The preparation and review of state environmental impact statements is governed by "Guidelines for the Preparation and Review of Environmental Impact Statements," issued by the Governor pursuant to Executive Order 1974-4.[7] Figure 8-4 illustrates the general flow of state environmental impact statements through the environmental impact review process, from a decision by a department to prepare an EIS to the transmission of recommendations on the proposed action to the Governor.

The Guidelines also provide for the preparation of abstracts and negative declaration statements by state departments. Abstracts are prepared on proposed actions when a department is unsure of the need for a full environmental impact statement. Negative declaration statements are prepared on major proposed actions when insignificant impacts on human life and the environment are expected.

Public involvement has been an essential ingredient in the review process from its inception and is now required under Michigan's "Open Meetings Law," Act 267, Public Acts of 1976. The provision for minority reports from INTERCOM reflects a concern that all points of view be considered in preparing final recommendations for the Governor, even though INTERCOM members adopt a majority report for consideration by the Environmental Review Board.

The entire review process takes a minimum of 60 days to allow for adequate public input and a maximum of 120 days, depending on the complexity

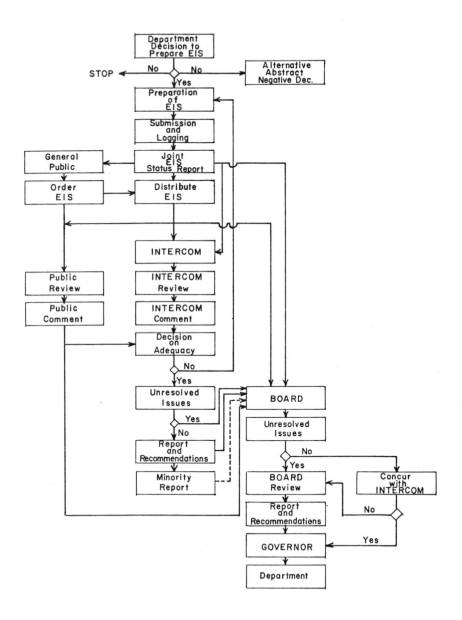

Figure 8-4. Flow diagram for state Environmental Impact Statements.

of the issues surrounding the proposed action and the adequacy of the environmental impact statement. To date, approximately 140 EIS's have been processed utilizing the two-stage INTERCOM/Board review process.

FEDERAL ENVIRONMENTAL IMPACT REVIEW PROCESS

In the same way that the state can be defined as a human ecosystem, so too can the nation. The United States has a population organized and possessing technology to derive sustenance from the environment within a given area. The state human ecosystem can be defined as a subsystem of the national human ecosystem, again without compromising the definition of a human ecosystem.

To assess adequately the impact of proposed federal actions on the state subsystem, the state must consider the impact of proposed federal actions within or affecting the state as external impacts on the human life and environmental units of the state ecosystem. For example, a decision to reduce the allocation of natural gas to the state by the Federal Power Commission would reduce the flow of energy to the state subsystem. Since Michigan imports 95% of its energy needs, the reduction would cause a severe impact on the human life unit of the subsystem in the form of an economic downturn and an attendant loss of business, employment and income.

In response to past reductions, the population, through its organizations (gas and utilities and the Public Service Commission) pioneered natural gas storage technology in an effort to balance out peak demands by storing natural gas in depleted gas fields during the summer months. Another response has been an organizational effort to increase the flow of natural gas from the state's environmental unit by applying advanced drilling technology to the development of domestic oil and gas reserves in the Niagaran Trend of Northern Michigan. Still another response has been an organizational effort to conserve energy within the human life unit, thus reducing the flow of hydrocarbons from the environmental unit. An external action by the federal government caused an internal response by the state to attempt to stabilize the state subsystem.

When a proposed federal action is preceded by a federal draft environmental impact statement (FDEIS), an opportunity is presented for the state's population, individually or collectively through an organization in state government, to assess the impact of the proposed federal action before it proceeds. Executive Order 1974-4 provides ample authority for the review of FDEIS's.[3] However, procedures for such reviews have only recently been adopted by the Interdepartmental Environmental Review Committee (See Appendix B). The forthcoming publication of an FDEIS on the proposed U.S. Navy Project Seafarer communication system in the Upper Penninsula

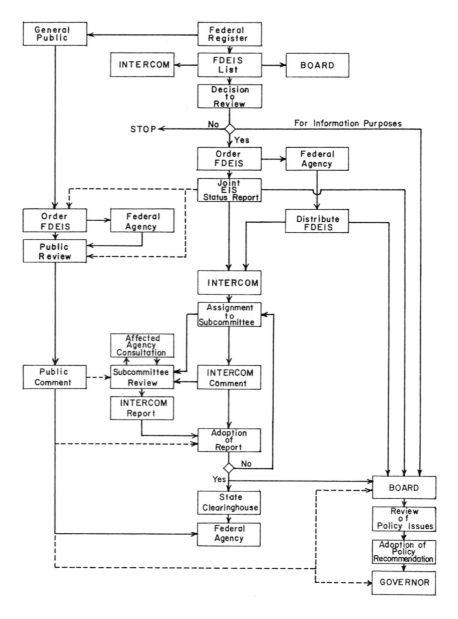

Figure 8-5. Flow diagram for Federal Draft Environmental Impact Statements.

of Michigan provided the necessary incentive to adopt FDEIS review procedures as did the awareness on the part of INTERCOM members that the state review of FDEIS's is not adequately provided for by the A-95 State Clearinghouse review mechanism.

The technical review of FDEIS's is conducted by the Interdepartmental Environmental Review Committee. The Board has responsibility for addressing major policy issues and potential state-federal policy conflicts associated with proposed federal actions. Once the review of FDEIS's is complete, the results of the review are forwarded to the Governor and to the State Clearinghouse for transmittal to the initiating federal agency. Public involvement is encouraged at the state level but cannot substitute for a direct response by citizens to the federal agency. A flow diagram of state FDEIS review process is illustrated in Figure 8-5.

It should be noted that the state review of FDEIS's can rarely be completed within the established 45-day review period. The INTERCOM review can be completed within a 34-62 day period following publication of the availability of the FDEIS in the *Federal Register*. Board action on the FDEIS may take 18 additional days to complete. The entire timetable for review depends on how quickly federal agencies respond to requests for copies of the FDEIS.

The Governor has asked that a broad human ecological approach be taken in formulating environmental policy and establishing an environmental impact review process in Michigan. A human ecological approach would appear to be superior to a classical ecological approach due to man's influence over the environment. The flow of resources and wastes between the human life and environmental units of the human ecosystem provides a focal point for decision-making, leading to the formulation of environmental policy and the establishment of an environmental impact review process. The value of the human ecological approach is that it serves as a sophisticated thought-ordering process when assessing the impact of state and federal actions on the environment and human life units of the state human ecosystem.

REFERENCES

1. State of Michigan, Executive Order 1973-9, July 26, 1973.
2. Milliken, W. G., Governor. Letter to Dr. Howard A. Tanner, Chairman, Michigan Environmental Review Board (December 7, 1973).
3. State of Michigan, Executive Order 1974-4, May 3, 1974. The full text of Executive Order 1974-4 appears in Appendix A.
4. Odum, P. *Fundamentals of Ecology* (Philadelphia, Pennsylvania: W. B. Saunders Company, 1971), p.8.
5. Duncan, O. D. "From Social System to Ecosystem," *Sociol. Inquiry* 31:140-149 (1961).
6. Duncan, O. D. in *The Study of Population,* O. D. Duncan and P. M. Hauser, Eds. (Chicago, Illinois: University of Chicago Press, 1959), p.684.

7.   Michigan Environmental Review Board. "Guidelines for the Prepara-
     tion and Review of Environmental Impact Statements under Executive
     Order 1974-4 " (Lansing, Michigan: Department of Management and
     Budget, 1975).

APPENDIX A

STATE OF MICHIGAN

Executive Office * Lansing

Executive Order
1974 - 4

Establishing the Michigan Environmental Review Board

WHEREAS, the quality of the environment of Michigan is of great concern to all citizens
of the state; and

WHEREAS, there is a need for the Governor to obtain a continuing review of state policies
and actions in terms of their impacts on the environment and associated impacts on
human life; and

WHEREAS, the Department of Natural Resources has been given new responsibilities
which involve decisions affecting the lives of all the state's citizens; and

WHEREAS, there is a need for a special body to advise the Governor on environmental
matters and carry out the responsibilities embodied in Executive Directive 1971-10, the
environmental impact review procedure;

THEREFORE, I, WILLIAM G. MILLIKEN, Governor of the State of Michigan, pursuant
to the Constitution and Laws of the State of Michigan, do hereby ordain and establish
the Michigan Environmental Review Board which shall be charged with the following
duties and responsibilities:

1. To provide advice to the Governor and state agencies on environ-
    mental issues.
2. To make recommendations to the Governor, Director of the Depart-
    ment of Natural Resources or other state agencies on environmental
    policy issues as may be requested by the Governor.
3. To conduct public hearings or conferences at the Governor's request
    for receiving recommendations on state environmental policies
    from the general public.
4. To assist the Governor in reviewing federal and state environmental
    impact statements and to identify actions of state agencies that
    should be suspended or modified if such actions should seriously
    threaten the quality of the environment or human life.

The Board shall consist of 17 members, appointed by and serving at the pleasure of the
Governor, of whom 10 members shall be appointed from the general public and 7 members as follows:

The Attorney General
Director, Department of Agriculture
Director, Department of Commerce
Director, Department of Natural Resources

Director, Department of Public Health
Director, Department of State Highways and Transportation
Director, Department of Management and Budget

The Governor shall designate a Chairman and a Vice-Chairman of the Board from among the general public members and members of the Board may designate an alternate to perform their functions in the event of the member's unavoidable absence. The Department of Management and Budget shall provide an Executive Secretary for the Board and additional staff support as may be determined to be necessary to fulfill the duties of the Board.

The Michigan Environmental Review Board shall forward to the Governor for his consideration within 60 days, interim guidelines for the preparation of environmental impact statements by state agencies including procedures for the timely review of such statements. Before December 31, 1974, the Board shall forward to the Governor for his consideration finalized guidelines after allowing sufficient public review and comment.

Further, I hereby order that each agency of State Government forward to my attention an environmental impact statement on each proposed major action within their jurisdiction that may have a significant impact on the environment or human life. If such a statement must be prepared pursuant to federal or state statute or regulation, that statement will comply with this requirement. Environmental impact statements not required by federal or state statute or regulation shall be prepared as succinctly as possible in accordance with guidelines to be issued by me. Each statement shall contain the following:

1. A description of the probable impact of the action on the environment, including any associated impacts on human life.
2. A description of the probable adverse effects of the action which cannot be avoided (such as air or water pollution, threats to human health or other adverse effects on human life).
3. Evaluation of alternatives to the proposed action that might avoid some or all of the adverse effects, including an explanation why the agency determined to pursue the action in its comtemplated form rather than an alternative.
4. The possible modifications to the project which would eliminate or minimize adverse effects, including a discussion of the additional costs involved in such modifications.

State agency environmental impact statements received by my office will be forwarded to the Environmental Review Board in accordance with my approved guidelines. The Board shall forward each statement for review to an Interdepartmental Environmental Review Committee which shall consist of one member appointed from each state department in a manner prescribed by my guidelines. The Committee shall be Chaired by the Executive Secretary of the Board who shall forward the Committee findings on each statement to the Board for its action as set forth in my guidelines.

Environmental impact statements must be completed by the agency within the constraints of statutory deadlines, rules and regulations in sufficient time to permit an adequate review of the statement and consideration of alternative courses of action if necessary to protect the environment and human life.

State agency environmental impact statements will be circulated by the Board to appropriate local agencies, public and private organizations and by request to interested citizens for their review and comment under provisions to be included in my guidelines. The

Board shall provide a forum for public comment on any major action if it determines that the public has not had sufficient opportunity to be heard.

Whenever a draft federal environmental impact statement prepared pursuant to the National Environmental Policy Act is received by the State Clearinghouse, it shall notify the Board. The Board may request copies of the statement and may review it in a manner consistent with the review of state agency environmental impact statements as provided for in my guidelines. The Board may forward a summary of its actions on the statement to the State Clearinghouse.

For the purpose of this Order, environment shall be defined as the natural resources of the State, including air, water, land, mineral and energy resources and the flora and fauna (not including human beings). Human life shall be defined as the citizenry, possessing unique demographic, socio-economic and cultural characteristics, socially organized and possessing a repertoire of techniques (technology) to obtain sustenance from the environment.

This Order shall supersede the provisions of Executive Directive 1971-10 dated September 30, 1971 and Executive Order 1973-9 which are hereby rescinded.

APPENDIX B

PROCEDURES FOR THE REVIEW OF
FEDERAL DRAFT ENVIRONMENTAL IMPACT STATEMENTS
(Excerpt)

Federal Draft EIS (FDEIS)

1. The following are general assigned responsibilities in the review of FDEIS's:
    a. FDEIS's shall be reviewed utilizing the same criteria as for the review of EIS's. INTERCOM shall place special emphasis on the review of the impacts of a proposed major federal action on the environment and human life within the State of Michigan. The Board shall place special emphasis on preparing policy recommendations for the Governor on policy issues raised by INTERCOM and the general public following a review of the FDEIS.

    b. Public involvement in the INTERCOM review of FDEIS's may include forwarding written comments on the statement to INTERCOM or making a brief appearance before INTERCOM offering verbal comments on the statement. Public comments for State review purposes shall be limited to those which will assist INTERCOM in the review of the statement or which raise major policy issues. Public comments on major policy issues shall be forwarded to the Board for further consideration. Public comments received by the Board or INTERCOM shall not substitute for direct public comments to federal agencies.

    c. The Chairman of INTERCOM may establish two or more 4- or 5-member subcommittees which, if established, shall be assigned FDEIS's selected for review as they are received. The subcommittees shall prepare a draft report on FDEIS's for consideration by INTERCOM. The report shall include an abstract of the FDEIS, general observations, a critique of the statement, recommendations, and a listing of major policy issues. INTERCOM may adopt the report or return it to subcommittees for

necessary revisions. The Chairman of INTERCOM shall forward copies
of the report to the State Clearinghouse and to the Board.

d. The Board shall review the FDEIS, the INTERCOM report on the FDEIS,
public input and other appropriate information, and shall forward to the
Governor its recommendations on major policy issues resulting from the
review of the FDEIS.

CHAPTER 9

THE ENVIRONMENTAL ASSESSMENT PROCESS IN MINNESOTA

John L. (Jock) Robertson

Vice President
National Biocentric, Inc.
St. Paul, Minnesota

Joseph E. Sizer

Director of Environmental Planning
Minnesota State Planning Agency
St. Paul, Minnesota

Arnold W. Blomquist

President
National Biocentric, Inc.
St. Paul, Minnesota

LEGISLATIVE HISTORY

Minnesota has a history of concern for the protection and effective management of the environment. This has frequently resulted in legislation dealing with specific problems in the environment.

One of the more notable actions of the past 10 years was the 1967 creation of the Minnesota Pollution Control Agency, with responsibilities for regulating the quality of the air and water. The Agency is also charged with the implementation of a solid waste management program and a noise abatement program.

Legislation to control the development of the shorelands surrounding our lakes and rivers and legislation designed to limit the development of floodplains and floodprone areas was enacted. An act to remove abandoned automobile hulks from the state was established, and an Environmental

Rights Act was passed to ensure Minnesotans the opportunity to review actions they felt would degrade the environment. Each action played a prominent role in the continuing effort to manage the resources of the state.

The 1973 state legislative session marked the climax of environmental awareness and environmental legislation in Minnesota. One of the most significant laws passed in this session was the Minnesota Environmental Policy Act (MEPA). The main purpose of this law was to complement the earlier environmental legislation that had been enacted and to establish a framework for the design of future environmental programs. It was drafted in a manner to make it compatible with the National Environmental Policy Act of 1969 (NEPA) and to fill in the gaps not covered by NEPA, including actions of state and local governments not covered under the provisions of NEPA.

In previous decades, Minnesota, like many other states, had accumulated many special-purpose environmental regulatory programs, such as mining and mineral extraction, water withdrawal, and pollution control regulations. However, 1973 saw a new chapter written in the state's approach to environmental management through more sweeping and comprehensive programs in addition to MEPA. These included the Power Plant, High Voltage and Transmission Line Siting Act; the Critical Areas Act, which provides for the review and planning of areas of more than local, significance; and the Wild and Scenic Rivers Act that permits the planning and management of recreational rivers. This year also saw the creation of a state Environmental Quality Council (EQC) conceived initially as a governor's cabinet to coordinate the environmental management activities of various state agencies in the natural environmental management area (Figure 9-1).

The Minnesota statute and program is generally complementary to the Federal Environmental Policy Act. The acts are basically the same, and the Minnesota program and rules recognize and accept the federal process. However, there are several differences that supplement the federal program.

MEPA CONTENT

The Minnesota Environmental Policy Act of 1973 was originally intended as an outline of a long-range state environmental management plan. The Act sets forth a series of goals and policies for achieving and maintaining environmental quality in both the urban and rural sectors of the state. It applies to both state agencies and local units of government, and the language implies that these bodies are responsible for ensuring that the various plans and programs for which they are responsible should be brought into compliance with MEPA.

Figure 9-1. Membership of state Environmental Quality Council.

The original draft of MEPA contained no explicit authority or mechanism to ensure that the plans and programs of state and local government were actually brought into line with its goals and policies. An implementation section was added from a separate pending bill setting up an environmental review process very similar to that established by NEPA, in which the implementation of various programs could be reviewed on a case-by-case basis through the use of environmental documents. As a result, the state undertook to implement long-range environmental management goals, not through the leadership mechanism of an explicit planning program, but rather through the reactive process of reviewing individual projects or actions resulting from previously adopted plans and policies. Four years later, the reactive case-by-case approach to environmental management is now generally recognized as being insufficient and the state government is becoming increasingly aware of the need for a more leadership-oriented planning program.

The Minnesota environmental review process is basically very similar to that set up by the National Environmental Policy Act of 1969. The Minnesota Law states: "Where there is potential for significant environmental effects resulting from any major governmental action, or from any major private action of more than local significance, such action shall be preceded by a detailed statement prepared by the responsible agency or, where no governmental permit is required, by the responsible person . . . ."

Clearly, the legislators intended that this environmental review process should apply to both public and private action and that the group responsible for the action was also responsible for preparing the environmental review document. The procedure which has evolved in the program can be described as a five-step process (Figure 9-2):

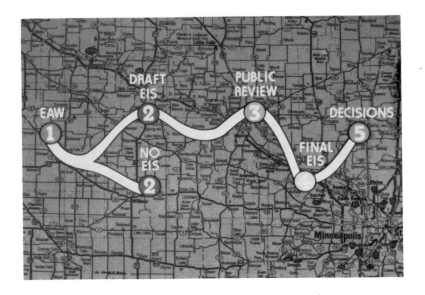

Figure 9-2. Steps in the environmental review process.

1. When a large development project is first proposed, an agency fills out an Environmental Assessment Worksheet (EAW). This helps officials decide if there is potential significant environmental effect, and if, therefore, an EIS is required. Most projects do not require an EIS and the process is completed after affected parties have had 30 days to review the EAW. Where no governmental action is required, the project sponsor is required to file an EAW with the EQC.

2. If an EIS is needed, the agency is responsible for preparation of a draft EIS.

3. The agency then holds a public meeting or hearing for other agencies and citizens to comment on the draft EIS.

4. Questions and responses to the draft EIS are added, and the final EIS is prepared.

5. When the final EIS is completed, agency officials decide to approve, modify, or turn down the proposed project. The EIS is intended to describe the probable environmental effects of a proposal before a decision is made.

In addition, the law provides a stopgap measure in the event that the responsible agency fails to initiate the environmental review process. One of the provisions states: "Upon the filing with the Council of a petition of not less than 500 persons requesting an environmental impact statement on a particular action, the Council shall review those petitions deemed by the Council to involve potential for significant environmental effects or to concern an action of more than local significance, and where there is material evidence of the need for an environmental review, require the preparation of an environmental impact statement in accordance with provisions of this section" (Figure 9-3). This petition provision, together with

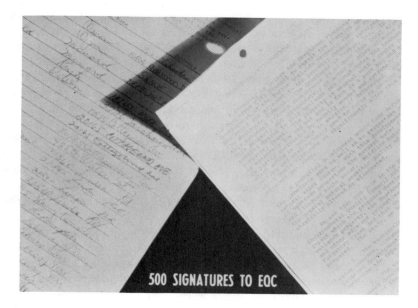

500 SIGNATURES TO EOC

Figure 9-3. Petition requesting an Environmental Impact Statement.

the notification and public hearing processes, was intended to ensure that state agencies and local units of government carried out the requirements of MEPA.

Thus, the intent of the environmental review provisions of MEPA was to provide environmental information to decision-makers before they take action on proposed projects. This implies that public and private agencies should, over time, become more informed and sensitive on environmental constraints and in the future make more environmentally sound decisions, and also that citizens should become more environmentally aware and discriminating.

Since the inception of the program in August of 1973, more than 220 proposed actions have been reviewed through the Minnesota environmental review process.   Approximately one half of these projects were located in the seven-county Twin Cities Metropolitan area.   The largest category of projects reviewed was residential development; the second largest category was industrial development projects.   By the end of 1976, the EQC had ordered environmental impact statements to be prepared on 49 projects.

Recent Modifications to Program

By mid-1974 it became clear that certain administrative aspects of the initial program were unnecessarily cumbersome and frustrating.   The EQC, originally intended to be a policy-coordinating body, was being called upon at its monthly meetings to make a multitude of decisions involving ordering the preparation of environmental assessments and impact statements and ruling on their adequacy.   Besides being time-consuming to the point of almost completely diverting EQC from its original purpose, this centralized administrative approach was found to have another major defect which worked against an original purpose of the law—the need to initiate environmental review at the earliest possible stages of a proposed action.   Centralization, with the EQC in St. Paul, the state capital, tended to encourage local governments and even state agencies to ignore environmental review unless the project came to the attention of EQC, and then usually at the eleventh hour, after most of the environmental design considerations had already been committed.

The EQC therefore decided to decentralize the environmental review process.   This decentralization put the responsibility where it belonged, according to law, on those government units responsible for the ultimate decisions on projects.   It gave local governments and state agencies more freedom and responsibility to decide when environmental review is required and when to initiate it (Figure 9-4).

The EQC encourages local units of government and state agencies to seize the opportunity to start environmental review in the early stages of a project rather than to wait for monthly EQC meetings.   In addition to cutting costly time delays, this earlier review should increase the possibility of modifying a project that could damage the environment before the project gets too far along and irreversible decisions are made.   Finally, the decentralized approach frees EQC from the burdensome administrative procedures of reviewing every potential action and gives it time to do what the legislature originally intended—to coordinate the environmental policies of state agencies (Figure 9-5).

The new rules also give state agencies and local governments an interesting option for meeting the environmental review responsibility of MEPA:

Figure 9-4. Responsibility for the environmental review process.

Figure 9-5. Decentralization of the environmental review process.

instead of reviewing each proposed action separately, a comprehensive plan, with an environmental management element, may be submitted as a related actions EIS for a geographic area (Figure 9-6). It is significant to

Figure 9-6. Environmental Impact Statement prepared for single-project or comprehensive plan.

note that the plan itself becomes the environmental review document, a separate EIS is not written on a comprehensive plan. It is hoped that rapidly growing communities can use this method to review anticipated development as a whole. This is designed to eliminate the repetitiveness of reviewing a series of single-project reviews.

Since the passage of MEPA in 1973, the question of who pays for the environmental review process has been raised frequently. The original statute made no explicit provisions on this matter, but implied that the cost of environmental review should be a part of the normal planning and design budget of a project. For public works, this means the cost of preparing environmental documents in a part of the initial design budget. For private projects requiring governmental permits, several different methods have been used by local governments and state agencies to require the private developer to help cover the costs of environmental review. These include requirement of data in draft document form, fee schedules and charge-back rules (Figures 9-7, 9-8 and 9-9).

Figure 9-7. Developer may submit draft environmental document.

Figure 9-8. Developer may pay advance fees for preparation of environmental documents.

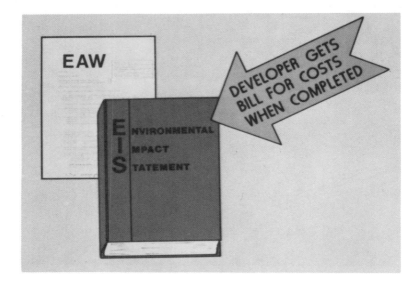

Figure 9-9. Developer may be billed for preparation of environmental review document.

The petition provision still does not work consistently. The experience of the EQC during the last three years indicates that what was intended as a stopgap measure is being widely misused as a free "appeals court." EQC has been barraged with petitions for maginal issues, including the cutting down of six trees for a new bridge abutment, relocation of a downtown bowery mission and sale of a theater license to a buyer who allegedly was going to show X-rated films. In these cases, the petition process has been used to delay projects for obvious nonenvironmental reasons and the EQC rejected the petitions after lengthy public meetings. One concept currently under discussion is to set up a "loser pay" process. Under this concept, rather than the EQC paying for a required hearing, the petitioner or the agency being challenged would pay for the hearing if its opinion did not prevail. This underlying theory is that over time, this would tend to discourage petitioners from filing frivolous environmental petitions. A counter argument is that this is a powerful deterrent to impoverished community groups.

The concern with providing an expedient and fair review or appeal process is especially relevant to the long-range need to monitor the effect of the environmental review process. Such monitoring is necessary to judge whether the ultimate legislative goal is reached, that is increasing environmental awareness and environmentally sensitive project design and execution in both the public and private sectors.

An interesting problem may occur in the future if the goal of environmental awareness is achieved. As presently outlined in MEPA, the environmental review process takes place in an adversary arena in which the proposer of the action, either private or public, essentially must prove "environmental innocence." If future development programs become more environmentally sensitive, one may hypothesize a situation in which a developer, such as an electric utility, must purposely propose a less environmentally favorable power plant site to preserve the environmental advocate role of the state regulatory agency—that of picking the more desirable site, which the utility actually desires also. To eliminate this deception, Minnesota may be required to modify the adversary roles to cooperator roles.

Compatibility of State and Federal Programs

The Minnesota environmental review process is basically the same as that set up by NEPA and therefore allows reasonably compatible processes and products. The Minnesota program recognizes the federal process. Therefore, when a federal document is produced under NEPA, the EQC recognizes the federal document as a draft state document. In such cases, when a federal agency is preparing a federal EIS and MEPA also applies, EQC will designate a responsible state agency.

The Minnesota program does differ from NEPA in several minor ways. Although EPA's final regulations on the preparation of environmental impact statements do not contain a definition of either action or environment, these rules go on to list applicability of the EIS to a rather wide range of administrative and legislative decisions. By contrast, Minnesota specifically defines those actions for which the process is applicable to "the whole of a project which will cause physical manipulation of the environment directly or indirectly. The determination of whether an action requires environmental documents shall be made by reference to the physical activity to be undertaken and not to the governmental process of approving the activity."

On the definition of environment, EPA refers to actions significantly affecting the "human environment." Here again, Minnesota has adopted a more specific definition. Environment is defined as: "the physical condition existing in the area which will be affected by the proposed action including land, air, water, minerals, flora, fauna, ambient noise, energy resources available to the area, and man-made objects or natural features of historic, geologic, or aesthetic significance."

The content requirements of a federal EIS are included in the Minnesota state EIS requirement. However, the following requirements are added to a state EIS:

1. "The impact on the state government of any federal controls associated with the proposed action. Federal actions pending which may affect the final outcome of the project should be discussed, including those actions which may result in the expenditure of additional state funds.
2. The multistate responsibilities associated with the proposed action. Impacts of the proposed action upon multistate responsibilities shall be discussed including the environmental effects of the action upon adjacent states."

Also, under MEPA, EQC has the option to stop the proposed action of state agencies, although the law implies that EQC cannot compel a state agency to initiate an action. This section applies only to state agencies and not to local units of government and, interestingly, has not yet been used since the passage of MEPA.

A final potential difference may occur if MEPA is modified to exempt the review of power plants and transmission line facilities which is already covered under a more specific and restrictive state statute.

Conflicts with Federal Programs

Because the state and federal programs are so similar in concept, conflicts between them arise out of minor procedural differences and are troublesome mostly to the parties of an individual case. One such procedural difference concerns the HUD "early start" provisions in the federal EIS review period. These conflict with the mandatory stop of construction under Minnesota statutes when a state EIS has been ordered. In several instances, a developer has been caught in the middle between HUD trying to expedite the provision of low- and moderate-cost housing and neighborhood pressure on the EQC to ensure that the project does not proceed until the state EIS has been completed and exhaustively reviewed. At first glance, this conflict can only be resolved by completing the state EIS process before the federal EIS process.

The second instance of procedural conflicts has been the reluctance of some federal agencies to use the state EQC to give notice and receive responses from state agencies. The Rock Island Office of the U.S. Army Corps of Engineers has, in the past, requested separate and direct response from state agencies. The response has been limited to the positions of individual agencies. As a result, the state has less opportunity to respond in a coordinated manner to this federal agency.

SUMMARY

The purpose of the Minnesota Environmental Impact Statement is to provide a reliable information document that examines environmental issues early in the planning process so that mitigating measures may be implemented to make the proposed project environmentally sound. This position is consistent with NEPA.

The state will accept a federally prepared EIS, with modifications, to assure that the results will meet the standards of the state product. The Minnesota EIS process covers proposed plans, projects and actions of local government and private developers not covered by NEPA.

The citizens of the state are given several opportunities to become involved in the review of the significance of a proposed action and the evaluation of the adequacy of an EIS required of a proposed action.

State agencies and local units of government are required to evaluate the environmental significance of a proposed project through the mechanism of the Environmental Assessment Worksheet. This forewarns interested agencies and citizens of impending actions, so they may raise concerns early in the process and it also makes the action of the responsible agency more predictable.

The creation of the "charge-back" provision of the EIS program places the responsibility for funding on the proposer and provides the responsible agency with funds to prepare necessary EIS in a timely manner. This fund source is particularly valuable to the local unit of government with limited technical and fiscal resources.

The related actions EIS option directs attention back to the planning process and the adequacy of the environmental element of a comprehensive plan by reviewing the plan rather than a separate EIS document. This is appropriate since the stated purpose of the EIS program is to ensure that environmental effects of a project are fully assessed and mitigated.

Finally, it has been demonstrated as a workable concept that an organization of key officials of state government could adopt procedures to evaluate the environmental implications of state and private actions and decide on environmental significance of a project and the effectiveness of various state programs. Perhaps the greatest benefit from EQC to date has been the increased understanding of programs by the leaders of the several state agencies whose actions most directly affect the environment.

CHAPTER 10

IMPLEMENTING THE ENVIRONMENTAL ASSESSMENT
PROCESS IN VIRGINIA

Susan T. Wilburn

Assistant Administrator
Council on the Environment
Richmond, Virginia

STRUCTURE AND METHOD

Within the framework of the National Environmental Policy Act of 1969 and Virginia's Environmental Impact Statement Law of 1973, Virginia's Council on the Environment administers an Environmental Impact Statement review process. The Council operates within the Office of Virginia's Secretary of Commerce and Resources, who reports directly to the Governor and is the agency in Virginia with ultimate responsibility and authority for implementing Virginia's Environmental Impact Statement program.

Approximately 15 other state agencies, including those directly charged with protecting the environment (such as the state Air Pollution Control and the Water Control Boards), are also involved on a daily basis with the review of environmental impact statements. The Council coordinates this review and prepares a consolidated state response for each project. A procedures manual for the review and guidelines for the preparation of environmental impact statements has been published and is available to anyone interested.

During the past three and one half years the Council on the Environment has coordinated the review and evaluation of over 250 environmental impact statements for federally sponsored projects affecting Virginia. By far the greatest number of these were submitted by the U.S. Army Corps of Engineers, followed by the United States Department of Agriculture, the Department of Transportation, and the Department of the Interior, with the remainder sponsored by various other agencies including, most frequently, the Nuclear Regulatory Commission, the Environmental Protection Agency, the Federal Power Commission and the Federal Energy Administration.

Additionally, during this period the Council has coordinated the review and evaluation of environmental impact statements submitted for well over 200 facilities proposed for state funding. Some of these have been for groups of related projects at a given site, *e.g.,* a university campus. Proposed construction activities at universities and community colleges, as well as park developments, comprised the major portion of the number cited.

Although Virginia's law is patterned after the National Environmental Policy Act, it affects only certain categories of projects sponsored by state agencies. No privately sponsored development projects are included at this time.

In addition to the review function, the Council has responsibility for assuring the orderly and effective preparation of environmental impact statements by those state agencies sponsoring activities covered by the state law. A process approach to EIS preparation, stressing informal, day-to-day consultation and cooperation between the agencies preparing the environmental impact statements and other interested parties, both in the private and public sectors, is the heart of our system, and we believe this ultimately determines its usefulness as a management tool. A key element, stressed by the Council to make the process an effective decision-making mechanism, is the participation of citizens with their contribution of knowledge and the expression of their values. We have also placed a major emphasis on fiscally conservative practices.

One significant means of reducing the costs related to the preparation and review of EIS's for state-sponsored projects, has been the use of what we call the "preliminary environmental impact statement." In contrast to many of the federal environmental impact statements we review, the state preliminary environmental impact statement usually is less than a dozen pages long. While following basically the same guidelines directing substantive content, the abbreviated state document does not contain lengthy discourses or listings of pertinent facts regarding the environmental features potentially affected by the proposed project or the project itself. Since, ideally, the project sponsor has already communicated with the pertinent regulatory agencies and other interested parties prior to preparation of the environmental impact statement, reference to the compliance of the project with the applicable laws, regulations or standards is usually sufficient. Therefore, only issues that have not yet been resolved require further elaboration or study.

For example, if a project, as planned, will meet our air quality standards, and the state's Air Pollution Control Board does not consider it to be a problem from their perspective, the applicant need only tell us of this in their environmental impact statement, and when the Air Pollution Control Board staff reviews the environmental impact statement, they will assure us of their intent to approve the project. Only if any agency or other interested party reviewing the preliminary statement discovers that such prior discussions have not taken place, or that the project as described is not acceptable to them, or that issues crossing agency lines remain to be resolved satisfactorily, will the requirement for a full environmental impact statement be invoked. And even in those cases, often potential problems or conflicts in isolated areas can be worked out through face-to-face communications, without a full document. Obviously, we have saved a great deal of paper, time and general shuffle in this manner.

PROBLEMS ASSESSED

Of course, we have experienced a number of problems associated with the process, both regarding state and federal environmental impact statements. Some of these problems are unique to one or the other of these requirements, and some reflect incompatibilities between state and federal requirements, particularly with respect to the EIS process vis-a-vis the state and federal permitting requirements.

We have tried to give careful consideration to determining which of these problems are procedural and which are substantive; and then, if they can best be handled administratively, legislatively, or judicially.

The most obvious problems have been associated with the process for federally sponsored projects. Basically, the weaknesses have been related to the timing, content and general usefulness of the documents submitted to the state for review.

Timing

The timing of the review of environmental impact statements is too often out of phase with the decision-making process at the state level, *i.e.,* environmental impact statements are not available until after agencies have been required to make decisions regarding the issuance of state permits. Therefore, environmental impact statements often are not prepared early enough to be useful as a decision-making tool on the state level.

This is a problem because several of the state regulatory agencies prefer to reserve judgment on issuing a state permit or certificate until they review an environmental impact statement addressing the proposed project as a whole. Since there is no legal basis for the state to require an EIS on most major projects in Virginia, because of the limited applicability of our law, the only environmental impact statement available is that prepared by the sponsoring federal agency. However, current law does not require an applicant to make application for a permit to the pertinent federal agency simultaneously with making application to state agencies. In practice, most applicants prefer to obtain necessary state permits prior to applying at the federal level. The result is that often many months, or even years, after a state agency has issued a permit for a project based on limited information, an environmental impact statement becomes available and they are locked into a position or run the risk of subjecting the applicant to "double jeopardy."

Content

The content of environmental impact statements is too often inappropriate. Many are verbose and contain superfluous material, in many cases focusing on technical details rather than substantive issues. While this increases the amount of paperwork and "bureaucratic shuffle" involved, and often taxes to the limit the resources of those in the state interested in reviewing environmental impact statements, the environmental impact statement may, nevertheless, fail to include the very minimum of factual data necessary for examination by the various interested participants evaluating the project. In some cases, requests made to a federal agency for additional data or project changes have gone unheeded.

Another weakness in the content of environmental impact statements is their occasional attempt to obscure or gloss over possible serious impacts, or to assign dubious benefits to a project for use in a cost-benefit analysis to justify a project. This leaves a lot of room for skepticism.

Review Process

The review process is too often segmented so that the impact of one part of a large project, as it relates to other components of the same project, is not clear; *e.g.,* an environmental impact statement may be prepared addressing a pier extension, which is only one part of a petrochemical complex. Without knowing what the future plans for the whole complex are, and how the pier relates to them, it is difficult to evaluate the potential impact of only the pier. This reflects little concern for land-use planning.

We have been able to avoid some of the weaknesses cited above, which have grown out of the federal process through recognition of these pitfalls in the review process for projects proposed by Virginia state agencies. For example, as mentioned earlier, we have encouraged the preparation of preliminary environmental impact statements very early in the decision-making process to assure their usefulness. Also, we have requested, and are reviewing, master plans and programmatic statements to which individual projects are keyed later on, in order to see the full scope of possible impacts.

OPPORTUNITIES AND PROSPECTS

During our three and one half years' experience with both federal and state environmental impact statement processes, we have explored a number of options for remedying these problems and have submitted our recommendations to the President's Council on Environmental Quality, the National Governor's Conference and our state authorities. Our own procedures and guidelines were updated and improved last year.

Timing

One possible solution to the timing problem, which we have studied and which was recommended by the state Land Use Council, would be a *state* requirement for environmental impact statements for certain types of major projects. Legislation to effect this is now under consideration by the Virginia General Assembly. If passed, the needs of the state regulatory agencies would be met and the applicant's responsibilities would be clarified. It is intended that this requirement would not materially affect the amount of effort now required for major projects, as the applicant presently must prepare the same data to submit to the sponsoring federal agency when it applies for federal sponsorship. The submission of the report would simply be required by the state at the time the state review takes place as well as forming a part of the application for federal sponsorship. Since the state agencies would have an earlier opportunity to assess the total project and document their concerns, the state's evaluation from a total perspective would facilitate the federal agency's task of addressing the appropriate issues and making its decision regarding sponsorship. Another layer of review by the state would not be necessary when the federal document becomes available, as the state's position would already be on record, unless, of course, the parameters or specifications of the project itself changed.

Process Changes

The Council on the Environment has made a number of procedural recommendations, including establishment of a mechanism to assure that comments offered by interested participants are given appropriate consideration.

The Council has recently completed a study on the monitoring of projects subject to the environmental impact statement process in Virginia. A number of recommendations involving federal-state communications and cooperation resulted from that study, again aimed toward integrating the federal and state environmental impact statement process with the permitting process on both levels.

In the coming year, we hope to continue to improve and streamline our state environmental impact statement and permitting procedures, as well as to discuss our recommendations for specific procedural changes with various federal agencies to bring the two sets of laws into closer harmony. We are optimistic that this can be done.

CHAPTER 11

WASHINGTON STATE ENVIRONMENTAL POLICY
—WHERE WE'VE BEEN AND WHERE WE'RE GOING

David W. Heiser
    Chief, Environmental Coordination
    Washington State Parks and
        Recreation Commission
    Olympia, Washington

INTRODUCTION AND BACKGROUND

Human interdependence with the natural environment was first recognized officially at the federal level with the adoption in 1969 of the National Environmental Policy Act (NEPA). A key requirement was that environmental values be exposed and considered in federal decision-making.

The State of Washington quickly adopted the same principle. The State Environmental Policy Act of 1971, known as SEPA, requires *all state and local governmental agencies to develop procedures to assure that environmental values are given appropriate consideration in decision-making.* This includes all public and private activities which require local or state approval of any kind. The original enabling legislation of SEPA contained a large number of broad policy statements and was written in general terms. There was no state body similar to the federal Council on Environmental Quality nor was any agency given direction to write guidelines or directives on how the Act was to be implemented. However, in Washington, we have the state's Department of Ecology which was created in 1970 as a superagency responsible for most aspects of environmental protection including air, water and solid waste regulation implementation. Because of that key leadership role and the fact that many state and local agencies were grappling unsuccessfully with how to comply with SEPA, the Department of Ecology created suggested

115

guidelines in 1972 for implementation of the Act. Those guidelines were construed to be merely advice and had no legal force.

Initial compliance with the mandates of SEPA was very weak. Many agencies of both the local and state governments refused to recognize the Act and expected that it would disappear if they paid no attention to it. However, some agencies did make a substantial effort to comply.

Sensing the lack of direction, the Legislature in 1974 created the Washington State Council on Environmental Policy, composed of members of the Pollution Control Hearings Board, to write rules to interpret and implement SEPA "in a manner which reduces duplicative and wasteful practices, establishes effective and uniform procedures, encourages public involvement and promotes certainty. . . ."

After 18 months of statewide hearings on three drafts, those rules were adopted by the Council as the official SEPA guidelines. Under the Administrative Procedures Act of Washington, the rules became effective January 16, 1976. Thereafter, state agencies had no more than four months, and local governments no more than six months, to adopt their own rules consistent with the guidelines. The rules adopted by agencies are to integrate both the policies and procedures of SEPA into all the various programs under their respective jurisdictions.

Model ordinances for the assistance and use of local governments were prepared by the Department of Ecology, after consultation with other state agencies and with city and county officials.

The Council on Environmental Policy continued to refine the rules slightly until June 30, 1976, when the Council legally ceased to exist and all authority was transferred to the Department of Ecology.

THE SITUATION TODAY

Because of the strong legal background of the Council on Environmental Policy and its staff, the guidelines tend to be quite specific and legalistic. However, in my opinion, this is what was required at this point in the evolution of our guidelines in Washington. Many county planners and other decision-makers, as well as state agency heads, first complained about the complexity of the new SEPA guidelines, but as their familarity with and knowledge of those rules increased, so did acceptance. We have seen many counties adopt model ordinances or the state rules by reference and we are seeing a much wider acceptance of the basic principles of environmental disclosure. The Department of Ecology, by whom I was employed for several years during the initial SEPA development stages, is now specializing in very brief, terse impact statements of 8-20 pages. This is in response to the almost unanimous objection to long, detailed statements, which often include numerous appendices.

The Council on Environmental Policy had fairly wide-ranging authority; it set up a rather complex system which establishes categories of actions related to the natural environment. The first of those is classed as a "non-action" under SEPA. Basically, these are governmental actions that have no direct effect on the environment.

Once a project has been determined to be an action under SEPA, the next step is to establish if it is categorically exempt from further analysis. Many types of minor, new construction and renovation and repair of existing structures are categorically exempted. When the decision-maker discovers that the proposed action is categorically exempt, he makes note of that in his SEPA Public Information Center and the SEPA process is complete.

Should the proposed action not be categorically exempt, the responsible government official must then prepare an Environmental Checklist and Declaration of Significance/Nonsignificance. While the Council has not defined what is significant, it has provided the format of an 8-page Environmental Checklist to help in that decision-making process. After the responsible official has completed a checklist on the proposed action, he must then decide whether the action will have a significant adverse effect on the environment. If he concludes that it will not, then a Declaration of Nonsignificance is prepared and circulated among all the agencies with jurisdiction and to private individuals who have requested the opportunity to review that document.

If the responsible official should find, on the other hand, that the action will have a significant adverse effect upon the environment he must then prepare a full-scale Draft Environmental Impact Statement using the rather detailed directions supplied in the guidelines.

The results of this evolutionary process are shown in Table 11-1. In the early days of SEPA, you will notice that fairly substantial numbers of Draft Environmental Impact Statements under both SEPA and NEPA were reviewed within Washington State. By 1974 we saw the evolution of the process continue to the point where more Negative Declarations, or Declarations of Nonsignificance as they are now called, were produced than Draft Impact Statements. That overall trend has continued up to the present. Since implementation of the SEPA guidelines, there have been large numbers of guideline inquiries, indicating a high degree of involvement by both local and state government officials in a decision-making process. The Action Notices indicate that a state-level response is required from the State Department of Ecology. SEPA petitions of 50 or more signatures require an EIS hearing. Local tranfers indicate that a local agency which initiated action has transferred the lead to the state.

It is the opinion of the Department of Ecology, and the other government officials within the state of Washington who review environmental documents, that the overall quality of documents reviewed has increased substantially.

Table 11-1. SEPA-NEPA—Five Years of Environmental Reporting in Washington (based on documents received by the Washington State Department of Ecology, which is responsible for storing all documents)

Year	Draft EIS (SEPA-NEPA)	Document or Activity					
		Negative Declarations	Action Notices	General Guideline Inquiries	SEPA Petitions	Local Transfers	Environmental Consultation Requests
1972	175	24	a	a	a	a	a
1973	310	333	-	-	-	-	-
1974	384	487	50	-	-	-	-
1975	250	262	192	-	-	-	-
1976	217	369[b]	456	532	20	4	16
5-Year Total	1336	1475	698	532	20	4	16

[a] No data were recorded.
[b] Total includes 199 proposed and 170 Final Declarations of Nonsignificance.

In fact, most of the impact statements received recently show a high degree of sophistication and clarity. We also note that actions of limited environmental effect have been properly relegated to the exempt or nonsignificant level and a process established to record those declarations appropriately.

FEDERAL-STATE COOPERATION

In the early days of SEPA implementation within Washington State, we basically had a situation in which the federal government said "we'll do our statement and you do yours." This led to substantial duplication and wasteful government practices. When the Council on Environmental Policy drew up the new guidelines, it incorporated a provision allowing the responsible state governmental official to bypass the requirements of SEPA if a NEPA impact statement has been prepared covering the subject actions in sufficient detail.

Within the last year, most of us in state government have noted a higher degree of cooperation between state and federal decision-makers in the production of a single environmental impact statement to cover a multiplicity of government actions. As an example, the agency I represent, Washington State Parks and Recreation Commission, participated in the production of a NEPA statement together with the U. S. Department of Interior, Bureau of Outdoor Recreation, and the City of Bellevue, Washington. Because of the cooperative nature of the acquisition, development and operation of this particular facility, it was evident that a cooperative effort should be involved in the preparation of the environmental document; and I must say that it was a successful effort. The statement received good reviews and the project is now being implemented.

FUTURE DIRECTIONS

It has been said by some that the state of Washington has gone too far in the development of environmental regulations. These regulations go far beyond those described here. They include the State Shoreline Management Act of 1971, which regulates all shorelines, land within 200 feet of the shorelines, major rivers and streams, and wetlands and marsh areas. Washington also has a strong hydraulic law, administered by the state departments of Fisheries and Game, and which is designed to protect the anadromous and resident fish populations. Recently, the Legislature passed the Forest Practices Act, which strongly controls that aspect of the natural environment.

As a result of this relatively strong environmental package, Washington was the first state to receive federal Coastal Zone Management approval of its entire plan and the funding to implement it. That program and those funds are administered by the Department of Ecology to perform basic environmental research and to establish environmental preserves at several locations within Washington State.

However, I am not suggesting that all has gone smoothly in Washington State, regarding environmental law. In fact, the environmental regulations and rules imposed have caused substantial changes to the lifestyle and ways of doing business in Washington. That, in turn, has caused substantial resentment by some elements of society, particularly the building trades. We also see a substantial amount of apathy and even outright hostility on the part of the general public toward any further environmental rules at this time. I believe it is significant that the Washington State legislative committees concerned with the environment are treading extremely lightly, lest the existing environmental regulation be wiped out on the floor of the Legislature. For these reasons, I believe it is incumbent upon everyone engaged in environmental analysis to do the best possible job, to be objective in impact analysis, expeditious in environmental review and as fair to all parties concerned as possible.

CHAPTER 12

THE ENVIRONMENTAL REVIEW PROCESS IN A LARGE CALIFORNIA CITY

Selina Bendix
Environmental Review Officer
City and County of San Francisco

THE SAN FRANCISCO OFFICE OF ENVIRONMENTAL REVIEW

In San Francisco, there were several primary considerations in setting up local implementation[1] for the California Environmental Quality Act (CEQA). One aim was to depoliticize the environmental review policy, as far as possible; another was to centralize it in the interests of efficiency and consistency. By removing the certification of environmental documents from the elected Board of Supervisors and placing it with the Planning Commission, we were able to remove a considerable amount of political pressure from the environmental review process. It is true that the Mayor appoints the Planning Commissioners who do the certification; however, actions before the Planning Commission don't take on the political aspect of matters handled before the Board of Supervisors.

Environmental review for all agencies, departments and commissions of the City takes place in a single office, with a single exception, to be discussed later.

Integrated Planning

The third aim was implementation of the intent of CEQA, which is like the intent of the National Environmental Policy Act (NEPA), that the environmental review process be integrated into the project planning process. This was achieved by putting the Office of Environmental Review into the

Department of City Planning; in fact, there is a considerable amount of overlap between traditional planning functions and the functions of the Office of Environmental Review. In many of the simpler cases, environmental review staff (most of whom have planning degrees) handle all the planning aspects of a project in addition to the strictly environmental review aspects of the project; in this fashion, separation of the planning process from the environmental review process is avoided. This organizational pattern minimizes the number of people the project sponsor must deal with in obtaining necessary permits.

NEPA review of Department of Housing and Urban Development-funded Community Block Grant projects, pursuant to the delegation of federal environmental review powers in Section 104h of the Housing and Urban Development Act of 1974, is also handled by the Office of Environmental Review, as is environmental review of 701 projects.[2] When we were faced with the problem of how to set up a procedure to implement NEPA review of Block Grant projects, the process was set up to duplicate our CEQA review process on every point the law permitted. Utilization of the CEQA review model made possible rapid establishment of Block Grant review procedures.[3] We soon had a feedback relationship between NEPA and CEQA review, which improved both processes and facilitated consolidation of review of projects subject to both state and federal review.

The one thing that does not go on in the Office of Environmental Review. is one type of what I shall call a "level of clearance decision." Under CEQA, there are essentially three possibilities for a project: it may be exempt from review; it may be a project which investigation shows not to have any significant environmental effects, in which case it would receive a Negative Declaration (comparable to a federal Notice of No Significant Effect), or it may be a project with potential significant effects, which requires an Environmental Impact Report (EIR) (California counterpart of the federal Environmental Impact Statement). Obviously, every time a water pipe to a home is replaced, we are not interested in having to look at it to find out if issuance of the permit would have a significant effect; neither are we interested in putting a piece of paper in the file which says "yes, this is categorically exempt." So, the first level of clearance decision, "is the project exempt or isn't it," is made by the operating department that approves the permit. The Office of Environmental Review makes all level of clearance decisions on which projects are going to receive Negative Declarations and which will be required to have EIR's. To avoid potentially costly level of clearance decision errors, as well as to centralize publicly available information about environmental review, a recent Code change requires the issuance of a Certificate of Exemption from Environmental Review by the Department of City Planning for all exempt projects costing over $100,000.[4]

Evaluating Changing Projects

In March 1977, new amendments were made to the San Francisco environmental ordinance. These amendments were designed to address the problem of "What do you do when a project changes?"

It is desirable to institute environmental review as early as possible in the development of a project. The earlier it is done and completed, the more likely that something is going to change: as the project proceeds down the line, more details emerge, availability of materials changes, and new constraints emerge. Then what do you do? CEQA requires reevaluation of a project in certain situations after the project has been found to be exempt, after a Negative Declaration has been issued, or an EIR prepared and certified; it does not say how.

Most agency people feel that, in the absence of specific instructions on how to amend an environmental document, it is very hazardous to do it. There is a resulting tendency to feel that, once environmental review has been completed, the project is frozen or that one must sweep under the rug all the changes, because one does not know how to deal with them. I feel that this is hazardous both to the project's sponsor and for the approving jurisdiction. It's an invitation to litigation, because there is a vacuum; we have tried to fill this vacuum by amending our local ordinance to specify what happens when a project changes.

These amendments provide for reevaluation of a project when there is:

"1. a substantial change in the proposed project;
2. a substantial change with respect to the circumstances under which the project is to be undertaken; or
3. a substantial change in relevant information available for use in evaluation of the project."[5]

A project that is found to be exempt from review must be reevaluated and a new Certificate of Exemption from Environmental Review issued, if appropriate. When a Negative Declaration has been issued for a project, staff must determine whether the change would result in a substantive change in the environmental effects of the project: if not, this is noted in the case record, and no further action is required. If a substantial change would occur, the project must be reevaluated as if it were a new project.

When an EIR has been certified for the project, there are three possible actions.

1. If there would be "no substantial change in the environmental effects of the project as a result of such modification, this determination and the reasons therefore shall be noted in the case record, and no further evaluation shall be required."[6]
2. In cases "where the modification relating to the project could result only in a clearly defined change in the environmental effects of the

project,"[7] the previous EIR may be amended according to a defined
procedure.

3. More sweeping project changes require a new EIR.

Informing the Public

Level of clearance decisions are noticed in various ways: one of the most
important is an informal one—an advantage of our operation within the Department of City Planning. This Department has a system of what is called
"area liaison planners." The City is divided into districts, largely on the basis
of people's perception of themselves as constituting communities, to which
liaison planners are assigned. It is the responsibility of these area liaison
planners to be familiar with publicly active groups and vocal citizens (hopefully the not-so-vocal citizens too, but realistically it is hard to contact the
latter). The liaison planner should note projects proposed for his/her section
of the City, contact community leaders, and say "we think that you might be
interested to know that such and such a project is proposed for your area.
Do you think you might be concerned about it? Would you like to see the
building plans? Would you like to have someone come and tell your group
about it? Would you like to come down to the office and see the file record
on it?" That kind of personal contact will do more, when it is effective, than
all the public notices we issue.

Legal notices of Negative Declarations, decisions to require EIR's, etc. are
scheduled for each Friday. If deadlines require publication on another day
of the week, the notice is republished Friday so that the person who checks
Friday notices will see all the notices. Copies of the legal notice are posted in
the area of the proposed project site, at the library and the San Francisco
Ecology Center, and are sent to a mailing list and to any persons expressing
interest in a particular project.

One or more public hearings are held on each EIR. There are provisions
for administrative appeals, both of the decision to issue a Negative Declaration
and of the decision to require an EIR. These appeals result in a public hearing
at which the Planning Commission decides whether to uphold the staff level
of clearance decision. *Fewer than 1% of level of clearance decisions are
appealed.*

Achieving Objectivity

The project sponsor, private or city department, is allowed to select an
EIR consultant. Office of Environmental Review staff take responsibility for
ensuring that the document meets our standards. Administrative guidelines,
the "Format and Guidelines for Material Required for Draft Environmental
Impact Reports," are provided to aid consultants in their work. Project
sponsors and consultants are told that preparation of an advocacy document
simply delays the project by requiring additional editing.

We don't think that an EIR is a decision document. A strenuous effort is made to maintain neutrality and objectivity. One of the techniques we use, a difficult one to achieve but a standard that can be met with some experience, is that we do not allow any impact to be described as "significant," "insignificant," "big," "little," "positive," "negative," or any other such modifier implying a value judgment. There is always some way of describing that impact, if not quantitatively, then qualitatively, and relating it to something familiar. For example, if I were to tell somebody that a noise level resulting from construction of a particular project is insignificant, I may not be believed. Instead, suppose I say: "This is how noise levels are measured, this is how noises you are familiar with are labeled in dBA (decibels corrected for the variation in frequency response of the typical human ear at commonly encountered noise levels–a physical, logarithmic unit of loudness) by people who like to quantify things; this is the distance from the construction site at which you will be able to perceive that noise above the background level; and these are the measurements we have made of the background level." Then I can set up a situation in which someone who had never heard of dBA before he read that report has a feeling he is in a position to judge whether he will be bothered by that impact.

How Much Is Enough?

We have also had to deal with the completeness issue and have always felt that a short EIR is a good EIR because decision-makers don't read them if they are too long. Moreover, the people who do read long EIR's get lost and confused, so we have always believed that one should deal with what appears to be significant and that *that* is where one is, in fact, making the value judgment. We don't label those impacts as insignificant, but in deciding what is going to be covered in the EIR we are making a professional judgment as to what is significant. This procedure has been in use in San Francisco for four years; 1977 amendments to CEQA have recognized its validity.

An example of how *not* to write an EIR is a case in which we had a consultant who wanted to be very complete; he thought we were being lax and that we were going to be legally challenged because we weren't complete enough in our EIR's. When a major office building was proposed in the center of the downtown business district (this involved tearing down another building–the only way to obtain such a site in San Francisco), this consultant informed us that one did not need to worry about the impact of the project on the development of mineral resources in our jurisdiction because there were no economically developable deposits of mineral resources under the main street of our downtown business district. That's my idea of "overkill." Developing mineral resources in this location would be like mining in the middle of Manhattan; it's irrelevant.

WHAT IS THE URBAN ENVIRONMENT?

One problem faced in San Francisco relates to the origin of environmental law. Much has come from a public desire to protect the wilderness from the dam and highway builders. San Francisco is, for all practical purposes, a 100% "built" city. We don't have a wilderness to protect, but it *is* a human environment; so the question becomes "What is it we are trying to protect in the urban environment? What makes it a suitable human environment?," and that's not always easy to define. Frankly, I think it is much easier to define what one is trying to protect in the wilderness.

Traffic Issues

One of the environmental issues about which San Franciscans are often concerned is traffic, and I would propose traffic and traffic-related issues as a prime example of the question of framework of reference in evaluation of environmental impact. My personal bias is that our society needs to be freed from the private-car dependence from which we now suffer. If a project is going to eliminate some street parking, I think that's desirable: if people cannot find parking spaces, they may use public transit, especially as we have an unusually good public transit system in San Francisco. On the other hand, the people who want to drive their cars and park them in that area will regard that as a negative impact, because they want to park. As far as I am concerned, that impact cannot be labeled in an EIR as a positive or negative impact. The EIR should say "there are this many parking spaces in a radius of so many blocks or feet from the site; the proposed project would remove this many spaces; the available parking would be decreased by this percent." You, the reader, must decide how you feel about that impact.

Some interesting mitigation measures have come up as a result of public concern over certain kinds of traffic problems. A residential development was proposed for a site where there were streets but whose steep lots had not been built on. The streets were narrow and the people in the area pointed out that if cars were to park on the streets, fire engines would not be able to get by them. When no houses were built on the street, nobody parked there, and the streets were wide enough for the city's fire equipment. Technically, we could put in a mitigation measure requiring that the streets be posted with signs saying "no parking," but how well would that be obeyed in a residential district and, realistically, would the Police Department have enough staff to monitor people who park on a residential streets? So, we could put up signs, but we know they are not going to be obeyed and that they are not going to be enforced. In practice, we have a fire hazard that we were not aware of until after the publication of the Draft EIR, when area residents, some of whom had seen a local situation in which a fire engine had to make four attempts at negotiating a corner from one narrow street to another, called it to our attention. The result was the development of a mitigation agreement with the project sponsor to change the lot lines so as to widen the streets by two feet. When this project is fully developed, the streets are going to be wide enough to permit parking *and* emergency vehicle access.

Density and Preservation Issues

Some of the other issues of concern in San Francisco are height, density and historic-site preservation. Generally, the Office of Environmental Review is concerned only about the impacts of proposals that exceed neighborhood norms for height, bulk or density. If a neighborhood has been undergoing a process of change for decades, we accept that as a characteristic of the site. Those residents of the neighborhood who wish to arrest that change process may wish to use the environmental review process to stop or alter the direction of that change. Is this a legitimate function of the environmental review process? Should we be developing information to help decision-makers deal with such issues? This is not a simple question and I do not offer an answer because I'm not sure that there *is* a general answer. At present, I deal with such issues on a case-by-case basis.

Interesting issues arise in connection with determining what constitutes a building of historic merit, such that it should be preserved. Many citizens who are concerned about historic site preservation do not consider nominations to the Federal Register of Historic Places as a satisfactory criterion. If a beautiful, but not unique, old building is a severe earthquake hazard, should one try to improve it structurally or give up and build a building that meets modern earthquake standards? In a city full of pre-earthquake safety code buildings, how does one justify removal of one potentially hazardous building? Opinions may be heated, and it is particularly important to have an EIR as an objective source of information for all parties in such disputes.

Wind Tunnel Studies

San Francisco is concerned about the effects of high-rise buildings on wind conditions at the pedestrian level. We have a prime example in San Francisco of a building no one would enter if it were not the Federal Building. It is so windy in front of this building that the decorative fountains often must be turned off to keep people from being drenched by the spray that blows across the entrance steps. This is not a desirable condition, and something we do not want to see repeated. San Francisco has been putting a considerable amount of economic effort into revitalizing its downtown area. It would be absurd to allow a new building which produced adverse pedestrian conditions in the area to which we are trying to attract people.

Wind-tunnel modeling tests of all high-rise buildings are now required to determine the effect of the building on wind conditions at the pedestrian level or in any open public plaza areas. The Office of Environmental Review does not use the Building Code definition of high-rise buildings (75 feet from street level to the floor of the top floor); each building is evaluated in terms of its location and the height of nearby buildings. In one case the Zoning Administrator denied a floor area bonus for provision of open public space because wind tunnel tests showed that conditions would be such that the space would not be used.

In another case, involving a prime downtown business district site, three different designs were proposed for the site, with vehement supporters of each. The architectural firm was anticipating a year or two of anguish in negotiation with the Planning Department, and the probability that it would have to design three buildings, so that when the decision was finally made they would have a building ready to go. When I heard about this, I said: "If you are seriously considering three different alternatives for this site, of course they will all have to be discussed in the EIR and all three will have to be wind-tunnel modeled. May I suggest that instead of worrying about how the decision is going to be made, you get the wind-tunnel study done now. You don't have to have detailed architectural drawings; you already know what the envelope would be for that building for each of those three proposed designs. You know enough to do the wind-tunnel modeling. Why not get that information, and while you are at it, get sun-and-shade studies (studies showing the shadows which would be cast by the building at different times of day for different seasons of the year) too."

It turned out that one of those three designs would produce the lowest wind speed at the pedestrian level—the one that was best from the wind standpoint also would cast the least shadow on the sidewalk during the hours people were most likely to be on the street. All of a sudden, the decision as to which design was going to be approved became perfectly clear; staff of the architectural firm came to me and said: "We never realized that this environmental review process could be helpful. Do you have any idea how much money you saved us because we didn't have to design three buildings?" This is an example of the benefits derived from interaction of the environmental review process with the early project development process.

THE EIR AUDIENCE

San Francisco has an active EIR audience. We are very concerned about writing our documents to meet the needs of that audience. The public and the decision-makers are not geologists, engineers, meteorologists, botanists, or any other kind of specialist that contributes to the preparation of an environmental document. It is very important that these documents be edited to a state in which they are meaningful to the audience for which they are intended. "Good engineering English" is not appropriate for an EIR, nor is biological language, such as the following examples from an EIS: ". . . concluded that species density patterns for polychaetes, gastropods, bivalves and ampeliscid amphipods which are residents of the subtidal benthos. . . ." I never did figure out a "sublethal description of physiological or behavioral activities."

We have a varied level of sophistication of response. Some members of the public will make comments such as: "The first thing that struck me is the complete misquotation of the Burton Act by which (ownership of) the Port was transferred (from the state) to the city. The EIR quotes the Burton Act as asking for maximum return when the Port declares land surplus. This was in the original Burton Act. It is no longer in the act. An amendment in 1972 has eliminated it specifically and replaced it with the words 'in the public interest.'" On the other hand, we had a situation in which a large sewer was going to go along two sides of a man's shoreline property and he came with an impassioned speech to the Planning Commission to say: "By making the cut through here, it's going to put these blocks virtually on islands and there is no reinforcement for those blocks. . ." He convinced the Planning Commission that he was being detached from the mainland and would slide into San Francisco Bay; I had to obtain a letter from a geotechnical expert to reassure people that it was not quite that easy to create an island. The text of the EIR must meet the needs of both the knowledgeable reader and the persons reading their first EIR to gain information about a project in their neighborhood.

Our decision-makers read the documents. The Planning Commissioners tell us when the EIR's are too long and when they can't understand what the EIR says, they make comments such as: "I would like somebody in the Department to read the wave section because I cannot understand it."

Sometimes the Planning Commissioners tell us they can think of alternatives not considered by the staff. In fact, perhaps we thought of them and didn't feel that they were meaningful alternatives; but we have learned that the technical expert's view of what are reasonable alternatives is not that of the decision-maker or of the public. One should deal with the alternatives that people think exist, even if they do not, because it will have to be explained why those are not viable alternatives. If there has been adequate advance contact with the public, the agency will find out about most such issues before publication of the Draft EIR.

THE WASTEWATER MASTER PLAN

One of the biggest San Francisco projects is a $2 billion, 20-year program for wastewater treatment facilities. This program has to deal with a variation from 100 million gallons per day (gpd) flow of dry weather sewage to 14 *billion* gpd maximum wet weather flow. (San Francisco has a combined sewer system in which the sanitary, dry weather flow and rainwater runoff travel in the same sewers.) Present facilities provide primary treatment for the dry weather flow. During wet weather, untreated sewage is spilled into San Francisco Bay and the Pacific Ocean. A Wastewater Master Plan has been adopted to correct this situation.

The environmental review process began with a joint EIR/S, meeting California and federal requirements, compiled together with the Environmental Protection Agency (EPA). The EIR/S answered the questions:

1. What was the problem?
2. What alternative generic approaches were there to solving the problem?
3. How should a decision be made as to what was a reasonable approach to a solution? and
4. What were the potential impacts of the selected concept and the alternatives?

Since then, we have been doing what we call "element environmental impact reports" under CEQA, and EPA has not required any further EIS's. The EIR/S on the Wastewater Master Plan was a thick document (400 pages), with much technical material (you can't talk about sewage treatment without getting technical once in a while). A glossary was provided, but most of the technical language was edited out of the summary, and we published 10,000 copies of the 10-page summary chapter.

This project affects one section of the city at a time. Most people really don't want to pay any attention to sewage treatment—it is unpleasant and not understood. People are not concerned about a 20-year plan for the whole pattern of sewage treatment in the city, but do become very concerned when we propose to build something in their part of town. There are always many good reasons why it ought to be built somewhere else. As we go into each section of the city, we give people the EIR/S summary to orient them on the whole Plan; then we give them the local element EIR discussing the construction impacts on their neighborhood. We have now published eight of these, covering different aspects of the program (Table 12-1).

Public Comment

Some EIR comments that have been received on Draft-element EIR's may give a feeling for the problem of trying to explain expansion of the sewage treatment system. The city proposed to upgrade a sewage treatment plant providing advanced primary treatment to a secondary sewage treatment plant. Advanced primary methods remove 40-50% of the suspended solids and from 25-28% of the BOD_5. BOD_5 is the quantity of oxygen used in the biochemical oxidation of organic matter in a five-day period, at a specified temperature,

Table 12-1. Wastewater Master Plan Element EIRs

Case No.	Implementation Program No.	Project Title	EIR Status
EE74.62	I	North Point Transport Project	Final EIR certified 5/9/74
EE74.158	II	Southwest Treatment Plant Dry-Weather Expansion and Interim Point Discharge	Final EIR certified 4/10/75
EE75.155	III	North Shore Outfalls Consolidation	Final EIR certified 12/18/75
EE75.421	IV	Richmond/Sunset Interim Improvements	Final EIR certified 4/22/76
EE75.179	V	Southwest Outfall	Final EIR certified 12/18/75
EE75.123	VI	Islais Creek South Side Outfalls Consolidation	Final EIR certified 5/6/76
EE75.122	VII	Channel Outfalls Consolidation	Final EIR certified 5/13/76
EE77.18	VIII	Land Use Changes and Drill Track Relocation near the Southeast Treatment Plant	Final EIR certified 3/10/77
EE75.304	-	West Side Transport	In preparation
EE76.389	-	Southwest Water Pollution Control Plant	In preparation

and under specified conditions. This is a standard test used to assess wastewater quality. Secondary treatment would provide approximately 90% removal of pollutants. These are quotations from the transcript of the public hearing on the Draft EIR (DEIR): "also adjacent to the preferred project is the San Francisco Produce Market. I feel this sewer plant would be too close to it. With all the fruits and vegetables exposed to the elements as they are, they surely don't need to be exposed to the smell and fumes of sewage." The primary treatment plant has been there for more than 20 years; the changes were designed to upgrade the quality of treatment.

"The project would ruin the environment with its pollution of the Bay. . . ." One of the purposes of the entire Wastewater Master Plan is to take San Francisco sewage effluent out of San Francisco Bay. This particular section of the project was designed to improve the quality of the existing discharge to the Bay from primary to secondary; ultimately, we will probably also remove secondary effluents.

"An alternative would be to put the plant under the Bay. If it was possible to build the BART tunnel (Bay Area Rapid Transit District Tunnel)
under the Bay, it should be possible to build the sewage treatment plant under
the Bay where it won't be in anyone's neighborhood." At the expense of a
major increase in technical difficulty, cost, energy consumption, time of construction, etc., it might be possible to do this. The prohibitive cost and technical complexity of this alternative were such that it was never considered;
however, the problems are not obvious to the nonengineer.

"Any doctor or medical establishment will tell you that such a sewage
plant will cause hepatitis and typhoid fever."

"Secondary treatment would not take all the bacteria out of the water,
according to the DEIR. People don't want that remaining 10% of bacteria to
go into water near their homes." The Wastewater Master Plan EIR/S does
discuss tertiary treatment (treatment of secondary sewage effluent to remove
pollutants characteristic of that effluent; the process used varies with the
nature of the pollutants remaining after secondary treatment), but the relevance of this discussion was probably not apparent to the commentator. In
any case, the present discharge does not even have secondary treatment.

All the misunderstandings should not be attributed to an uneducated
public. For example, the following comment was received on the same EIR
from the Regional Water Pollution Control agency: "Under 'Effects Upon
The Receiving Water' the statement that 'The effect of. . .any. . .process alternative. . .would be an improvement to the receiving waters in the vicinity of
the discharge. . .' ignores the effect of the 'interim point discharge' to Islais
Creek. The statement should be modified or deleted. . . . " The commentator
apparently didn't understand the project. We had to respond: "As present
untreated overflows would be replaced by secondary or near-secondary effluent, the statement in the DEIR is accurate as it stands," and called the agency
to clear up the misunderstanding.

There have been different probems with each section of the Wastewater
Master Plan. When we go into a commerical area, the merchants are very
concerned about what the construction will do to their customers' access.
When we approach a beach area, concern is about access to recreational areas.
Each EIR has to deal with local concerns. We anticipate that we are going to
go on with the program, issuing perhaps another half a dozen or dozen of the
element EIR's. One thing we hope to do, over a period of time, is to use
these documents as tools to educate the entire city about its sewage treatment and water pollution problems and solutions.

In the case of the more controversial segments of the program, we now
hold public information meetings while the Draft EIR is being written. This
enables us to find out early what questions the public wants answered, and
public response often brings out information that causes shifts in location of

elements of the system. The Alternatives chapter of an EIR for a project that develops in this fashion is much richer in detail about the consequences of alternatives considered and the reasons for discarding alternatives than is the Alternatives chapter of an EIR written after all the key decisions have been made.

The EIR can also be used to educate people on the public approval process. Not only does the public fail to understand who has authority over a project, many agency people do not know which other agencies are involved and what are the roles of the other agencies. We use our EIRs to educate everybody who has a role in the approval of the project. On occasion, this has resulted in private project sponsor discoveries about needed permits.

Selecting Consultants for City Projects

The consultant input to the Wastewater Master Plan EIRs has been a continuing problem through the first years of the program. Consultants were selected without participation of the Office of Environmental Review; consultant submissions tended to be excessively lengthy, technical and showed inadequate familiarity with the overall Wastewater Master Plan. Excessive in-house time was required to turn these submissions into publishable Draft EIRs, imperiling grant deadlines. These problems were alleviated by setting up a consultation-selection process involving all the city departments concerned with the proposed project. A decision was made to eliminate all design firms involved in the project from the EIR work.

Representative EIRs written by the consultants, a written proposal dealing with the current project, and résumés of the consultant staff team were evaluated in the first round. Those firms evidencing little past experience with large wastewater facilities, low engineering representation on the project team, and poorly organized proposals, with the use of obvious "boilerplate" material used in many proposals, were eliminated in the first round. An interdepartmental panel then evaluated oral presentations and interview responses for depth of familiarity with the environmental review process, understanding of the proposed project, and breadth of the interdisciplinary team, including proposed specialty subconsultants. Three finalists were then questioned in a second oral interview about administrative experience, current workload, scheduling plans, and past record on meeting deadlines and cost control. Telephone calls were made to other jurisdictions, given as references, to confirm the impressions of interviewing staff and to check that no problems had arisen of which we were not aware.

As a result of this selection process, firms have been obtained that do substantially better work, thus relieving stress on agency staff. After completion of the selection process, a meeting was held for losing candidates to inform them of our perception of their weaknesses and thus aid them in future competition for City EIR contracts.

CHANGE IS CONSTRUCTIVE

The environmental review process in San Francisco, as elsewhere, is in a continual state of flux. Useful ideas from other agencies, the professional literature and consultants, are incorporated into city procedures wherever they appear to improve the process. These procedures also change in response to alterations in state law. This state of change often makes it difficult for people to be familiar with current procedures. Rapid evolution is the norm for environmental review procedures across the country because of the newness of the endeavor. Many of the problems and frustrations of dealing with the environmental review process, from both the project sponsors' and the agencies' viewpoints, derive from this rapid evolution.

Despite the difficulties of dealing with a "moving target" due to advances in the state-of-the-art and legislative changes, I feel that the dynamic state of the environmental review process should be encouraged by environmental professions until a greater level of understanding of methods of optimizing the benefits of the process is achieved. There will be time enough to solidify the process after we have solved some of the remaining problems.

REFERENCES

1. San Francisco Administrative Code, Chapter 31.
2. The Housing Act of 1954, Section 701; Environmental review pursuant to 40 FR 36856 (1975).
3. In compliance with 40 FR 29992 (1975).
4. Section 31.22(a).
5. Section 31.35(a).
6. Section 31.35(d).
7. Section 31.36(a).

SECTION III

PUBLIC RESPONSIBILITIES—
PUBLIC ETHICS

Carol Ford Benson

Socioecological and Business Management Consultant
Washington, D.C.

The environmental professional (EP) is our conscience. He/she reminds us that short-range planning will be of no avail if we do not succeed in long-range planning to preserve a viable human environment. The ethics and intellectual honesty of the Environmental Professional matter not only today and tomorrow, but also in the next decade and the next century. We are trying to do the impossible—to extrapolate from insufficient data, to judge probable futures in the face of uncountable variables. Yet, we are the vanguard of the fight to ensure a future for the short-range planners, that we do not accidentally alter our climate so that we cannot raise enough food; loose toxic substances into our environment that accidentally sterilize us all; accidentally create a plague that affects people, wheat or rice; or otherwise accidentally create irreversible change on spaceship earth that eliminates us from competition with species less demanding of the earth's finite resources.

In our arrogance, we members of *Homo sapiens* often assume that the only limit on our ability to manipulate the environment and control it is that which man, the dreamer, puts upon his imagination. How flexible and adaptive are we? How much change, and at what rate, can people adapt? What are the selective effects of pollution?

Being a part of the conscience of society is not a comfortable role. The environmental professional must ask difficult and disconcerting questions. A problem worth serious environmental analysis inevitably turns up some unwanted information.

135

The environmental professional needs a strong sense of responsibility, a firm ethical gyroscope, to play this role, knowing that it is the right thing to do, yet without becoming self-righteous.

CHAPTER 13

MANNERS, BANNERS, EGOS AND ETHICS

Carol Ford Benson

Socioecological and Business Management Consultant
Washington, D.C.

We are the generation of transition. We are the evidence of change.
We are the result of the environmental activism of the 1960s. Our profession was legislated by inference in the National Environmental Policy Act of 1969, and defined by the Code of Ethical Practice of the National Association of Environmental Professionals in 1974.

Ours is the profession upon which others look with a little awe, a lot of sympathy, and a hearty disdain. We are whacked for providing evidence upon which environmentalists act. We are then attacked as sellouts to the establishment for providing data upon which they demur.

In choosing professionalism instead of activism, the best of us are working to institutionalize the environmental ethic, and the worst of us, for fear of losing livelihood, become biostitutes.

Vogue's Book of Etiquette and Good Manners says, "A conversation should not turn into a battle or a duel between two people. One never asks others to take sides and never does so oneself if urged. It is always possible to say, "I'm neutral, and want to stay that way.""[1]

Scientists say "science is value neutral." Bureaucrats say "don't rock the boat." Abe Lincoln reportedly said, "To keep silence when they should speak makes cowards of men."

Many environmental professionals appreciate that they finally have a professional designation. Our past NAEP president, W. Herbert Pennington, is listed in *Who's Who in America*[2] indicating his affiliation with the National Association of Environmental Professionals.

The challenge is to reach beyond the falsity and sham, to remove impediments to our own self-actualization, to liberate the concerned, informed, ethical person within each of us, before we find ourselves saying, in the words of Jeb Stuart Magruder to a Watergate judge, "Somewhere between my ambition and my ideals, I lost my compass."

We use the word *profession* incorrectly. It is not a status; it is a statement. It is a public affirmation, a profession of commitment and responsibility. A profession is made to avow the inherent obligations of special expertise. The common good depends upon a moral discharge of our responsibilities to society, especially difficult when this runs counter to the short-range interests of an employer.

It is unethical to claim that there are no adverse effects when we know there are. It is immoral to state there is no danger to health from the ingestion of Kepone, even if the fishermen of the James River can't sell fish. It is reprehensible to claim there is no significant damage to humankind and habitat when we bombard the air with pollutants or release radioactive materials, whose genetic implications are well enough understood by men of science, who are also men of conscience, to be forthrightly addressed, not swept under the appendices of a phlegmatic "impact assessment."

This may be unreasonable, but there can be a tendency to sidestep responsibility to one's self and to one's species, thinking that economics is more important than ecosystems, that "just once can't hurt anything."

I agree more with Lincoln than with Vogue. There is a genetic imperative to stop committing social genocide by yielding to the shortsighted greed of people who would increase profits at a cost of mutant children and chemically induced palsy. Human destruction is not measured in dollars.

My activist ego is fed by the beauty of live oaks grown mighty since my battle with the Base Commander to save them from the tree butchers 15 years ago. My professional ego is nurtured by the growing recognition and reputation of the National Association of Environmental Professionals and its sister societies in Michigan and California. My personal ego is gratified by being provided a podium from which to legitimately express my personal commitment to responsible ecosystem management.

When preparing impact assessments for proposed federal or state projects having potential significant impact, we are repeating our profession of commitment not just to the employer, but to uneducated workers exposed to toxic substances, to underprivileged children, breathing the foul air of the inner city, to underdeveloped Third World countries willing to strip themselves of resources to gain the advantages of affluence. We are responsible to unborn generations to pass on, through the practice of good husbandry, an earth habitat as rich and undefiled as possible.

We are obliged to take the long view as well as the short. We are obligated to live up to a stringent Code of Professional Ethics. I contend that humanity's most precious resource is the gene stream on an undefiled, habitable planet.

REFERENCES

1. *Vogue's Book of Etiquette and Good Manners* (New York: Conde Nast Publications, Inc. in association with Simon and Schuster, 1969), p. 17.
2. *Who's Who in America,* 39th edition (Chicago: Marquis Who's Who, Inc., 1976-1977).

CHAPTER 14

SOUND PRINCIPLES OVERCOME BY REALITY

Edward Bogdan

President
Quality Environmental Planning Company
White Plains, New York

The environmental movement took a large stride forward in 1969 when the National Environmental Policy Act and the Council on Environmental Quality were formed. Guidelines established by CEQ have forced all federal agencies to review and revise their environmentally related regulations, and to establish review procedures to comply with the intent of NEPA. The procedures established have, for the most part, been similar in nature. Individual agencies have performed initial assessments of their projects to determine whether they were major or minor in scope and significant or insignificant in their potential environmental impact. Minor, insignificant projects received a declaration of no significant effect. The major, significant projects were required to undergo a rigorous review and to be made public in an Environmental Impact Statement. The public, except for active environmental groups, was not made aware of the project or its potential impacts until the statements were published. Public participation usually did not take place until public hearings were held. Some projects considered insignificant by the sponsoring agencies, but damaging by some citizens, inevitably were allowed to be constructed due to lack of such public input.

Public participation in the environmental review procedure has been increasing each year. Strong environmental groups have been forcing federal and state agencies to heed NEPA. These agencies have lost numerous court decisions and consequently have been forced to prepare EIS's for projects they considered insignificant. The public has become more aware environmentally, and the large agencies have incorporated the environmental review into their project planning.

BLOCK GRANT REVIEW

The success of the environmental movement and the environmental review procedures specifically, depend, in part, upon such public participation, but there is a limit to its usefulness. Overexposure can, at times, be detrimental. An example of overexposure and environmental overkill is the stringent review procedures required by HUD, the U.S. Department of Housing and Urban Development, for its Community Development Block Grant Program. HUD has delegated the authority to act as the "Responsible Federal Official" to the Community Development (CD) project sponsoring Community Officials. In so doing, HUD has divested itself of the responsibility for the qualitative review of CD Block Grant projects, and forced the communities to review the environmental impacts of their proposed projects. These reviews usually have been performed by the Community Development Agency, the planning department or private consultants.

The basic principle is sound. The initiators of the projects are held accountable and must assess the effect on the environment. Then, where did the drafters of the review procedure regulations go wrong and why is the public overexposed? Why has this procedure become a burdensome chore to some, an impedance to large projects for others, and a program which has seldom accomplished the original goal of protecting the environment?

Excess Review

The first error made by HUD was ignoring the lack of environmental relevancy of most CD projects. The agency has required an assessment for almost every type of project. Social programs, such as food for needy school children, public works improvements and even the Administration of the local CD program were required to receive environmental clearance prior to the request for funds. It was not until the second CD year, 1976, that local program administration was exempted from the review procedure.

Public Overexposure

The aforementioned error has been compounded with that of the requirement for full exposure of each assessed project to the public. The entire annual local CD program must first be put through an A-95 Clearance process independent of the environmental review process.* The A-95

---

*In some states NEPA and A-95 Clearance processes are integrated (Ed.).

review includes multiple public hearings and approvals from interested agencies. It provides the public with the first generalized look at the proposed community development program. The actual projects are proposed at a later date, as many communities have not been able to plan for each project at the beginning of the CD year. Hence, most projects are introduced to the public when conceived, which is throughout the year.

The review process, and the environmental assessments for each project specifically, result in either a declaration of no significant effect or of significant effect upon the human environment. The vast majority of CD projects are determined to have no significant effect and thus do not require an EIS. The clearance procedure for those projects requiring only an assessment is as follows:

> First a 15-day notice of no significant effect is published in the local newspaper and distributed to interested agencies and individuals. This is the second exposure of the public to the CD program and its review procedure. At the end of the 15-day comment period, a second notice is published in the local newspaper informing the public that funds for the project will be requested from HUD in 5 days. If substantial opposition to the project is raised during either the 15-day or 5-day comment period, a public hearing should be held. The determination of need for a hearing, though, is ultimately left up to the local sponsoring agency. The last step is for the community to submit a formal request for funds and certification to HUD. Then HUD is required to entertain any objections to the community's procedural format during a 15-day comment period. Thus, another exposure of the public to the program.

This process must be adhered to for each and every nonexempted project. The public notices are being published ad infinitum. One for a social program, one for a minor public works project, etc. The significant impacts of most projects are almost always nonexistent. With such an onslaught of public notices and hearings, the relevancy dwindles and participation wanes .

Lack of Exemptions

Another error is the HUD requirement for a complete environmental analysis of all CD projects. Contents of the assessments must include sections on existing environmental conditions, impacts imposed by the project on the environment and vice versa, alternatives to the project, methods for mitigation of impacts and others. In other words, a mini impact statement is required for every CD project, regardless of its magnitude or importance. The quality of the assessments is most often poor, as they are usually being completed only to fulfill the requirement for funding. The attention given to an assessment of a social program often equals that given to one for the construction of a new neighborhood facility. This lack of differentiation is detrimental. It forces a flood of assessments having little environmental relevancy, hence reducing the quality of work. Consequently, the public becomes bored with the procedure and an agency is provided the opportunity to ram through an environmentally damaging project along with one of much lesser significance. There is no final arbiter in this review procedure. HUD is only concerned with the adherence to its procedures. If the public is not concerned, the assessment contents almost become irrelevant. The assessments are not reviewed by any agency routinely. EPA has requested submittal of all CD project assessments in some regions of the country, but has neither the staff nor time to devote to this program. Thus, a continuance of the flooding of irrelevant assessments will turn the public off to the entire review procedure and render it completely ineffectual.

The weakness of the HUD review procedure has been magnified, since its inception in 1974, by the poor economic situation. Participating communities have had limited funds. The larger, more meaningful projects have seldom been undertaken. Smaller projects, which required the minimum environmental review, were purposefully chosen to ensure a minimum of delay. The lack of funds and lack of significant projects has been accompanied by a common misunderstanding of the impact statement. To the novitiates of environmental review, an environmental impact statement signifies trouble. To some, the EIS means death to the desired project. In the few instances where a HUD CD project required an EIS, community officials have rushed to the forefront with suggestions and redesigns of the projects to have them "approved." This desire to make the project more palatable has been a positive outgrowth of the program, but not necessarily generated from an interest in the environment.

Project Delay

Misuse and misunderstanding of the environmental review procedure have not been solely the fault of local officials. Citizens have used the procedure to stall or kill projects distasteful to them but beneficial to others in the community. A New England city has attempted for several years to obtain community approval for construction of a new fire station. The residents living adjacent to the proposed sites have successfully banded together to oppose and halt construction. During the past two years, community residents have successfully used the lengthy review procedures required in the CD program to block construction on two different sites. The concerned citizens critiqued the environmental assessments and have opposed the notion that no significant impact would be imposed on the environment. The city has been morally obligated to respond to the objections and hold public hearings, although it has been made clear that the fire station would be opposed on any site within the area in need. This is a definite misuse of the right of public participation. The need for expanded fire protection in the subject area of the city is real. Fire stations do create uneasiness amongst nearby residents, and perhaps affect land valuations, but they are needed. The review procedures should be used to evaluate all possible sites and to provide the basis for choosing one site which is economical and meets with the least opposition. The constant use of the procedures to block a needed project is not beneficial to the city or to its residents.

REMEDIES

Now that it has been recognized that the environmental review procedures designed by HUD have been both misused and misunderstood and that the public is overexposed to these procedures, revision of such procedures could benefit everyone. What types of revision are needed? Are the lines of responsibility correct? Let's look at the available methods for making the entire program more manageable and meaningful.

Since HUD has decided to give the local agencies and officials the authority to act as the responsible federal official, HUD should also provide them with the ability to improve upon the program administration. The local agencies have now been administering the program for two years and have become all too familiar with its shortcomings. The environmental review procedure could be improved by permitting these agencies to propose updated procedures subject to HUD's approval. The local agencies should be given the opportunity to prepare a list of projects which they consider insignificant and worthy of automatic exemption from the review procedure. Thresholds are needed. Minor, insignificant projects, such as social programs, must be exempted. Once suggested exemption lists are provided, the area offices of HUD could review such lists and eventually propose an amendment to the CD environmental review procedures in the *Federal Register*. This would pave the way for a review procedure which assesses only the significant projects, and remove one which has become a generator of wasted action and needless report writing. Once approved, the list of exempted projects should be made public. At the onset of each new CD program year, the local agencies should publish a list of the specific projects that have been exempted from the review procedure.

A final arbiter should be established for projects that are contested by the public or by other agencies. Presently, the local agency is responsible for the preparations of the environmental assessments, receipt of comments on the assessments, the decision to hold or not to hold a public hearing, and the ultimate decision to proceed with the project.

The public participation process should be streamlined. The A-95 process and the environmental review procedure time periods should mesh to remove the requirement for excessive public hearings. Those hearings held during the A-95 process should provide for discussion of specific CD projects which have significant environmental impacts. Making such projects public at this early stage would provide an impetus for better planning and perhaps provide a method for alteration of the projects, thus making them environmentally acceptable. If this is done, such projects could be assessed properly, revised where needed, and perhaps be saved from the time delay required for the preparation of an EIS.

The concept of the Environmental Review Procedure developed by HUD is good. Its significant impact upon the environmental movement could be better. With time, and the necessary revisions, the procedure could actually accomplish the intended goal of protecting the environment.

15

THE RESPONSIBILITIES
OF ENVIRONMENTAL CONSULTANTS

John C. Henningson

Manager, Environmental Planning
Malcolm Pirnie, Inc.
White Plains, New York

The passage of the National Environmental Policy Act of 1969 fostered the requirement to bring together diverse disciplines to determine the impact of certain activities on complex environmental relationships. The Act also required that the impacts of a proposed action and its alternatives be clearly documented so that government agencies and the public would have the opportunity to review the decision-making process.

The examination of the broad, cross-disciplinary impacts of various actions has created the need for an environmental generalist, often a private consultant working for a larger planning or engineering firm, to tie together the input from specialists in various fields. The intended result is a statement which clearly presents the pertinent environmental issues to decision-makers and the public. A Code of Ethics and/or Rules of Practice are being developed to guide these activities. An examination of the complex responsibilities, both explicit and implied, of the private environmental consultant, are the subject of this chapter.

AREAS OF RESPONSIBILITY

The role of the environmental professional is only now being defined, and the viewpoint may differ depending on one's personal position, be it with a regulatory agency, as a public advocate, or a private consultant.

However, four possible areas of responsibility can clearly be defined: the public, the client, the consulting firm furnishing employment, and one's self.   A fifth area, the regulatory agency, might be considered, but may represent an overlap with the public and/or client.

It would be ideal if the consultant need only worry about the objective presentation of impacts.   However, since the significance of impacts is largely subjective, many diverse viewpoints and ancillary factors may influence the evaluation.   Obviously, the paramount concern is to limit adverse impacts and maximize the net benefits of a project, but compliance with applicable regulations and guidelines may be viewed by some as sufficient.   Other conditions influencing judgment may be related to factors such as future business development or the reputation of the consulting firm and the financial or political position of the client.   These various concerns need not be mutually exclusive.   However, at the very least, one must expect conflicts to arise which must be settled.   The key to settling diverse concerns is through communication and reasonable compromise.   But for such arbitration to work, all parties must view the issues objectively.   The adversary or "we-they" spirit which often exists must be modified so that development of a degree of mutual understanding and cooperation is facilitated.

RELATIONSHIP TO PUBLIC

The involvement of the public in the decision-making process has received increased emphasis since the passage of NEPA.   J. R. Quarles states in his recent book on his experience with the EPA, that without the potential force of public opinion, the environmental movement would lose much of its strength and influence.[1]   A recent article in *National Wildlife* suggested the Act serves as a process by which "rocks can be lifted" and the previously private decision-making process may be exposed to the "light of day."[2]   Public participation, including as a minimum a public hearing, is now required by most regulations governing federal projects.   Furthermore, as a result of many state laws spawned by NEPA, this process has been extended to many other activities.

The goals of public participation have been summarized quite well in the EPA regulations on Public Participation.[3]   In brief, public involvement is intended to: (1) achieve greater responsiveness to local concerns and priorities; (2) improve popular understanding; and (3) foster a sense of openness and mutual trust.   In a more practical sense, public involvement is necessary to avoid controversy, promote support and avoid costly delays or even abandonment of basically sound projects.

In spite of these noble objectives, explicit requirements and obvious advantages, the involvement of the public in the decision-making process has resulted in numerous difficulties. One of the greatest problems is that one cannot expect meaningful input unless there is a clear understanding of the issues. A second problem lies in the mechanisms by which the public becomes involved. Most public participation is through special-interest groups. The interest and participation of individuals is limited.[4] This situation may lead to a misrepresentation of the actual desires of the public at large. Furthermore, it leads to a third problem whereby environmental issues may be presented not out of sincere concern, but rather as an obstructionist tactic to cover other reasons for delaying a project. The issue often may reduce to the concept that a project may be sound but is unwanted in a particular state, town or backyard.

From a strictly professional standpoint the fact that most, if not all, projects involve some type of government regulation or funding means that the environmental consultant clearly must answer to the public. In addition, the consultant must recognize a social responsibility to utilize technical knowledge with concern for the public welfare.[5] The environmental professional often finds himself as an intermediary between diverse interests, one of which is that of the public. Instead of shrinking away from this role, the consultant should welcome the opportunity to foster a meaningful dialogue between groups.

The EPA has recently conducted a series of workshops throughout Region I (Air Quality Control Regions of Maine, New Hampshire, Vermont, Massachusetts, Rhode Island and Connecticut) to develop greater understanding for and improve the degree of public involvement. In at least one such workshop, strong statements were voiced by consultants in opposition to public participation. One consulting engineer felt that public participation was a big headache and that he would gladly give 5% of his fee to have someone else shoulder the responsibility. Another workshop participant complained that some means has to be devised to prevent "cuckoo bird" environmentalists from delaying projects. There was an apparent general feeling that public participation is the responsibility of the regulatory agencies or client, if a public official.

To achieve worthwhile public input, the participants must understand the environmental consequences of the action. To do so, the environmental consultant must present an accurate and full disclosure of associated environmental impacts. The consultant must seek to identify the real issues regarding the project so that local concerns are accurately reflected.[6] Complex issues should not be simplified to the point of giving a false sense of cognizance.[7] The intent should be to promote public understanding and not simply to satisfy requirements for public participation. It is also helpful to recognize the importance of so-called

community influentials in decision-making. The value of utilizing
public attitudes as a persuasive tool in achieving projects which consider
environmental costs, as well as profit and economic concerns, should
also be considered.[8]

In turn, the public must recognize its obligations to seek an active
role in project development, speak out from an informed position and
avoid the use of environmental issues to cover up other concerns.
Furthermore, the public must realize that if proposed projects must be
modified or dropped to accommodate the environment, society must
do likewise with its expectations. This means that the public must
recognize the difference between improved quality of life and extravagant
personal aspirations for amenities.[9]

RELATIONSHIP TO CLIENT

The environmental professional must recognize certain obligations
which go beyond the established narrow interpretation of client-consultant
relationships. In the past it was often assumed that the client was more
aware of the desires and needs of the public to be served. This relieved
the consultant of the responsibility to question the basic wisdom of an
action in a social context.[5] This type of relationship has been perturbed
by the current public exposure of decision-making to criticism, principally
by consumer or environmental interests. In many cases the client may
nominally represent the public sector but the decisions are based more
on politics than broad consideration of the public interest.

Decisions that are basically political may not withstand the scrutiny
of well-informed publics. Unfortunately, the technical specialist is often
the undeserving goat of criticism.[6] To limit liability, the environmental
consultant should insure that the client is fully informed and under-
stands the requirements and intent of environmental regulations and
the public participation process. The consultant should actively assist
in the development of public participation programs so that the client
may benefit fully from previous experience. To assure that decisions
are made from a fully informed position, the trade-offs between various
alternatives should be clearly delineated. It is also essential to realize
that objectivity is crucial during the planning stage, although at later
stages, after an environmentally sound project is assured, a position of
advocacy may be warranted.[7] Finally, the client should receive the
full benefit of the environmental consultant's technical expertise. The
recommendations should not reflect what the client is thought to want.
Rather it should represent the action that is the most cost-effective,
environmentally sound and implementable, considering many possible
diverse viewpoints.

The client must also appreciate the value of an open client-consultant relationship. The implementability of a project can be assured only when it can be demonstrated that the selection was made from an informed position and with public understanding. If a public representative, the client has a duty to assure adequate consideration of the views of various constituencies. As a minimum, a meaningful A95* review or similar process should be sought.

In the particular case of the private sector, the client must also meet certain social responsibilities and recognize the cost of valid environmental protection measures where public interests may be impacted.

RELATIONSHIP TO REGULATORY AGENCIES

Separation of regulatory agencies from the public and/or client may be inappropriate, since in many projects a public agency is the client by reason of funding, advocacy or permittance. This overlap has been criticized as akin to the "fox guarding the hen house."[10] Certainly the regulatory agency has the key responsibility for the environmental soundness of most projects. However, we must recognize that in almost all cases, agencies are considerably understaffed and often the reviewers are idealistic and relatively inexperienced. For these reasons it is imperative that the environmental professional present the issues clearly and concisely, yet provide sufficient background data to justify the subjective judgments regarding the estimated degree of impact. Consideration of several other factors may aid in expediting the review of a project. The consultant must work to develop a condition of openness and mutual trust commensurate with the espoused common goal of environmental soundness. It is helpful to establish at an early date an approved scope of study to avoid later confusion. Furthermore, the agency should be kept abreast of project developments through periodic conferences and timely notification of changes. It is the consultant's responsibility to keep up-to-date on changes in requirements and not fasten the blame for their ignorance on the agency.

The representatives of the government agencies must also shoulder their burden of responsibility, in spite of certain handicaps. Decisions on technical issues should reflect professional judgment rather than be oversensitive to the political climate or bureaucratic pressures. Administrative positions should reflect technical competence, where necessary,

---

*The A95 review process is required by federal regulation, if federal or state resources are involved, to ensure that the project is coordinated with state, areawide and local planning.

and not be just political plums. The agency must strive to clearly define requirements and be decisive and consistent in its administration. It should disseminate information on changes in a timely fashion and ensure accessibility of personnel. It must seek reasonable application of standards and regulations and resist undue recognition of limited interests simply because they cause controversy. A final, but very important, charge on the government agencies is to insist on a meaningful A95 or other review process wherein responsible officials do not merely sign off a project without giving it sufficient consideration in the planning process.

An additional comment regarding legislative responsibility may also be in order. At the federal level, and in states such as New York, considerable environmental legislation has been passed which has given the public a false sense of accomplishment and protection. Much of this legislation has not been substantially implemented because of grossly inadequate staffing and budgets. If substantial legislation is to be implemented, then the budgetary requirements of the administering agencies must be met.

RELATIONSHIP TO THE CONSULTING FIRM

Environmental professionals are often employed by consulting or planning firms to assess the impacts of projects which the corporation has been contracted to develop. As part of a multidisciplinary team, the environmental professional has a responsibility to delineate clearly the pertinent issues and to recommend means of mitigating adverse impact. The approach to identification of impacts must be reasonable, recognizing differences in magnitude and local importance. Areas of inadequacy in data or technical expertise must be admitted rather than allowing judgments to be poorly based. Keeping up-to-date on requirements is also critical since new developments occur quite frequently. The environmental professional should ensure that the accuracy of assessments is commensurate with the level of detail to which the project is developed. While it is important that an environmental evaluation of alternatives is begun early in the planning stage, detailed assessments often cannot be made until specific plans have been developed so that the locations of impacts are identified precisely. It must be realized that the final decision to recommend a project is highly subjective and must represent a compromise among several diverse considerations. As long as the decisions are made in full recognition of the potential impacts and public participation is provided for, the obligations of NEPA will be met.

Certain corporate responsibilities should also be addressed. If a consulting firm espouses the preparation of environmental evaluations through the employment of in-house staff, there must be a commitment to an environmental ethic throughout the organization. This commitment should be reflected by the utilization of environmental professionals at all phases of project development—from planning through implementation or construction. The firm must establish a broadly based staff with sufficient expertise to ensure adequate consideration of each critical technical area of a project. Recognition must be given to the fluid nature of the developing environmental field and time be provided to allow staff to stay up-to-date. In spite of the best efforts, environmental effects are often impossible to quantify due to an insufficient data base or variability in local conditions or values. Therefore, it must be recognized that environmental assessment is not a numbers game but represents highly subjective judgments, which require considerable contemplation. The firm should be sensitive to valid environmental protection/restoration costs and stand behind reasonable mitigating measures recommended to the clients by the environmental professional. A common occurrence is change in design subsequent to preliminary planning and environmental assessment. In such cases, the environmental professional should take part in developing the revised design and, if the changes and/or associated impacts are substantial, the public should also be reinvolved. Finally, the firm must assure that final recommendations are based on a full evaluation of all engineering, economic and environmental factors.

RESPONSIBILITIES TO SELF

This final area of responsibility is really the "nitty gritty" of the whole process. Clearly, any code of ethical behavior reduces simply to a personal resolution of one's own beliefs in his/her conduct as a professional.[11] The misrepresentation of issues, improper extrapolation of inadequate data or deletion of pertinent information are examples of actions that are clearly unprofessional. However, the determination when one is being used to justify a project as opposed to objectively evaluating its impacts is a personal issue. One must balance realism against idealism. The true magnitude of potential impacts must be placed in perspective. Objectivity means avoiding negative bias as well as premature advocacy. Furthermore, the importance of maintaining lines of communication and recognizing a reasonable compromise are part of maintaining our social order. One must always recognize that important decisions must consider a number of areas, one of which is the environment.

There are several ways by which the responsibilities of the environmental professional may be better clarified. We can work through both the older scientific societies and new organizations such as the National Association of Environmental Professionals (NAEP) to actively promote the status of the environmental professional and to define our professional and moral responsibilities more clearly. We should insist on a developmental role in project planning, rather than a post-project review, which fosters an adversary relationship. Finally, we should encourage the use of environmental professionals not only in the planning team but also during design, to specify realistic environmental protection and restoration measures, and as inspectors during the construction stage, to ensure that mitigation measures are properly implemented.

Earlier, reference was made to regulatory agency staff as the "fox in the henhouse." There are many who might view similarly the environmental professional working for a private consulting engineering or planning firm. However, if one subscribes to the thesis that environmental evaluations are best implemented in the early planning stage, the employment of dedicated environmental professionals within the design organization is an excellent means of establishing a true multidisciplinary development team. This role is complex and in many ways more difficult than that of the public advocate or the regulatory reviewer. There is clearly a need for environmental professionals working cooperatively in each of these capacities. Indeed, without such cooperation, the full realization of the goals of NEPA and other worthy environmental legislation may never be attained.

REFERENCES

1. Quarles, J. R. *Cleaning Up America—An Insider's View of the EPA* (Boston: Houghton Mifflin, 1976).
2. Houck, O. A. "How People Who Remember Clean Water are Using New Laws to Bring It Back," *Natl. Wildlife* (December 1976).
3. U.S. Environmental Protection Agency. "Public Participation in Water Pollution Control" (40CFR105), *Federal Register* 38(163) (August 23, 1973).
4. National Commission on Water Quality. "Public Participation, The Water Pollution Control Act 1972, Institutional Assessment" (Springfield, Virginia: NTIS, October 1975).
5. Turnick, T. L. "Public Versus Client Interest—An Ethical Dilemma for the Engineer," *Eng. Issues—J. Prof. Act.*, American Society of Civil Engineers (ASCE) (January 1975).
6. Spitko, J. E. "The Engineers Response to Non-Engineering Criticism of His Professional Work," *Eng. Issues—J. Prof. Act.*, American Society of Civil Engineers (ASCE) (October 1975).

7. Stever, H. G. "Professional Judgments and Personal Responsibility,"
    Proc. Energy Environ. Ethics Seminar (Washington, D.C.: George
    Washington University and NAEP, 1975).
8. Grecco, W. L. "Identifying Your Client," *Eng. Issues–J. Prof. Act.,*
    American Society of Civil Engineers (ASCE) (October 1975).
9. Clark, F. J. "The Engineer's Role," *Eng. Issues–J. Prof. Act.,*
    American Society of Civil Engineers (ASCE) (April 1972).
10. Gouatos, G. C. "Social Responsibility Within the Present Code of
    Ethics," *Eng. Issues–J. Prof. Act.,* American Society of Civil
    Engineers (ASCE) (July 1975).
11. Reynolds, A. F. "Institutionalization of the Environmental Ethic,"
    Proc. Energy Environ. Ethics Seminar (Washington, D.C.: George
    Washington University and NAEP, 1975).

16

ENVIRONMENTAL CONCERNS IN PLANNING
AND DEVELOPMENT AT THE LOCAL LEVEL

Philip Barske

Consultant
Fairfield, Connecticut

Developers and local decision-makers face significant environmental concerns in planning for a local project.[1] Each group operating in any community has certain environmental responsibilities. The modern developer is faced with an awesome array of federal, state and local environmental laws and regulations. The local government agencies are faced with decision-making that has significant social, economic and environmental implications. Most of the state's environmental programs are carried out at the local level. Here, lay citizens are given the important responsibility to administer environmental laws and regulations equitably.

Modern understanding and the demand for environmental concern have been basically accepted by most people and are now a part of a developer's cost of doing business. We now, and in the future, will experience increasing numbers of environmental controls and regulations. This will affect the developer, the community and the individual— particularly at the local level.

The National Environmental Protection Act of 1969 (NEPA) laid the foundation for environmental regulations at the federal and other levels of government. Actually, some federal and state actions and local environmental regulatory programs predated NEPA, but the passage of NEPA solidified and set the pattern for what has become a nationwide, even global, movement. By 1976, environmental laws had been enacted throughout the many government levels, involving 36 states, 3,000 countries, 18,000 municipalities and 17,000 townships.

Nearly three-quarters of the states have followed the National Environmental Policy Act with statewide environmental control acts. Some of the nation's towns have established local controls that exceed those of the state. It can be assumed that within a decade all states and all levels of government will be operating under a variety of environmental restraints.

BACKGROUND

Good buildable land is relatively limited. Until recently, we have used our prime lands without concern for future generations. Productive farm lands too often had to retreat before marching rows of homes (Figure 16-1). Man has put his imprint almost everywhere on the land, sometimes wisely, but often without a thought for the environment. Before environmental concerns became an integral part of a building concept, homes were sited and constructed without a thought to the surroundings. "Cookie cutter" homes were strewn over the landscape. (Figure 16-2.) For too many years, marshes were dredged and filled by government agencies and developers. Shorefront homes

Figure 16-1. The conflict of development and farm land.

Figure 16-2. The imprint of man on the land.

have become extremely popular during the past three decades. Thousands of productive marshlands are now industrial and residential sites.

It is no longer necessary to make major blunders in local land use through lack of ecological knowledge (Figure 16-3). It is no longer necessary to sacrifice long-term environmental values for short-term economic needs in any sort of project. It is generally possible to reconcile the conflicting demands upon land and resources so that irreparable damage is avoided and human populations can enjoy meaningful benefits.

PLANNING WITH ENVIRONMENTAL CONCERNS

This chapter follows the general steps and sequences that the developer, the planner and the local community governing body would go through from inception to local acceptance of a master building plan for a small community project of 200-1000 acres. This process involves the traditional business and local regulatory commitments and requirements, but we now must add the new phase and costs of environmental impact analysis and public involvement.

Modern environmental impact reports and conceptual site planning presentations become highly involved technical reports, and generally

Figure 16-3. A development with long-term environmental values.

it is a layman board or commission that must make important land use decisions. Over the past several years of environmental impact reports, one fact stands out and that is the complexity, involved technical data and verbosity of such reports. It is almost beyond the ability of many board or commission members to truly comprehend the volume of ecological-social data that some environmental studies include. Yet, decisions must be made that influence land use, economics, land values and other external aspects. Every board and commission member is not a trained ecologist, planner or landscape designer, but these are the people who must make the decisions.

The Eco-plan process offers an important means of integrating environmental concerns with the overall land use planning process (Figure 16-4). It is a new tool offering a significant advance in land use planning that, when properly used and understood, will permit continued growth and development of our communities with the minimal adverse impact on the natural resource base.

Planners and ecologists must be able to present the coordinated development concept to the decision-makers in a readily understandable form to overcome the understanding-comprehension barrier. It is essential to present relevant environmental data to all concerned persons

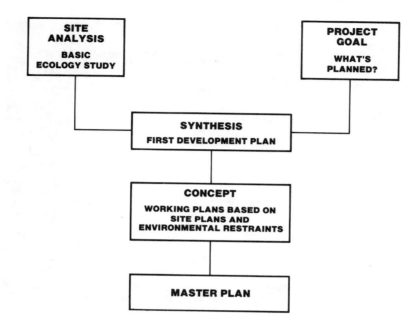

Figure 16-4. Developing the eco-plan.

and agencies. The report should not be a deep scientific treatise but
be presented in a written and graphic form that is understandable,
comprehensive and logical. The report should contain enough scientific
background and reasoning to satisfy experts within the field. A well-
planned and easily understood concept will go a long way to influence
decisions on the basis of facts derived from fundamental ecological
studies and evaluations.

A developer must be prepared to consult with a variety of resource
specialists (Figure 16-5), and should employ the services of a professional
land planner to integrate resource data into the proposed plan for
development. Decision-making in most towns is still divided between
the traditional agencies—typified by Planning and Zoning—and the many
new commissions and boards now involved in land use decisions.

SITE ANALYSIS PHASE

The first step in developing a logical Eco-plan is site analysis. The
limitations and opportunities of the site are evaluated in terms of
geology, soils, water, wetlands, vegetation, wildlife and historical concerns.

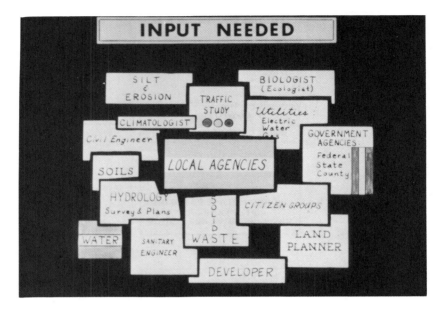

Figure 16-5. Resource specialists
whose inputs are needed for development planning.

The Land Use Pyramid (Figure 16-6) illustrates the variety of information needed. Starting at the bottom with the site maps and considering the biological, cultural and social concerns, this sequence will help those involved in the decision-making process arrive at sound land use judgments.

Consideration should be given to the existing vegetation in this first step of the eco-plan. Woodlands are aesthetically pleasing (Figure 16-7). They also help cleanse the air, reduce wind velocity, protect watersheds, support wildlife and perform other important ecological functions.

Old farm roads and trails usually followed natural contours (Figure 16-8). Often these roads can be utilized as a part of the proposed road system for the development project.

Wetlands are probably one of the most important siting factors. A basic function of wetlands is to store and absorb storm flow (Figure 16-9). Environmental evaluations must include a detailed study and analysis of this resource. Many eastern states have enacted inland wetlands laws and delegated regulatory responsibility to the local communities, giving them their first, basic environmental authority.

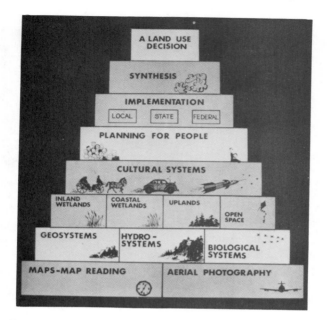

Figure 16-6. Information needed for sound land use decision.

Figure 16-7. Natural vegetation performs important ecological functions.

Figure 16-8. Old roads usually follow natural contours.

Figure 16-9. Wetlands store and absorb storm flow.

The site analysis provides pertinent information to support the development project and supply scientific data for an environmental impact report.

PROJECT GOAL

While the site analysis is being prepared, the developer must simultaneously define the project goal and identify basic plans for the area. What is the target purpose? Is it homes? Industry? Commercial? Or is it a combination of these? Building to meet social and economic demands should be the responsibility of both the developer and local decision-maker (Figure 16-10). Consideration should be given to who will be served—the young family? Minorities? The elderly or low income groups? The costs of housing are creating racial and economic segregation that is reaching a critical stage!

Figure 16-10. The project goal should meet social and economic demands.

SYNTHESIS PHASE

This third step of the eco-plan, synthesis, is land planner's use of the environmental analysis data gathered in the site and program plans. Here, the information is evaluated as it relates to the site and the developer's project goals. Now the land planner begins to blend environmental restraint and the forces that control land use and finally arrives at an economically sound and environmentally acceptable plan.

Scientific reports from the various resource specialists, basic maps delineating land capabilities and restraints, knowledge of existing building codes and regulations are brought to the table where planners, environmentalists and developers review development potentials (Figure 16-11).

Figure 16-11. Planners, environmentalists and developers review development potentials.

CONCEPT PLANS

From the synthesis phase, where environmental data have been evaluated and melded into the developer's program, we enter the concept stage where conceptual site plans begin to materialize.

At this stage of an eco-plan, formal meetings are held with the various local decision-making groups. These town boards and commissions actively enter into the evaluation of the project according to their separate responsibilities.

A series of charts, prepared by professional land planners, summarizes the presentation of data for local town agencies. This soils map (Figure 16-12) delineates the various soils types and indicates those lands most suitable for building purposes. A systematic approach to analyzing a site's major characteristics involves the use of a series of overlay maps that show the opportunities and limitations of the site for building purposes. An analysis chart is usually prepared which indicates basic environmental concerns, such as existing vegetation, steep slopes, rocky outcrops and vulnerable wetlands.

The synthesis chart (Figure 16-13) identifies the critical environmental restraints that would limit land use. At this stage, potential building sites begin to appear.

The concept map (Figure 16-14) is the first plan for development and delineates buildable land units and environmentally critical areas. The basic road system and location of utility lines can now be plotted.

The master plan (Figure 16-15) for any project is subject to regulated change, but environmental concerns must be maintained.

Environmental impact studies come in all thicknesses and in all degrees of quality (Figure 16-16). The environmental impact statement should be concise and factual. It is important to describe the area and list proposals for development, describe physical and biological features, identify probable impacts on the natural cultural and social environment, consider unavoidable adverse effects, indicate alternatives, and present short- and long-term relationship and enhancement and mitigation potentials.

Up to this point in development planning, most concerns have been environmental, but the economics of the program cannot be ignored. The cost factors of home building and purchasing have a direct impact on the social structure. Exclusionary and restrictive barriers are imposed when home costs exceed the purchasing power of the middle and lower income brackets. Today, local decision-makers and developers must face environmental, social and economic realities for any major development (Figure 16-17).

Town governments play an important role in resource protection by working in support of local, state and federal laws and regulations (Figure 16-18). As decision-making bodies, the commissions and boards must make choices based on personal knowledge, environmental impact reports and/or the advice of professional staff—when available. As a plan

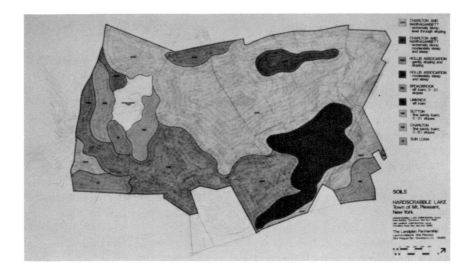

Figure 16-12. Soils map.

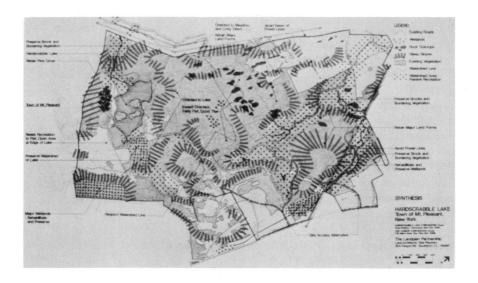

Figure 16-13. Synthesis chart.

Figure 16-14. Concept map.

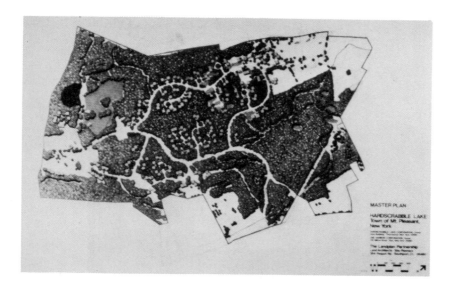

Figure 16-15. Master plan.

Figure 16-16. Environmental impact studies.

Figure 16-17. Facing economic realities.

Figure 16-18. Local decision-makers.

firms up, the local commissions and boards again become increasingly involved. Most decisions made at the town level are influenced by potential costs to the town, regulatory ordinances and tradition.

The success in society's demand for environmentally sound development depends on the proper understanding and administration by government decision-makers and the interested public. Since there is greater decision-making by boards and citizens, it behooves both groups to better understand, in layman's terminology, the environmental, social, economic and siting problems confronting any project. Once data are developed in response to environmental laws and local regulations, it must be interpreted so that those involved at the local level can understand the data presented.

MASTER PLANS

The conceptual plans have now been reviewed, revised and finally approved by the local decision-makers after the developer has included provisions to meet environmental requirements and site control features. Architects and land planners can now draw up detailed master plans. Professional land planners must work closely with the architect to ensure that all resource concerns and requirements are considered in the master planning stage. It is most important for the developer to negotiate and agree with the subcontractors to include all necessary provisions to meet all regulations for environmental protection. Many towns now require performance bonds.

The design team must consider the increasingly important need for energy conservation in the designing and siting of homes. Use of roof overhang, generous insulation, shade trees, and attached town houses are some of the measures to consider (Figure 16-19). Solar devices are being perfected to supply energy.

FOLLOW-THROUGH

During the follow-through stage of the eco-plan is the time to introduce enhancement and mitigation measures (Figure 16-20). Frequent inspections should be made by local government agencies and the developer as the project progresses. This will ensure compliance with all regulations and contract specifications. The developer should

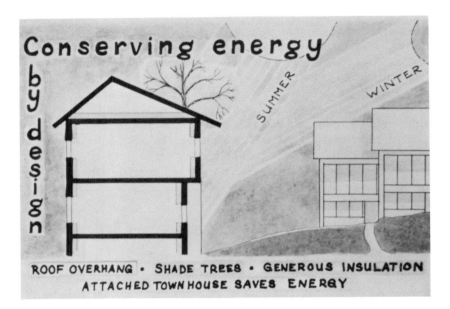

Figure 16-19. Conserving energy through design.

Figure 16-20. Enhancement and mitigation measures during construction.

assign at least one knowledgeable staff member to be responsible for environmental liaison between the regulatory agencies and subcontractors.

Soil erosion and sediment control are major environmental concerns. Towns are beginning to require on-site control measures for all development projects. Simple guidelines recommended by the United States Soil Conservation Service include such practical measures as keeping disturbed areas small, stabilizing them, controlling runoff, and retaining sediment. By instituting a sound program of storm water management, runoff can be temporarily retained and the degree of discharge effectively maintained in a range that existed prior to development (Figure 16-21). Natural features on the site can be retained and attractively blended into the siting and landscaping.

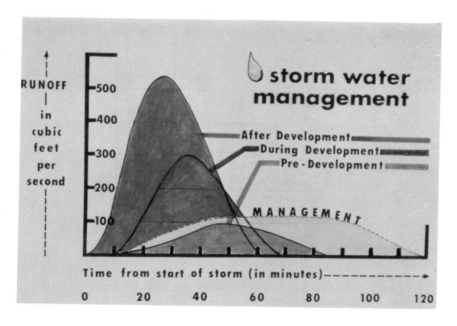

Figure 16-21. Water management as an environmental concern.

Today, progressive developers are capitalizing on environmental considerations and, in many instances, going beyond the basic environmental requirements (Figure 16-22). This is good business! Decision-makers need to know basic guidelines to be discussed as well as the proposed development site. They should study related information, seek technical help, and get answers to questions before making final

Figure 16-22.   Enjoying a life of quality.

decisions.   Sound planning by all professionals leads to environmentally compatible land use.   Innovative environmental action and continued concern by local decision-makers will permit coming generations to enjoy a life of quality in their homes and surroundings.

REFERENCES

1.   Barske, P.   "Environmental Concerns in Planning and Developing a New Community," an audio-visual overview for developers and local decision-makers, 1976.

CHAPTER 17

REGULATORY REFORM IN ENVIRONMENTAL ASSESSMENT: IS IT NEEDED? CIVIL AERONAUTICS BOARD (CAB) —TO BE OR NOT TO BE?

James M. Burger

Shaw, Pittman, Potts and Trowbridge
Washington, D. C.

CAB AND THE ENVIRONMENT

One might anticipate that the agency charged with granting airlines authority to operate jumbo jetliners from all U.S. points would be deeply involved with NEPA; however, this is not the case. The Civil Aeronautics Board reached that conclusion only after painful and expensive disruptions.

CAB's actions have minimal impact on the environment for at least four reasons. First, in 1969, the U.S. air transportation system was reasonably mature and the most that the CAB could do under its authority was tinker with the system. Second, the environmental models and instruments used to measure aircraft noise and pollution are not capable of accurately measuring the minimal impact of most new proposed services, assuming there is any impact. Third, the CAB has no legal control over schedules and aircraft types. Finally, the Federal Aviation Administration (FAA) and the Environmental Protection Agency (EPA) have decision-making authority which impacts on the interrelationship between the environment and commerical aviation.

CAB went through a considerable exercise to demonstrate this. From an economic regulatory point of view, the ability of an incumbent carrier to delay new entry on one of its lucrative monopoly routes by using NEPA as an anticompetitive tool was most interesting. That carrier, National Airlines, in the recent *Miami-Los Angeles Nonstop Competitive Case,*[1] received a short-term benefit of between $9 and $19.6 million, according to its own calculations, as a result of the delay in that case.

CAB AND FAA JURISDICTION

The Federal Aviation Act of 1958[2] (originally the Civil Aeronautics Act of 1938) prohibits air carriers from engaging in air transportation without a certificate of public convenience and necessity. Upon application, after notice and hearing, the CAB "shall issue a certificate" if it finds the applicant fit, willing and able to perform the transportation and the transportation is required by the "public convenience and necessity." The Board's ability to condition the grant of a certificate is severely restricted by Section 401(e) of the 1958 Act which states:

> "No term, condition or limitation of a certificate shall restrict the right of an air carrier to add to, or change schedules, equipment, accommodations and facilities for performing the authorized transportation and service as the development of the business and the demands of the public shall require."[3]

Schedules and equipment are the two most important variables which affect the environmental impact of air service. But the CAB is powerless to order a carrier to use more environmentally acceptable equipment or to operate during daylight hours when noise would be less annoying.

Of more importance, the vast majority of CAB route cases will not have any measurable impact on the environment. The CAB has been in the business of granting certificates since 1938. By June of 1969, 37 carriers held certificates, naming 1453 duplicated cities.[4] In 1976, 36 carriers were serving 1422 duplicated cities.[5] These figures indicate that little service to new points had been authorized by CAB since the passage of NEPA. Most sizable cities are connected by scheduled air service. Accordingly, CAB cases generally consist of granting authority to a new carrier to compete with an incumbent over an already-served route, or to connect two cities nonstop which are currently served one-stop or by connection. It is rare that a CAB case could mean significantly increased aircraft operations at any given city.

The actions of other federal authorities and local airport authorities do have a significant impact on the environment. The Secretary of Transportation and his delegate, the Administrator of the FAA, are empowered to take actions which will have a pervasive impact on the environment. One of the most important powers granted to the FAA is the issuance of type certificates for aircraft.[6] Under this authority, the FAA can require changes in the noise and pollution characteristics of aircraft or deny a type certificate all together. In 1968, the Federal Aviation Act of 1958 was amended to include a provision empowering the FAA to revoke any certificates, including type, production and individual aircraft airworthiness certificates, if the aircraft failed to comply with noise standards.[7] This mandate was tempered by a requirement that the FAA determine "whether any proposed standard, rule or regulation is economically reasonable, technologically practicable and appropriate. . . ." The FAA has recently proposed noise standards that would call for an overall reduction in the noise of aircraft and airline fleets. In addition, the Noise Control Act of 1972 mandates the FAA, with EPA consultation, to provide:

> "for control and abatement of aircraft noise and sonic boom
> including the application of such standards and regulations in
> the issuance, amendment, modification, suspension, or revocation
> of any certification authorized by this title."

FAA power over airports is exercised in two ways: the grant of funds to construct or improve airports and pervasive control over the movement of aircraft. With the exception of Washington National Airport and Dulles International Airport, the FAA acts in few instances as a landlord. Instead, under the Airport and Airway Development Act of 1970,[8] the FAA is charged with overseeing "substantial expansion and improvement of the airport and airway system. . .to meet the demands of interstate commerce, the postal service and the national defense." Under this program, the FAA approves grants for construction of entirely new airports (*e.g.,* substantial funds for Dallas/Fort Worth Airport were provided under the Airport Development Aid Program) or for the improvement of existing airports (runway extensions, new electronic landing aids, etc.). These actions will have a substantial impact on the environment, not only in the immediate sense, *i.e.,* dislocation of the local ecology, but will have a significant effect on the operation of aircraft in the immediate vicinity. Thus, the FAA routinely prepares environmental impact statements under NEPA.

Under Section 307 of the Federal Aviation Act:

> "The Secretary of Transportation is authorized and directed to
> develop plans for and formulate policy with respect to the use of
> the navigable air space; and assigned by rule, regulation or order,
> the use of the navigable airspace under such terms, conditions
> and limitations as he may deem necessary in order to insure the
> safety of aircraft and the efficient utilization of such air space."

The FAA Administrator establishes landing and takeoff patterns at airports, controls the movement of aircraft in those patterns, establishes landing and enroute radio navigational facilities, and controls the movement of aircraft enroute between airports. Accordingly, all the CAB can do is authorize an air carrier to extend its routes to another city. That city is almost always a medium or a large hub airport, which numerous commercial aircraft already serve. The CAB cannot dictate to the carrier what type of equipment is permissible or how frequently it may or may not exercise that authority. The FAA has exclusive jurisdiction over the type of aircraft manufactured and used, the path through the sky the aircraft will fly, and when and how that aircraft will land at a given airport. Thus, to determine whether its actions would have any impact on the environment, the CAB would have to speculate on the actions of both the air carrier and the FAA, over which it has no control. In fact, however, the CAB has done just that.

ENVIRONMENTAL ISSUES

CAB'S concerted response to NEPA did not actually occur until the Autumn of 1973. This increased concern, surprisingly enough, was not generated by an environmentalist group. Instead, it was generated by National Airlines in an attempt to thwart or at least delay competitive service on its lucrative Miami-Los Angeles route. Prior to 1973, CAB essentially gave pro forma treatment to NEPA.

Pre-NEPA

Prior to the enactment of NEPA, the U.S. Court of Appeals of the District of Columbia Circuit held that "questions relating to environmental impact of proposed services upon persons and property lying below the routes are substantial and clearly relevant to CAB's certification inquiry."[9] In that case, CAB had denied full party status to a citizens' group alleging a keen interest in reduction of noise, air pollution and safety hazards attendant to air traffic above their property. The CAB had granted the civic organization the right to participate in the proceeding, as somewhat less than a full party. The Court did not overturn CAB's decision granting a certificate for scheduled helicopter service in the Baltimore-Washington area, but labeled as "folly" the thought that consideration of environmental impact was not a proper issue before the CAB. Civic associations wanted the CAB to deny the application for the proposed service or reopen the record for additional environmental evidence. The CAB refused to do either and held that:

> "... new service ... is required by the public convenience and necessity despite the fact that some additional noise might result. Where there is a showing on the record of unusual noise by an opponent of the service, a different result might be indicated."[10]

CAB's First NEPA Rules

In June, 1970, CAB adopted implementing policy regulations, which essentially paraphrased NEPA, and stated that if a proceeding might result in a major federal action significantly affecting the quality of the human environment, the CAB order setting the proceeding for hearing would contain possible environmental consequences. The threshold test for a major federal action was:

> "Primarily but not exclusively, those licensing activities which result in authorization of air transportation
> (i)   to an area not previously served by air transportation; or
> (ii)   to be operated under conditions or with equipment which might result in changes significantly affecting noise or air pollution levels."[11]

In cases where the threshold test was triggered, the regulations required that the record include sufficient data to prepare an environmental impact statement. However, the rule failed to define what significant or unusual noise or pollution would be. Thus, it was essentially left up to the individual participants in a proceeding to allege that CAB's threshold had been crossed. Furthermore, CAB did not specifically delineate the nature of the additional evidence to be adduced if the proposed action might result in a significant impact on the environment.

Prior to the *Miami-Los Angeles Case,* CAB rarely invoked its NEPA regulations. Two of the few examples involved:

1. CAB's proposal to authorize vertical takeoff and landing-type services in the northeast corridor;[12] and
2. Wright Air Lines' proposal to operate aircraft between the downtown airports in Cleveland and Detroit.[13]

In the *VTOL Investigation,* an environmental decision was not reached because that case never proceeded to a final CAB decision. In the Wright Air Lines proceeding, CAB's Administrative Law Judge found that the proposed operations would have no adverse effects on the environment.

In two cases, civic or environmental groups attempted, without success, to induce CAB to act. In one case, Inglewood, California asked CAB to revoke the authorization of one or more air carriers serving Los Angeles International Airport.[14] Inglewood alleged that this would decrease current congestion and, accordingly, be environmentally beneficial. In denying Inglewood's petition, the CAB noted that even if it had the power to accomplish the requested changes, the disruptive consequences would outweigh any potential benefits. The CAB's statutory authority to revoke authorizations is severely limited: it can revoke a certificate only "for intentional failure to comply with any provision of [the act] or any order, rule or regulation," and must give the offending carrier the opportunity to correct its behavior. CAB pointed out that "Inglewood's primary goals of air and noise pollution abatement are the subject of continuing efforts by other agencies (*e.g.,* Federal Aviation Administration and the Environmental Protection Agency). . .".

In a second proceeding, the National Resources Defense Council (NRDC) requested an investigation of CAB's implementation of NEPA.[15] NRDC alleged that CAB failed to consider the conflict between NEPA and the provision of the Federal Aviation Act preventing CAB from restricting schedules and aircraft types and failed to consider the inconsistencies between NEPA and CAB's statutory mandate to promote air transportation. NRDC requested CAB to revise its report to the Council on Environmental Quality, stating that CAB's current statutory authority was entirely adequate to comply with NEPA and that no basis existed for proposing corrective legislation to give the CAB additional power to comply with NEPA.

"After careful deliberation" NRDC's complaint was dismissed. CAB found that its inability to control aircraft types and scheduling was not a "deficiency." Instead, CAB found that its actions in other cases, such as the *Domestic Passenger Fare investigation,* were designed to discourage excess scheduling and had been based, in part, on environmental considerations. CAB noted that other than route certification, its actions did not "often rise to the NEPA standards. . .". CAB said it encouraged participation in all cases by interested parties in assisting in the formation of a "meaningful record" on "environmental impact," and concluded that this position on participation by interested parties and its NEPA regulation would "insure 'that presently unquantified environmental amenities and values may be given appropriate consideration in decision-making along with economical and technical considerations.'"

Miami-Los Angeles

It was not until the *Miami-Los Angeles Case* that CAB took a hard look at newly authorized service. The origin of this case can be traced to 1951. In that year, a number of carriers sought authority for direct service between the two points, but in 1951 only 11.2 passengers per day traveled between Miami and Los Angeles. The CAB denied all applications for direct service, authorizing interchange service among several carriers.[16] An interchange is an arrangement that provides single-plane service over a long route, without involving additional competitive carriers over one or more segments of the route. On a given interchange flight, a plane of one of the interchange partners flies the entire trip, but the crew is changed so that each carrier flies only over its own route segment. Most interchanges involve only two carriers, although occasionally there are three. The route's value increased as the southeastern and southwestern United States grew economically, so that the CAB authorized National Airlines to operate nonstop between Miami and Los Angeles in 1961.[17]

In 1969, CAB found National's monopoly service inefficient. It granted Miami-Los Angeles authority to Northwest Airlines, the weakest trunk carrier, to strengthen the carrier.[18] Some suggested the carrier only desired the route for a bargaining chip in merger negotiations.[19] CAB affirmed the award "after Northwest categorically advised the CAB that the carrier did not contemplate any merger. . .".[20] Six days later, Northeast announced merger negotiations with Northwest Airlines.

In the subsequent merger case, the CAB excluded the Miami-Los Angeles route from the merger. Northwest backed out of its agreement to merge with Northeast. Subsequently, Delta Air Lines and Northeast signed a merger agreement. CAB approved the merger without the Miami-Los Angeles route. This time the acquiring carrier accepted the decision.

Northeast's relatively ineffectual competitive service ceased in July, 1972. In August, CAB instituted the *Miami-Los Angeles Competitive Nonstop Investigation.*[21] No environmental findings were contained in CAB's instituting order.

By 1974, 623 passengers a day traveled between Miami and Los Angeles. Accordingly, Pan American World Airways, and every trunk carrier (except United Air Lines) seriously prosecuted their applications for authority to compete with National between Miami and Los Angeles. Each of the nine carriers seeking the route argued that its competitive proposal would most benefit the public. Of these carriers, Pan American submitted the strongest case for award of the route. It argued that it would divert only $2 million per year from National Airlines, that it needed the route for strengthening purposes more than any other carrier, and proposed to operate the largest number of seats in the market.

Seven months after the proceeding had been instituted, after close of the record, National's brief to the Administrative Law Judge alleged that CAB had failed to comply with NEPA because authorization of a competing Miami-Los Angeles carrier would be a major federal action significantly affecting the quality of the environment. Therefore, National claimed that without the preparation of an environmental impact statement, any award would be invalid. National maintained that the only way CAB could authorize a competing carrier would be by reopening the record for environmental evidence.

The Administrative Law Judge found that the public convenience and necessity required authorization of a competing carrier and that Pan American should receive the route. The Judge did not give National's eleventh hour argument a warm reception:

"National has had a full opportunity to present evidence with respect
to the environmental issue. The carrier, however, offered no evidence
dealing with this matter. National's tardy enthusiasm for environmental matters has, of course, effectively deprived all other parties of
any opportunity to comment on brief with respect to National's
contentions."

The Judge then specifically responded to National's environmental claims,
finding that the small increased use of fuel, if any, and the relatively small
additional operations at Miami and Los Angeles would in no way have a
discernible impact on the environment.

Under its regulations, the CAB exercised discretionary authority to review
the Judge's decision. National reiterated its environmental argument. The
CAB had a visceral reaction that the maximum three additional round-trips
between Los Angeles and Miami could not "significantly affect the quality
of the human environment," but was troubled by the fact that it did not have
a detailed environmental record demonstrating this judgment. It decided
"to give the fullest consideration to the environmental questions raised by
National."

"While the CAB does not believe that further procedures in this case
are necessarily required under the judicial decisions interpreting
NEPA, we are nonetheless desirous of complying with the spirit as
well as the letter of the statute."

CAB instructed its staff to prepare a statement regarding environmental
matters. More than 14 months later, CAB staff issued a "final statement of
environmental assessment." Some two years and nine months after the Judge
issued his Initial Decision, the CAB granted competitive authority, not to
Pan American, but to Western Air Lines. One interesting result is that National
managed to forestall competition by alleging environmental impact. Later,
National joined other carriers in seeking a solution to the technical difficulties
raised by the NEPA issue, since National itself was seeking new authority in
other cases. It has been estimated that National's short-term gain due to lack
of competition was between $9 and $19.6 million.

CAB'S NEW ENVIRONMENTAL REGULATIONS

CAB's action in halting the *Miami-Los Angeles Case* for the preparation of
an environmental statement had a far-reaching impact. Not only was that
case brought to a halt, but numerous others that were pending or in the process of hearing were similarly affected. Many of these cases were as, or more,
important than the *Miami-Los Angeles Case,* such as the *Transatlantic Route
Proceeding,*[22] *Capacity Reduction Agreement Case*[23] and several more route
exchange cases.

Initially, CAB staff had serious difficulties in preparing a request for environmental evidence because it was composed of legal and economic experts and did not have a single environmental expert. It turned, in part, to experts in the Department of Transportation. CAB staff's first attempt at a request for environmental information was exceedingly cumbersome.

Noise Thresholds

American Airlines, which was eager to successfully complete two route exchange cases, engaged outside consulting firms to prepare the environmental evidence. These route exchange cases were essentially simple operational changes, switching carriers with very minor increases and decreases in frequencies. After considerable effort and expense, American submitted a 142-page volume, which contained 31 oversize graphics and a 29-page, separately bound, conclusion. The American effort involved an analysis of existing flights and newly proposed flights with regard to fuel burn, pollution and noise. Noise—the most difficult to calculate—was handled by an analysis of the potential flight paths at each airport and calculation of the daily noise exposure. A change in noise exposure was determined by the use of the Aircraft Sound Description System. The conclusion was that there would be no discernible impact. This effort, analyzing six cities for two carriers, cost $50,000.

In the larger *Transatlantic Route Proceeding,* there were some 28 domestic cities and some 13 carrier applicants. The transatlantic carriers were determined to find an alternative approach to environmental impact. Their conclusion was reinforced by a recent EPA study which showed that even with a 20% reduction in flights at a hub airport, there would only be minimal or imperceptible impact on aircraft noise levels.[24] In the *Transatlantic Case,* even the largest proposals would only result in fractional increases.

At the same time, Pan American, on behalf of the carrier applicants in *Miami-Los Angeles,* was working with Bolt Beranek and Newman Inc. to develop a noise screening analysis. This analysis was based on the noise exposure forecast method (NEF) which is an average noise level over a 24-hour period, expressed as contour lines, surrounding a given airport. Basically, NEF is a planner's tool. While livable, the geographic area between the NEF 30 and 40 contour lines will not be comfortable for all persons. The area closer to the airport, wholly contained within the NEF 40 contour, is considered unacceptable for any uses other than those that can accommodate high levels of noise.

The carriers' and their consultants' problem before the CAB was the formulation of a defensible criterion to indicate whether there would be perceptible changes, as opposed to defining what the actual change would be.

There was a need for a threshold test showing whether a discernible change would occur if a carrier's proposed service plan was in fact operated. If a perceptible change was indicated, only then would it become necessary to use more precise tools to determine the local effects of that change.

Bolt Beranek and Newman developed a mathematical model[25] that predicted airport noise contours including adjustments for (1) night operations, (2) older, less-quiet, four-engine aircarft, and (3) long-range operations.[26] The model developed by Bolt Beranek and Newman computes the relationship between the NEF contour area and operations at the airport as follows:

$$\text{Area of Contour} = A_o \cdot 10^{\frac{[10 \log N + 24 - NEF + C]}{15}}$$

where A_o is a constant related to fleet mix and NEF contour, N equals the number of operations, NEF is the contour value, C equals the adjustment factor for day vs night, 4-engine Low Bypass-Ratio (LBPR) and short- vs long-haul operations. The Bolt Beranek and Newman formula was used in the screening analysis to compare the area between the NEF 30 and 40 contours before and after the implementation of the airlines' proposal. EPA studies have shown that even an increase of five NEF units caused complaints; and an increase of two NEF units might cause complaints.[26] A single unit of NEF change was picked as the threshold above which a detailed analysis would have to be prepared.

Air Pollution Thresholds

Meanwhile, R. Dixon Speas Associates prepared a pollutant analysis screening test to determine when an airline proposal would justify closer analysis of its environmental effects. The standard was developed using pollutant dispersion analysis techniques applied to EPA emissions data. The threshold was established below the relevant units of the National Air Quality Standards determined by EPA. The screening standards for pollutants resulted in an order of magnitude estimate of particular pollutant concentrates at airport boundaries. If the proposed aircraft operations resulted in increased total pollutant emissions, but the change at the airport boundary were less than 1% of the air quality primary standards, no further pollutant emission analysis would be required. If the threshold level were exceeded, additional analysis, accounting for specific local conditions, would be required.

Both the noise and the pollutant screening tests were used in several cases, including *Miami-Los Angeles* and the *Transatlantic Route Proceeding,* and accepted by CAB's staff. In virtually all cases before CAB, these relatively simple and inexpensive tests showed that no discernible impact would result.

ENVIRONMENTAL ANALYSIS RESULTS

A great deal of time, energy and expense resulted from CAB's environmental exercise. The conclusion was what most environmental experts, the CAB and the carriers had assumed: a change of several flights at an air carrier airport would not have any discernible environmental impact. The question remains, was it worth it? This author concludes that it was not. All that CAB action generally accomplishes is to give a carrier a new point or more flexibility operating between points it already serves. The FAA and the EPA have direct control over the noise and pollution resulting from aircraft operations, as well as the construction and operation of airports. Thus, in upholding the decision of another agency with similar types of powers not to examine environmental impact, a U.S. District Court found that a detailed environmental analysis was not required where "the federal action will *possibly* allow others to set into motion projects which *possibly* will affect the local environment."[27]

REFERENCES

1. CAB Order 76-3-93 (March 15, 1976) (Hereinafter referred to as *Miami-Los Angeles*).
2. 49 U.S.C. §1301 *et seq.*
3. 49 U.S.C. §1371.
4. Civil Aeronautics Board, FY 1969 Report to Congress.
5. Civil Aeronautics Board, FY 1975 Report to Congress.
6. 49 U.S.C. §1423.
7. 49 U.S.C. §1431.
8. 49 U.S.C. §1701 *et seq.*
9. *Palisades Citizens' Association, Inc. v. CAB,* 420 F.2d. 188, 191 (D.C. Cir. 1969).
10. 49 C.A.B. 346 (1968).
11. 14 C.F.R. §399.110(b) (1975).
12. *Northeast Corridor VTOL Investigation,* CAB Order 71-1-74 (January 15, 1971).
13. *TAG-Wright Case,* CAB Order 72-2-52 (February 14, 1972).
14. *Petition of the City of Inglewood for Decertification,* CAB Order 72-2-41 (February 11, 1973).
15. *Complaint of the Natural Resources Defense Council,* CAB Order 71-7-140 (July 26, 1971).
16. *Southern Service to the West Coast,* 12 C.A.B. 518 (1951).
17. *Southern Transcontinental Service Case,* 33 C.A.B. 701 (1961).
18. *Southern Tier Competitive Nonstop Investigation,* CAB Order 69-7-135 (July 24, 1969).
19. Lowenfeld, *Aviation Law* (1972) at I-203.
20. CAB Order 70-12-162/163 (December 31, 1970) at 5.
21. CAB Order 72-9-95 (August 23, 1972).

22. CAB Docket 25908.
23. CAB Docket 22908.
24. Shumann, W. "Airport Noise Unaffected by Flight Cuts," *Aviation Week Space Technol.* 29 (February 4, 1974); Nozick, H.J. "Possible Consequences of Fuel Allocation Program on Aircraft Noise," *Information Brief* (January 24, 1974).
25. "Aircraft Noise Analysis for the Existing Air Carriers' System," Bolt Beranek and Newman, Inc., Report No. 2218, prepared for the Aviation Advisory Commission (September 1, 1972).
26. Elrad, K. M. "Community Noise," Environmental Protection Agency (NTID 300.3) (December 1971).
27. First National Bank of Homestead v. Watson. 363 F. Supp. 466, 473 (D.D.C. 1973).

SECTION IV

THE REVIEW PROCESS - FERTILE OR FUTILE?

Robert P. Thurber

Environmental Program Analyst
Office of Environmental Affairs
United States Department of Transportation
Washington, D.C.

Rebecca W. Hanmer

Director
Office of Federal Activities
Environmental Protection Agency
Washington, D.C.

This session is based on two major premises. The first is that citizen input is just as vital to the environmental review process as agency input. One of the most prominent figures in environmental protection today, Jacques Cousteau, has pointed out the need to question assertions made by conventional decision-makers, whether in government or the private sector. He cites the difficulty of obtaining a truly unbiased judgment on the matter of acceptable risks and stresses the need for the average citizen to place greater reliance on his own judgment and to give utterance to them whenever possible. The Environmental Review Process provides one such opportunity, while yielding unbiased facts for the citizen to judge.

The second premise is that, like other facets of environmental assessment, the review process should be continuous in nature. As the planning process develops, and more facts are revealed, there should be continuous feedback to the planners of the citizens' judgment of these facts.

The chapters in this section address a wide span in the life of a proposal, from prediction of public response before a proposal is put forth, to public and agency review of environmental documents. The chapters also raise some important questions. Do some reviewers lose sight of the intent of the National Environmental Policy Act in their dogged determination to be procedurally correct? How does one minimize the enormous potential for misunderstanding other points of view? How does one balance the concerns of a team of specialists? What methods are being used to ensure that the citizen's judgment is heard?

CHAPTER 18

ACHIEVEMENT OF NATIONAL ENVIRONMENTAL POLICY GOALS*

Ruth Hamilton Allen**

Senior Environmental Planner
Department of Water Resources
Metropolitan Washington Council of Governments
Washington, D.C.

John S. Winder, Jr.**

Attorney Advisor
Noise Enforcement Division
U.S. Environmental Protection Agency
Arlington, Virginia

> The problem is that everyone knows the National
> Environmental Policy Act requires an Environmental
> Impact Statement, but no one remembers why![1]

Seven years after the passage of NEPA and thousands of impact statements, the goals of NEPA remain unchanged, and unfulfilled. This new policy can be more nearly achieved if the authors and reviewers of EIS's and environmental assessments focus more on the goals of NEPA and less on EIS procedures.

---

*The information presented herein represents the views of the authors and not necessarily the views of their respective agencies.
**Ruth Hamilton Allen is former Assistant Director, Environmental Impact Assessment Project (EIAP) of the Institute of Ecology; John S. Winder, Jr. is former Director, EIAP.

Section 101 of NEPA sets out the broad policies and goals of the Act. It declares a new national policy "to create and maintain conditions under which man and nature can exist in productive harmony." Section 101 also states that it is the continuing responsibility of the federal government to use all practicable means to "fulfill the responsibilities of each generation as trustee of the environment for succeeding generations . . . ." In addition, the Section confirms the Congressional recognition that "each person should enjoy a healthful environment and that each person has a responsibility to contribute to the preservation and enhancement of the environment."

These general principles provide evidence that the goals of NEPA transcend the preparation of Environmental Impact Statements. In fact, as early as 1974, the Council on Environmental Quality predicted that the continuing process of environmental assessment by federal agencies "will increasingly replace the current one-shot impact statement method."[2] A continuous assessment process is important because many projects and programs span decades. Long-term, cumulative impacts are overlooked if there is only a single assessment late in the planning process.

Notwithstanding this early CEQ prediction, the preparation of lengthy EIS's and the EIS procedure remain the central focus and achievement of EIS authors and reviewers.

ENVIRONMENTAL IMPACT ASSESSMENT PROJECT

During 1974 and 1975, the authors participated in the Environmental Impact Assessment Project (EIAP)–a Ford Foundation-funded project designed to focus on ways to improve the implementation of NEPA.[3] The primary goal of the EIAP was to stimulate improvement in federal environmental planning and assessment procedures mandated by NEPA, which requires all federal agencies to:

> ". . . utilize a systematic, interdisciplinary approach which will insure the integrated use of the natural and social sciences and the environmental design arts in planning and in decision-making which may have an impact on man's environment."

The Assessment Project used an interdisciplinary approach to EIS reviews in an effort to improve environmental decisions as well as the review process.

The Assessment Project was an ambitious and timely effort to review selected environmental impact statements. This two-year project was organized by The Institute of Ecology, and the objective was to bring scientists, citizens and policy experts from many disciplines directly into the Federal NEPA review process. Planners of the EIAP assumed that well-organized and well-publicized reviews would help promote the preparation of more efficient and more scientifically accurate environmental impact statements, and thereby help safeguard environmental amenities. The two phases of the Assessment Project were EIS review and substantive guidelines preparation. Each phase lasted about one year.

Reviews

The Assessment Project initially planned to review about 25 environmental impact statements. Selection of impact statements for review was made by an advisory board of scientists, economists and lawyers. The EIS's focused on highway construction, wastewater treatment plant construction, energy development, forest management and stream channelization. Very large projects, such as the Garrison Diversion Project, the Oil Shale Leasing Program and the Federal Coal Leasing Program, were selected and reviewed because of the associated potentially significant, widespread adverse impacts. Smaller scale projects, including a highway expansion in Vermont, a stream channelization in North Carolina and a wastewater treatment plant in Nevada, were also reviewed in an effort to uncover piecemeal effects and to broaden the scope of substantive guidelines.

Teams of 15-30 reviewers uniformly produced enough text for comprehensive reports, but teams of fewer than 15 people ran into problems reviewing massive EIS's in a short period of time. Also, the geographic separation of reviewers created problems of coordination between review teams, team leaders and EIAP staff. Some reviews were stalled, ten reviews were completed, and six reviews were finally published.[4-8]

The review process was successful in bringing a wide range of disciplinary input quickly into focus. Reviewers noted data inadequacies and inconsistencies. They also noted that EIS's failed to consider alternatives adequately. Cumulative and long-term impacts were singled out for further analysis. The scope of impact analyses and the analytical methods used to produce estimates of impacts were questioned. In program level impact statements, level of detail questions were raised repeatedly.

The major conclusions from the ten EIS's reviewed were that time constraints and poorly prepared EIS's make independent, team reviews very costly. Also, volunteer reviewers had different reasons for participating in EIAP reviews. Some reviewers exhibited high idealism and altruism toward natural environments. Some reviewers, mainly in academic institutions, were reluctant to "rock the boat" by involving their scientific reputation in controversial policy recommendations. Some reviewers wanted to stop programs or projects. Many reviewers wanted more information on local conditions and field visits to project sites. Many reviewers wanted more information on the lead agency's personnel, organizational structure, mission statement and legal requirements. Some reviewers wanted more expense money, paid team leaders, earlier group meetings and a better definition of their work tasks. Reviewers especially called for feedback and post-project evaluation. In short, despite good credentials and good intentions, volunteer help was sometimes out of synchrony with rigid procedural and time requirements of federal EIS reviews. Yet, volunteer reviewers did bring fresh insight into the NEPA review process. Reviewers did make constructive, substantive recommendations on EIS content. Projects and plans were improved as a direct consequence of team reviews. Furthermore, hundreds of citizens participated in the NEPA review process, and published reviews continue to educate the general public.

Substantive Guideline Preparation

Guideline preparation required a systematic analysis of lessons learned by the production of 10 EIS reviews. Because most of the reviews related to energy development and water resources projects, guideline preparation focused on these areas. Western energy development case material was subsequently used for a four-day workshop on substantive guideline development. Thirty-six review team members, agency officials and environmental leaders worked together in small, diverse task groups to draft a preliminary framework for substantive guidelines. Prior to the workshop, 19 working papers,[9] on EIS preparation and review guidelines were prepared by participants.

Substantive guideline development was partially successful. It was fertile in what it uncovered. For example, there is a near absence of post-EIS project monitoring. There is a real need for ecosystem level impact analysis. EIS formats should include a clear, concise statement of project goals and objectives. Impact statements should contain clear policy alternatives for decision-makers and the public. Major statements should be written with their long-term utility in mind so that future projects can be compared with similar past projects. There is great redundancy in EIS's, and what is learned from one environmental impact assessment should educate future impact statement writers and reviewers.

Ironically, perhaps, one of the basic conclusions which emerged from the EIAP is that overemphasis on the EIS document itself resulted in EIS authors and reviewers alike losing sight of the basic goals of NEPA and of the role of the EIS in the whole NEPA scheme.

There is a great danger that new EIS guidelines will make the EIS more encyclopedic and less effective as either an analytical tool or a decision document. The trend of longer EIS's appears to be an overreaction to actual and anticipated NEPA lawsuits against federal agencies. Therefore, public and private efforts to improve EIS guidelines should focus on the total NEPA process, rather than on the EIS document alone. Such efforts should seek to analyze and improve the way in which the EIS furthers the goals of NEPA within the total agency decision-making process.

NEPA GOALS AND THE EIS PROCESS

Implicit in the goals of NEPA Section 101 is the need to focus on mitigation of the most adverse environmental impacts. The balancing of human needs and desires with the requirements of long-term environmental quality is a major challenge to leaders of government and business. The stewardship of the environment by this generation on behalf of the next generation, wide-ranging beneficial uses of land and water, preservation of natural and cultural diversity and uniqueness, balance between population growth and resource use, and the increase of recycling of materials—all these important goals mean little if they are not translated into action. Moreover, full public participation and public understanding of decision criteria are essential to the achievement of NEPA goals.[10]

Post-Project Monitoring and Evaluation

The EIAP reviews reveal a clear need for comprehensive post-project monitoring. Monitoring must be conducted specifically to assess the long-term effects of energy and water resources development projects. There needs to be much more coordination on what parameters are monitored, where and by whom. The objective should be to create a monitoring process capable of being used by many sources to assess the actual outcomes of planned actions. Do projected impacts of major water and energy development projects actually occur on site? Do unpredicted synergistic effects appear? The piecemeal nature of many of the projects reviewed suggests that realistic safeguards have to be added via a post-project monitoring phase.

Ecological Impacts

Mere description of ecosystems is necessary but not sufficient to predict dynamic responses of communities and functional ecosystems. Complex environmental stresses, such as sublethal toxic chemicals, noise and intermittent habitat disruptions, alter basic life processes. Embryonic life, both foodstuffs and future citizens, is especially vulnerable. If the aim of environmental impact assessment is to predict long-term, system-level changes, population dynamics, ecosystem diversity, or the carrying capacity of stressed systems, then more direct observation, modeling and experimental studies are needed.

Western energy development case material calls attention to the ecological impacts of reclamation after surface strip mining. Authors of EIAP working papers are concerned about how soils, plants and animals respond to reclamation. Reclamation is viewed as ecosystem reconstruction.

Water resources EIS reviews and working papers from the Workshop on Substantive EIS Guidelines highlight the ecosystem consequences of watershed manipulation and runoff changes. Downstream runoff changes cause interrelated ecological and social impacts. Abundant, high-quality water has many beneficial uses and direct economic value. Reviewers showed that, in semi-arid, mineral-rich western states, domestic, recreational, agricultural and industrial water users are often in competition.

If society is to realize the goals of NEPA to any significant extent over the next 100 years, there must be more credance given to the simple fact that we are *of nature* rather than *above it.*[11]

Data Handling

Data handling is often a critical problem. Scientific reviewers recommended that measurement units be consistent within the EIS. For example, the use of Btu-adjusted values should be used to compare coal from different areas. The political reality of using confused and incomplete data,[12] because something had to be written or decided before there was time for proper field studies, was objectionable to reviewers. The purpose or intent of EIS data should be stated clearly and explicitly. Actual sampling techniques and information on their validity and reliability should be included as a separate appendix to the EIS or otherwise made available to the public. Not all readers want this level of detail, but it should be readily available for those who wish to evaluate the impact analysis.

Adequate documentation and consultation with a wider range of experts in university, government and business was recommended by many EIS reviewers and seems to be improving with the state-of-the art in impact statement production. Perhaps the most significant recommendation links data handling to long-term monitoring. Data should be collected and presented in a convenient form for use by the next generation of impact assessors. The expense may be great, but it is often less expensive than having to start again with each new project assessment. Environmental problems are not easy to solve, and we need the benefit of cumulative insight into the magnitude and intensity of specific local and regional environmental problems.

Format

Diversity of EIS formats is readily apparent to all who review a substantial number of environmental impact statements. Reviewers complain of a morass of detail in EIS's. They claim the details are less than useful when analysis is weak. Rigid adherence to agency format outlines results in redundant, nonanalytical EIS's, which thus far fall far short of the goals of NEPA.

Reviewers wanted more variety in EIS formats, according to the scope and purpose of particular projects or programs. At the same time, they expected more concise presentations of environmental impacts and mitigation measures. They wanted concise data on the relative cost and effectiveness of proposed mitigation measures. As a result of misleading format guidelines, too often the most significant potential impacts are completely overlooked.

As a rule, environmental impact statements should be shortened. A briefer document with full citations and a concise summary of the impacts and policy considerations would be more useful both to scientists and to decision-makers.

NEPA GOALS AND THE PLANNING PROCESS

One outcome of the Assessment Project is the clear realization that NEPA goals must be interjected into the early planning process. A wider range of alternatives are often suggested by consideration of these goals.

The planning process is the sum total of seemingly trivial decisions by an amorphous set of people. The plea for impact assessment during the planning process is often only lip service to environmental amenities. Assumptions, wishes and decision criteria remain vague. Even after application of supposedly objective computer programs, too many plans are mere wish lists. Explicit assessment in the NEPA tradition is quite new in planning circles. Too often, experts think only within the narrow boundaries of their professional training.

In the areawide water resources management planning efforts, under Section 208 of the 1972 Federal Water Pollution Control Act Amendments, impact assessment is required in the initial two-year planning process. In the range of 10 or 15% of the generous 100% of federal wastewater management funds are to be spent on impact assessment.

So far, one problem is that planners and engineers are reluctant to admit that there are any long-range social, economic and environmental impacts of sewerage expansions and advanced waste treatment. Assessment requirements are poorly understood. A holistic overview of individual local decisions is rare. Federal dollars are welcome; federal NEPA requirements are burdensome. There is a clear need for sensible amalgamation of local and state authority with regional priorities.

If a spirit of cooperation and compromise can be fostered, then alternative pollution control strategies can be devised and tested. Realistic final demands for goods and services can be matched with environmental quality standards.

In conclusion, the goals of NEPA serve as a benchmark. Their achievement reflects the nurturing and care people give to maintain future generations.

> In these bewildering circumstances, only one prediction can be made with certainty. Man, the child of Mother Earth, would not be able to survive the crime of matricide if he were to commit it. The penalty for this would be self-annihilation.[13]

REFERENCES

1. Wright, V. C. "Problems in the Preparation of an Energy EIS—A Conservationist's Viewpoint," in *Proceedings of Regional Energy EIS Seminar,* D. H. Wayman, Ed. (Denver, Colorado: Denver Federal Executive Board, 1975), p. 98.
2. "Environmental Quality," *Fifth Annual Report of the Council on Environmental Quality* (Washington, D.C.: U.S. Government Printing Office, 1974), p. 412.
3. Winder, S., Jr., and R. H. Allen. *The Environmental Impact Assessment Project: A Critical Appraisal* (Washington, D.C.: The Institute of Ecology, 1975).
4. Fletcher, K., and M. F. Baldwin, Eds. *A Scientific and Policy Review of the Prototype Oil Shale Leasing Program Final Environmental Impact Statement* (Washington, D.C.: The Institute of Ecology, 1973).
5. Applegate, R., and M. F. Baldwin, Eds. *A Scientific and Policy Review of the Draft Environmental Impact Statement: Crow Ceded Area Coal Lease Westmoreland Resources Mining Proposal* (Washington, D.C.: The Institute of Ecology, 1973).
6. Smythe, R. B., Ed. *A Scientific and Policy Review of the Draft Environmental Impact Statement Wastewater Treatment and Conveyance System North Lake Tahoe-Truckee River Basin* (Washington, D.C.: The Institute of Ecology, 1974).
7. Fletcher, K., Ed. *A Scientific and Policy Review of the Draft Environmental Impact Statement for the Proposed Federal Coal Leasing Program* (Washington, D.C.: The Institute of Ecology, 1974).
8. Winder, J. S., and C. Lochner, Eds. *A Scientific and Policy Review of the Draft Environmental Impact Statement for the Proposed Federal Coal Leasing Program* (Washington, D.C.: The Institute of Ecology, 1974).
9. Pearson, G. L., W. L. Pomeroy, G. A. Sherwood and J. S. Winder, Eds. *A Scientific and Policy Review of the Final Environmental Statement for the Initial Stage, Garrison Diversion Unit* (Washington, D.C.: The Institute of Ecology, 1975).

10. The Environmental Impact Assessment Project. *Working Papers on Substantive Guidelines for Improving Environmental Impact Statements* (Washington, D.C.: The Institute of Ecology, 1975).
11. Allen, R. H. *Approaches to Environmental Quality: NEPA and the Evolution of Biosocial Criteria for Environmental Impact Analysis.* (New Haven, Connecticut: Yale University, Institute for Social and Policy Studies, Center for the Study of the City, WP73-40, 1973).
12. Marsh, G. P. *Man and Nature* (Cambridge, Massachusetts: Harvard University Press, 1965).
13. Toynbee, A. *Mankind and Mother Earth* (New York: Oxford University Press, 1976).

CHAPTER 19

THE MARYLAND WATER RESOURCES
ADMINISTRATION'S EXPERIENCE WITH
THE EIS REVIEW PROCESS

Roger A. Kanerva

Deputy Director for Operations
State of Maryland
Department of Natural Resources
Water Resources Administration
Annapolis, Maryland

To address my personal concerns, I must expand the scope of the title "The Review Process-Fertile or Futile?" Thus, in keeping with the alliteration already provided, I offer the word "fetal" as an addendum, based on my belief that the EIS review process is just in an early stage of development in my agency. While I cannot back it up with hard experience, I would also hazard the guess that the description of "fetal" might also apply to the review efforts of many other agencies at federal, state and local levels of government.

Keeping this keynote thought in mind, this chapter presents our agency's experience with the Environmental Impact Statement review process, from my professional point of view as a "generalist."

BACKGROUND

The passage of NEPA in 1969 signaled the beginning of the formal EIS process at the federal level. It is my impression that several years were necessary for federal agencies to gear up for this activity. As could be expected, even more lead time was involved in bringing states into the

EIS process. Speaking as a state bureaucrat, I can honestly say that during its early years NEPA was mostly a foreign entity, as far as the day-to-day operations of our agency were concerned.

Then in 1973, the Maryland General Assembly passed the "Maryland Environmental Policy Act." Suddenly each state agency was involved to one extent or another in the EIS process. It was about this same time that we began to see significant numbers of federal EIS documents coming through various channels for review and comment. Mixed in with this review activity was an increasing demand by those preparing environmental assessments for a wide variety of basic resource data from state agencies. Looking back on this period, I must admit that many of us held a rather dim view of EIS's. It seemed like much additional work without meaningful results. It is clear now that initially we did not really understand this program.

One bright spot during these early times was the A-95 Clearinghouse procedure. This activity was firmly established in Maryland and provided an organized means of carrying out the review process. The Department of State Planning was the central Clearinghouse agency. It routed EIS documents to sister departments for review and coordinated comments received for submittal to the applicants. Documents received by the Department of Natural Resources were, in turn, assigned to a lead agency within the Department. Because of our wide range of resource management programs, the Water Resources Administration was often placed in this leadership role. It was our responsibility to further distribute documents to sister agencies such as the Fisheries and Wildlife Administrations.

While the mechanics of review existed, the quality and extent of review were certainly open to question. For one thing, the assignment of Project Review Officer for A-95 was hardly viewed as a "bureaucratic plum." Rather, it was considered more of a routine chore involving a cursory review of projects that were well on their way toward implementation. The prevailing mood was that these matters should and would be addressed via the existing regulatory programs when applicants came in for the required licenses and permits.

The inadequacies in the review process were further compounded by the attitude of some of the parties responsible for preparing EIS documents. We were often given the impression that this was just a paperwork exercise to clear another procedural hurdle. Undoubtedly, this initial attitude was fostered by the retroactive nature of NEPA which caught many projects well along the implementation pipeline.

REVIEW RENAISSANCE

Now that I have described what amounts to the "dark ages" of EIS review in our agency, I would like to note some key experiences that have significantly affected that review process. The "review renaissance" began in 1975.

It was during this year that we became involved in a controversial sewage treatment plant project in Southern Maryland. In one form or another this project had been under study and design for nearly 10 years. During this time, other state agencies and several local agencies had issued various permits or approvals for the project. We were faced with issuing the last permit for part of the project which affected a floodplain. What started out as a routine permit case ended up as a hotly contested appeals case with angry parties on all sides. In response to citizen group pressure, EPA was forced to take another look at the project in terms of EIS requirements for grant projects. To assist EPA, we gathered background information on all the state and local actions, studies, plans and permits relative to the project for use by EPA in preparing an environmental assessment.

Although sometimes we have trouble admitting it, this effort was a real eye opener. While we had often been exposed to poorly coordinated, piecemeal actions of government, we seldom had the opportunity to pull together all the loose ends of a major project. Suddenly we were face to face with a major example of fragmented decision-making. The lesson was clear enough—*there definitely was a need for some type of comprehensive evaluation of a project as early as possible.* Without really noting it at the time, we had experienced a basic tenet of the EIS process.

This experience sent us back to the bureaucratic drawing board. How could we prevent another situation such as was just described? What mechanisms were available to deal with these problems? Again, the A-95 Clearinghouse procedure turned out to be a positive starting point. As Project Review Officer for our agency, I started paying closer attention to those 3-6 inch EIS documents. Some of the better ones attempted to undertake a comprehensive evaluation of projects and their impacts. I also began to notice a subtle shift in the attitudes of the agencies preparing EIS's. For example, new environmental staff of the State Highway Administration seemed to be making a sincere effort to address our comments and incorporate our concerns in initial project planning.

We were making progress by early 1976, but were far from pulling things together. During this critical period, I received a brochure providing information on the National Association of Environmental Professionals (NAEP). Its Code of Ethical Practice struck a chord, and I joined

NAEP. Subsequently, I took a short course in EIS preparation at George Washington University and did some additional reference reading on environmental analysis. With these and other aids we were finally on the road to effective EIS review.

What I have presented here is, of course, experience limited to one agency within a single state. However, I cannot help but suspect that similar situations exist in many parts of the country at many levels of government.

CURRENT THINKING

We have had our awakening to the meaning and potential impact of the EIS process. This has, in turn, led us to critical evaluation of the adequacy of our agency's review activity. This evaluation has demonstrated the need to improve our review process in four specific areas.

Organization of Review

Our review efforts were rather informally structured around the A-95 procedure. The Project Review Officer would decide what other agencies and internal staff would review an EIS document. Usually, each agency and individual staff would review the document from its specific perspective in an independent manner. The Officer would then consolidate the comments into a single reply for the department.

The shortcoming involved here was the failure to consider the review staff as an integrated professional team. No designed effort was made to pull the staff together into an open forum to discuss and evaluate the documents. *Thus, it was concluded that the review effort must be formally organized around the concept of a review team.*

Utilization of Reviewers

Fortunately, we had routinely involved competent professional staff in the EIS review process. However, we did discover a weakness in the way in which expertise was being applied.

For example, while we had a fisheries biologist reviewing the documents, upon close scrutiny he might have been trying to assess some aspects of the engineering data and conclusions. At the same time, we had civil or sanitary engineers reviewing the documents without clearly directing their efforts at the engineering aspects. *Thus, it was concluded that we must be concerned with both the specific professional qualifications of review staff, and with the integrated application of that expertise to various aspects of EIS documents.*

Quality and Extent of Review

Once we became more cognizant of the EIS process, we found ourselves asking a seemingly simple question. What should be the nature of our initial review of EIS documents? This basic query grew into a complex series of questions. Should we focus our attention on the base data? Should we concentrate on the estimations of specific impacts or should we evaluate the larger picture, the overall analysis of major issues?

A final conclusion has not been reached on this issue. However, I can report on the current thinking regarding this matter. Contrary to some bureaucratic instincts, we believe that an attempt should be made to minimize duplication of the efforts put forth by those preparing EIS documents. *This approach leads in the direction of placing maximum emphasis on the analytical aspects of an EIS.* In other words, given the data provided and the estimations of potential impacts, does the EIS present a reasonable and justifiable analysis of the project or program for the final decision-maker?

This is by no means an unwarranted lessening of review responsibilities. The hurdle from facts to analysis is indeed a critical phase of the EIS process. It involves judgments that can be as subjective as they are objective. In support of this position, we offer experience which shows that some EIS's present analyses that are not justifiable based on the information provided in the same documents. There could be many reasons for such anomalies, ranging from prior commitments to projects to simple misunderstanding of data. The key point is that this step in the process is a crucial one which we feel deserves dual evaluation by both preparers and reviewers.

It would be a valid criticism of our thinking to cite the inherent danger of accepting outright the data base for EIS documents. We propose to minimize this danger by helping to provide data inputs to the preparers early in the EIS process and spot-checking the final information utilized in the documents.

Monitoring of Results

An aspect of our EIS review that was clearly inadequate was the follow-up monitoring of results, or lack thereof. It was quite easy to consider the review job completed once comments had been furnished to the applicant. This was not enough. It did not provide for meaningful feedback.

We concluded that at a minimum the staff must check final EIS documents to determine the disposition of our review comments. Simple insertion of our written statements on page 200 of a 300-page appendix is pretty meaningless. We must ask if our comments actually resulted in changes or improvements in the nature of the final EIS analysis. If not, then we should follow up with the applicant.

The next step we will consider is some type of joint follow-up monitoring of field results. Hopefully, we will be able to address concerns such as the following: Were all the areas of significant impact considered? Were the estimates of the nature and magnitude of the impacts accurate? Were the mitigating measures implemented? How successful were they? Was the overall analysis valid, or did an entirely different result ensue? This area may be the most significant activity with respect to the EIS process during the next few years.

Our agency does not pretend to have all the know-how involving EIS review. However, we can speak as practitioners struggling to play our part effectively. As such, we are convinced that we are involved in something that has the potential to improve human decision-making and reduce adverse environmental impact.

CHAPTER 20

PUBLIC INVOLVEMENT TECHNIQUES UTILIZED IN HIGHWAY TRANSPORTATION PLANNING

William M. Wood

Social Scientist, Office of Environmental Policy
Federal Highway Administration
Washington, D. C.

This chapter describes community involvement programs utilized by highway agencies in transportation planning, and discusses how different techniques and planning processes are used to produce effective citizen participation during project development and in the EIS review process. Background information was obtained from Action Plans, documents which describe the individual state highway agencies' process for managing the development of federal-aid highway projects, and from correspondence with these transportation agencies.

PUBLIC PARTICIPATION SURVEY

Action Plans define, in general terms, the organizational arrangements, the assignment of responsibilities, and the procedures to be followed in developing projects, including the involvement of other agencies and the public in the planning, location and design of highways. These documents were prepared by highway agencies in response to Section 136(b) of the 1970 Federal-Aid Highway Act, which identified the need to assess social, economic and environmental effects of federal-aid highway projects.

With the assistance of other members of the Federal Highway Administration (FHWA) Office of Environmental Policy's Community Involvement Branch, I prepared summaries outlining public participation contained in the

Action Plans of the 50 states, Puerto Rico, the District of Columbia, and the FHWA Offices of federal highway projects. These summaries were circulated to FHWA field offices and state highway agencies to verify the accuracy of the information. Reviewers were asked to identify individual techniques or basic participatory programs which had worked well in their application. Comments from respondents concerning the Action Plan summaries and correspondence highlighting techniques and programs were used to supplement information found in the Action Plan documents.

The large number of techniques and the frequency with which they were referenced was impressive. The utilization of citizen participation techniques in all stages of highway development was encouraging, especially in light of the importance of systems level involvement. Some states traditionally considered to have limited participation programs, were found to utilize innovative techniques for public information, *e.g.,* billboard advertising.

STUDY FINDINGS

Intended Audiences for Techniques

Analysis of the 53 Action Plans and the comments submitted by the highway agencies revealed approximately 30 separate techniques for involving and informing the public (Table 20-1). The techniques are divided equally among those used to involve the public and those used to inform them. Techniques that involve one-way communication have been classified as "information" techniques, while those that utilize two-way communication and participation are "involvement" techniques.

These types of public involvement and public information techniques can be further subdivided based on the size of the audience to which the technique is directed. Involvement programs that are open to participation and discussions with the population at large include such techniques as public hearings, information meetings, televised planning discussions and project field reviews with citizens. The aforementioned techniques are also time-specific in their application, that is, they occur at definite points in time during the project's development. The remaining public involvement techniques rely more on the participation of individuals and generally occur over a period of time. These involvement techniques include citizens' committees, project field offices and telephone hotlines.

By determining which population segments they want to reach, highway agencies utilize information techniques appropriate to dissemination of project-related materials or notices to a variety of audiences. Widespread exposure to diverse segments of the public may be achieved through techniques such as mass media advertisements, news releases and audio-visual presentations.

Table 20-1. Public Involvement Techniques Identified in Action Plans

Technique No.	Technique
1	Public Hearings
2	Information Meetings
3[a]	Legal Notices
4[a]	Mass Media Advertisements
5[a]	Mailing Lists
6	Citizens Committees
7	Speaking Engagements With Interested Parties
8[a]	Circulation of Project Reports
9[a]	News Releases
10	Pre- and Post-hearing Meetings
11	Conduct Surveys
12	Public Workshops
13	Direct Contact With Affected Property Owners
14[a]	Response Forms
15[a]	Newsletter
16	Personal Interviews
17[a]	Audio-Visual Presentations
18	Public Forum
19	Project Field Office
20[a]	Publish Project Development Schedule
21	Telephone Hotlines
22	Televised Planning Discussions
23	Project Field Review With Citizens
24[a]	Mass Mail-outs
25[a]	Citizen Band Radio Announcements
26	Resource Base Analysis
27[a]	Announcements on Local Bulletin Boards
28[a]	Public Information Displays
29[a]	Billboard Advertisements Near Project
30[a]	Press Conferences

[a]Public information techniques.

Project-related announcements which may be directed at more well-defined neighborhood populations include billboard advertisements near the project, announcements on local bulletin boards, and public information displays. Notices of highway development activities and project data are often exchanged between highway agencies and specific individuals, groups or institutions. These notices may be conveyed through circulation of project reports and newsletters. Techniques for informing the public may be implemented at virtually any time during the project development process.

Frequency of Technique Utilization

The frequency with which the individual techniques are used is an important variable. As seen in Table 20-2, there are some techniques that are used nationally, some which are used by fewer states, and some implemented by only one state during one phase of highway development. The category of occasional use in Table 20-2 includes those techniques mentioned in correspondence with highway agencies but not referenced in the Action Plan documents. The reference totals for a technique are cumulative through the three

Table 20-2. Action Plans Listing Public Involvement Techniques by Planning Stage

Technique No.	Systems Planning	Corridor Location	Design	Occasional Use	Reference Totals
1	30	53	53		136
2	49	42	32	1	124
3	17	53	53		123
4	25	29	25	2	81
5	23	28	23	1	75
6	40	12	7	2	61
7	11	19	13	2	45
8	15	14	9	2	40
9	13	11	6	3	33
10	4	13	12		29
11	14	4	3	7	28
12	6	5	3	5	19
13		4	10		15
14	3	4	3	2	12
15	8			3	11
16	4	2	4		10
17	1	1		6	8
18	5	2			7
19	1	2	2	2	7
20	3	2	1	1	7
21	2	1	1	1	5
22	2			2	4
23		2	2		4
24				3	3
25		1	1	1	3
26	1	1			2
27		1	1		2
28		1	1		2
29				1	1
30				1	1
Reference Totals	277	307	265	52	901

stages of planning (*i.e.,* systems planning, corridor location and design) and notations in highway agency correspondence; the documentation of a technique for one state may range from one to four separate references. Each highway agency utilizes an average of seven or eight different techniques in its planning process.

Action Plans merely provide the framework for public involvement programs and the lack of reference to a technique in an Action Plan or in correspondence from a highway agency does not preclude its use by that agency. The frequency with which these techniques are mentioned does give insight into how the existing involvement programs are constructed and will provide a benchmark for future analysts who may wish to measure the rate of implementation of selected new techniques.

An interesting implication of the data displayed in Table 20-2 is that grouping techniques according to frequency of use does not emphasize any particular stage of the highway development process. The number of references to different techniques is roughly equal across all three stages of development. The philosophy of implementing continuous and balanced public involvement programs during project development appears to have been proven in practice. Although the concept of citizen participation in systems planning is relatively new, highway agencies apparently utilize many public involvement techniques during the systems planning phase which are similar to ones used during the corridor location and design phases.

When the Process Guidelines calling for the development of Action Plans were officially issued on September 21, 1972, highway agencies already possessed a highway development framework upon which public involvement programs could be built.

Many of the techniques discussed were modified by agencies to conform to their individual highway development program or to the needs of a particular project. Rather than discuss the diverse ways in which techniques are defined and implemented, this chapter will attempt to provide a general perspective of why these techniques are used and what makes them effective.

Systems Planning Implementation

Working agreements between highway agencies and local municipalities are built, in part, on federal requirements known as the 3-C process. This process calls for continuous, cooperative and comprehensive planning activities between highway agencies and planning authorities in urban areas of over 50,000 population. A review of all existing economic, population and land use studies is required to promote more effective transportation planning.

Analysis of Action Plans reveals that many of the community participation programs in the systems planning stage are the result of close working relationships between highway agencies, municipal governments and local or state planning authorities. Opportunities for public involvement and public information are often jointly conducted and administered among the sponsoring governments and agencies. This operational arrangement has a number of advantages, not only from the standpoint of citizen involvement/awareness, but from the standpoint of multiagency involvement/awareness as well. By stressing the continuous, cooperative and comprehensive nature of planning, agencies are able to discuss issues from a variety of perspectives and present current, accurate information to the public. Planning offices, local governments and highway departments also minimize misunderstandings and outdated communications by this process.

Information meetings were referenced in 49 Actions Plans during the systems stage, partly in response to the call for public involvement in the 3-C planning directives. "Information meetings" is a general term for informal public gatherings where citizens and agency personnel discuss project-related information. These meetings emphasize spontaneous, personal, two-way communication between the public and the highway agency.

Forty states utilize citizens' advisory committees during systems planning to provide a consistent, well-informed body of people to serve as liaison between the highway agency and the public. Citizens' committees serve to advise highway agencies of the consequences of their programs from the viewpoint of the values and social structure of the communities from which the membership of these committees are drawn. Citizens' committees serve in an advisory capacity to create an awareness among decision-makers of the unforeseen impacts that their decisions might have. Citizen committees may also serve to interpret and disseminate an agency's policies in their respective communities.

Systems planning should include input from the public at large, and Action Plans reference techniques for accomplishing this through mailing newsletters. Newsletters often can give more detail about project development than do ordinary news articles, and the information they present can become increasingly technical as the audience's familiarity with the project grows. While the highway agency, or a designated representative, is responsible for publishing the newsletter, its content often includes articles, letters or editorials written by the public.

The systems planning phase marks the beginning of efforts to identify project impacts, compile inventories of affected agencies and community groups, and determine the general scope of the public involvement program. A multifaceted, open approach to defining important issues minimizes charges that the environmental analysis and project design reflected the perspective of the sponsoring agency and not that of the public. This approach also brings issues to the forefront so citizens have an opportunity to provide timely and effective input. As information concerning these issues is obtained, trends of thought may be identified which will influence the selection of public involvement techniques necessary in future stages of highway development.

Corridor Location Implementation

Public participation programs implemented during corridor planning emphasize slightly different techniques and involve a more narrowly defined set of participants. After the proposed project is established within the transportation plan, participation in corridor location development by the highway agency and the general public involves those individuals more directly associated with that particular project. The number of feasible project alternatives and their general consequences become more well defined, thus allowing the process to focus on a more specific set of issues.

Public workshops are meetings in which citizens are provided with basic transportation requirements and constraints and are then asked to offer a solution. A public workshop gives the public an opportunity to experience the complexities of transportation planning and provides the highway agency with the public's perception of areas sensitive to highway development. Public workshops often convey more than general impressions of public reaction to highway proposals. Many times they contribute actual design characteristics which should be incorporated into the final planning.

Public hearings, pre- and post-hearing meetings, and legal notices are frequently implemented at this stage. Public hearings are formal proceedings conducted by agencies to inform the public of proposed plans and to receive and document public reaction. They are both historically and currently the most commonly used method of public involvement. Although public hearings have shortcomings as a participatory technique, they do perform essential functions through their legal documentation.

Referring to Table 20-2, corridor location participation programs have more references (307) to more techniques (25 different techniques) than either the systems planning or design stages. This finding may represent that development of corridor locations is an extremely sensitive stage in the planning process. Extensive studies of alignment and potential social, economic and environmental impacts are initiated at this stage. The culmination of this effort produces project-related information which is incorporated into the environmental impact statement.

In the corridor location planning stage, Draft and Final Environmental Impact Statements must address technical issues which require a certain degree of design-level information. The early involvement of the public will hopefully provide them an opportunity to influence the design elements of a project. Most of the basic design characteristics (elevated versus depressed roadway, number of lanes, etc.) should be identified in the Draft Environmental Impact Statement (EIS) which is available for public review. After receiving citizens' input on the Draft EIS, the Final EIS should so adequately address their comments that new challenges from the public would ideally be eliminated.

Design Implementation

This stage represents the last period during the participatory process in which the public has an opportunity to influence project design. It is a time when all project information, including that derived from public involvement, is summarized before the decision to build, not build or reconsider the project. Careful attention is given to details of design, to continued and more specific analysis of actions and their impacts, and to considerations of individually significant community or social problems. The finalization of the development process is shown in Table 20-2, where the design stage has fewer references (265) to techniques than the two other stages.

The public is informed of involvement activities and project developments primarily through legal notices, mass media advertisements and mailing lists. A more specific segment of the public—those persons whose property will be taken or affected by the project, may be contacted directly by the highway agency. All persons and groups having final recommendations concerning the project submit them for consideration. Public hearings and pre- and post-hearing meetings mark the formal end of the public involvement process.

Post-Design (Construction) Implementation

Most highway agencies do not terminate the opportunity for public input on a project at the end of design planning. Relocation assistance programs, monitoring project construction for adverse effects, and unforseen project developments may warrant additional contacts with the public. Citizen involvement at this stage is usually limited to specific issues affecting a particular segment of the population. Comments regarding these impacts will continue to be received even after the Final EIS is approved. This is a sensitive communication period, the importance of which should not be underestimated.

Public involvement activities often reflect the strengths and weaknesses of the highway development process. Public hearings are similar to environmental impact statements in the sense that both are legally required, fairly inflexible, and often frustrating. The EIS, like the public hearing documentation, provides a summary of the events, assessments, and conclusions which transpired in the planning process. Public hearings and environmental documents represent requests for final input prior to making an action decision.

If the public involvement prior to the public hearing and work on the EIS was comprehensive and well planned, then the last review of the final documentation should produce no surprises.

Public involvement and environmental assessment are dependent on continuous and open communication with affected agencies and citizens. The development of the environmental assessment and participatory program is incremental, focusing attention on specific issues as they are reviewed by citizens and the sponsoring agency. As a general rule, it is difficult to have an acceptable environmental assessment if either the public involvement or the EIS is deficient. They are mutually reinforcing.

CHAPTER 21

PREDICTING PUBLIC RESPONSE TO
URBAN SYSTEMS PLANNING

Laurence Sherman

Director
IBI Group
Toronto, Ontario

This chapter discusses the potential for introducing an advance step in the review process of a planning project. It is actually a *pre-review* step. In Canada, we are presently experimenting with a systematic attempt at *predicting* how the public may react when introduced to the idea of new technologies and their effect in the urban environment.

Our intent is to be involved as urban designers in a give-and-take dialogue with the planners and engineers at the earliest possible stage in the project to identify those design characteristics that are likely to have serious environmental implications and thereby result later in a high risk of public unacceptability.

We feel that our task is determination of how to translate measurable factors of environmental impact, both quantifiable and nonquantifiable, into measures of likely public response. This is a significant step forward in the planning of urban systems. More often than not, planners and engineers have first solved all their technical problems and then gone to the public to explain why those solutions were, within available funds, the best approach with minimum environmental impact. Public reaction has been time-consuming and frustrating to both the planner and the citizen. Government has been caught in the middle. In the process however, we all have become more capable and more sensitive. We have learned that *getting the plan accepted is, in fact, an integral part of the technical design solution.*

APPLICATION TO TRANSPORTATION PLANNING

In 1973, the Government of Ontario established the Urban Transportation Development Corporation (UTDC) to research and develop new forms of urban mass transit. UTDC is currently in the early stages of perhaps its most pioneering project to date—the design and development of an elevated Intermediate Capacity Transit System (ICTS) that can operate in existing street rights-of-way. A design team has been assembled of UTDC transportation planners and engineers, consulting engineers from Canadair Ltd., KVN Ltd. and ABAM Engineers Inc. for guideway and vehicle design, and staff of the Toronto Transit Commission for station design.

UTDC recognizes that elevated transit may be much more cost-effective but much less environmentally acceptable than subways, particularly where applied to existing built-up areas in Canada's major cities. They therefore appreciate that to develop an acceptable elevated transit system over existing streets, they must first concentrate on minimizing the environmental impact of the guideways and stations. The initial design work has therefore focused on trade-offs between operational requirements and the obtrusiveness of guideway and station structures. Urban designers were added to the research team to assess the potential impact of alternative guideway and station concepts and thereby attempt to predict their likely public acceptability. By working as partners from the inception of the work. this time the planners will be able to take proposals to the public which have already been exposed to a first cut at assessment of environmental impact and public reaction.

Conclusions of the urban design assessment have been fed to the planners and engineers throughout the process so that the technical results already reflect a number of revisions to the first proposals for guideway massing, alignment and aesthetics; station massing, location and access; integration of the guideway and the station into the streetscape; and major redevelopment opportunities.

Given the preliminary state of this planning, we were faced with obvious limitations: we were asked to "measure" the likely acceptability of an idea which is specific (*i.e.,* elevated ICTS) but did not as yet have specific form, location or time frame. Since it was premature to fix a guideway or vehicle design or select specific corridor alignments at this early stage, it was not possible to survey the actual people who would be affected. Instead, we have postulated various categories of potential interests (*i.e.,* users and operators; adjacent homeowners and tenants, property owners and businessmen; and local officials), and have tried to anticipate their respective concerns based on collective experience in similar cases elsewhere. Using this empirical information as a base, we have devised a method whereby the potential acceptability of alternative guideway and station concepts can be predicted by measuring their environmental impact within a range of typical street conditions.

The method is not only of use to the planners and engineers at the early stages of the project to identify potential acceptability in typical situations; the same basic methodology can be used in specific corridors by applying site-specific data, and can be used continually throughout the later stages of the project as more definitive information becomes available and as dialogue can be established with actual interest groups.

The steps undertaken to evaluate the environmental impact and acceptability of elevated transit are shown in Figure 21-1. The environmental impact of alternative guideway and station concepts in typical urban settings was measured in terms of noise, effects of scale and massing of the structure, effects on vehicular and pedestrian circulation, the extent of daylight eliminated and shadows created, the proximity to adjacent buildings, the resulting invasion of privacy, and the possible effects on adjacent property value (Figure 21-2).

Our analysis demonstrated graphically how guideway and station designs could be accommodated under the various conditions, applying a sequence of three design stages: first, the structures over the street without modification; then adding amenities such as street furniture, landscaping, wires and street lighting within the structure; and finally showing what could be achieved by integrating guideway and station structures into adjacent building developments, such as sidewalk arcades under the guideway, off-street stations within commercial buildings, and air-rights development over stations. The urban designs illustrate both the nature and severity of the resulting environmental conditions, and how, by taking urban design initiatives, positive advantages can be taken and negative impacts reduced in certain situations.

It has been essential that this design process between the designers, transportation planners and engineers be iterative rather than sequential. The give-and-take within the team has achieved the necessary early trade-offs between systems design and environmental impact and has provided the valuable feedback required to narrow the variables, modify the designs and refine the evaluation as the work progresses.

MEASURING ACCEPTABILITY

While there are numerous examples of systematic measurement of the environmental impact of urban systems, the translation of such data into measures of how acceptable or unacceptable the designs may be must

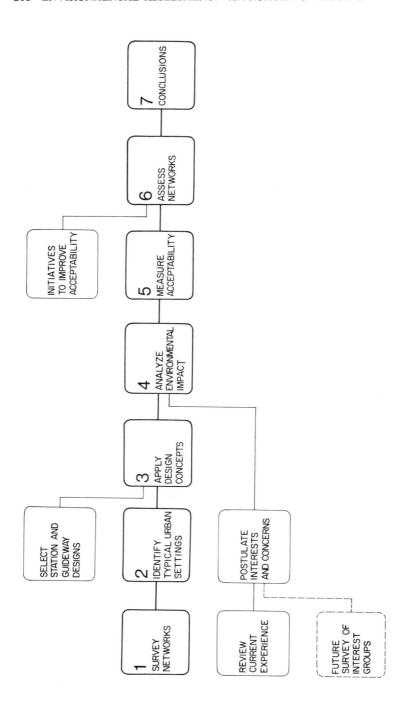

Figure 21-1. Steps for evaluating environmental impact of elevated transit.

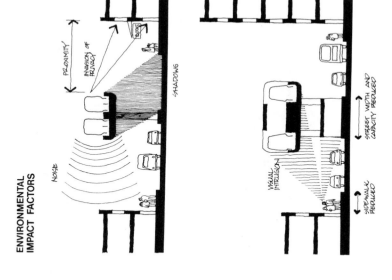

Figure 21-2. Factors for evaluating environmental impact and acceptability of elevated transit.

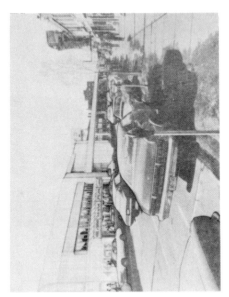

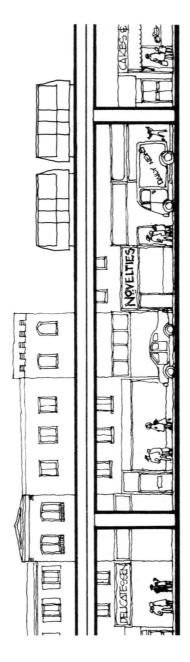

Figure 21-3.   Alternative urban designs for elevated transit.

rely largely upon sound judgment based on practical experience. For example, while an estimate can be made of how many more or fewer people may walk past a shopping area as a result of elevated stations, reasonable judgment must be relied upon to determine how this may affect business and thus how tolerable or intolerable it may be to the adjacent merchants.

It is possible, however, to apply these judgments within a systematic format so that the relative acceptability of competing alternative designs can be compared, and trade-offs then made between acceptability, operational effectiveness and cost. Our approach has been to establish "threshold" limits of environmental impact in the case of each design alternative in each typical urban setting. This has provided the basis for then predicting the acceptability of one alternative design relative to others. While the results are not absolute, they do provide an effective tool in the decision-making process which the team has carried out in narrowing its options towards a design concept that can be reviewed publicly.

CONCLUSIONS

The conclusions of this early assessment will need to be reviewed with various levels of government, with transit operators, and with the public, to assess more directly the level of support that might exist for implementing elevated ICTS. In cases where the planning concept is relatively new, support is gained by involving the interested parties in constructive review and refinement of the system as early as possible in the process. To this end, we have prepared a series of dimensioned drawings and sketches over photographs, showing each typical setting under alternative conditons to compare both negative and positive impact (Figure 21-3). This provides the ability to reapply the method and modify the conclusions as interested parties have the opportunity to respond.

THE URBAN DESIGNER'S ROLE

As part of the initial research team in this project we, as urban designers, have participated in two capacities:

1. as design analysts providing technical feedback to the transportation planners and engineers; and
2. as design negotiators attempting to resolve conflicts between technical cost-effectiveness and the interests of those various groups that are potentially affected.

This dual urban design role as a member of the interdisciplinary team runs counter to the tradition of the individual who imposes the "solution." For both social and technical reasons, this tradition must be replaced. The problems are just technically too complex for the individual, and at the same time, the participatory planning process is outgrowing the days of raw conflict between planner and user. We now find that concensus building between the many valid, and still often conflicting, interests is both achievable and effective. In our experience, the creativity of the designer is being stretched to combine analytical understanding of basic relationships between urban systems and built form, with understanding of human needs, behavior patterns and values as they are affected by these basic relationships.

We must determine through research and development the delicate balance between technological innovation and people's motivations for locating in certain places, for accepting certain disturbances and for rejecting others. While surely in this project we have not acquired all the answers, we can show the public that we have thought of many of the questions and anticipated many of the objections that predictably will arise. We have two basic objectives: better solutions and more effective (and speedier) public review.

CHAPTER 22

CONCLUDING REMARKS
REGARDING THE REVIEW PROCESS

Rebecca W. Hanmer

Director
Office of Federal Activities
U.S. Environmental Protection Agency
Washington, D.C.

The Environmental Protection Agency has been involved in the EIS process, on the review side, about as long and intensively as any agency in the United States. We were created in December 1970; the day after, I raised the issue of what kind of environmental review program we were going to have, and was told we were a pollution control agency. However, we managed to convince a few people, the Administrator included, that we should have some kind of review program. In the meantime, EIS's such as the Trans-Alaska Pipeline statement and a few others, were beginning to come in. The Administrator recognized this as a political process, so it was decided to centralize things, having six or seven people, mostly lawyers, sit in a room to produce comments in a highly pressured atmosphere. After only a few months, we recognized how necessary it was to get the documents out into the field. Now EPA review is done almost entirely in our field offices, with coordination from my office. We make a maximum effort to involve in this effort the technical people who are working in the areas affected.

As a federal agency, of course, we are not everywhere: We are in 10 regional cities and sometimes those people are almost as remote from some of the areas that are covered by impact statements as the people in

Washington. One hopeful sign is that states like Maryland are beginning to come into the EIS review process with us, to join us and the concerned citizens, which appears to be strengthening the process.

Our thinking is very similar to that of many other agencies discussed in this book. We are in fact trying to stress what we call *pre-EIS liaison* (or what was also called Pre-Draft consultation), which is the only long-term solution. We are finding that our resources are very stretched by the pre-EIS liaison concept, particularly when people request our help in writing the EIS and request a lot of data. Since our agency covers six pollution control areas, that would be a great deal of data. So we have to be much more selective about providing technical assistance to other agencies, and are concentrating on those projects that have the most significant adverse impact on the environment. In our view that includes water resource projects, the energy development projects, and some of the other major development projects.

We made something similar to what Laurence Sherman just mentioned in Chapter 21—a set of EIS review guidelines for major categories of projects, such as nuclear power plants, impoundments, or channelization. This is guidance both for our reviewers and for people who are writing environmental impact statements, because it gives them at least some idea of where we, as the pollution control agency at the federal level, are coming from. We are trying to be very discriminating about information requests.

Some critics have said that the review process and the court cases have led to the problem of those 17-volume environmental impact statements that contain masses of trivia. I agree with the State of Maryland that we should stress the analysis: once you work through 6 or 7 volumes of data, one should not have half a paragraph or half a page analyzing a particular alternative—that is really the test of that EIS.

We are trying increasingly to use the environmental impact statement as an early look at our new source enforcement reviews. I might say that we have had some difficulty in getting our enforcement people into the review process, because they have traditionally been oriented toward looking at projects that were in the latter stages of design, just ready to operate; this is the very worst time to take your first look at a project to decide whether it is environmentally acceptable.

Because there are so many of those projects, the regulatory people are so overworked, with 40,000 permits that must be issued, they do not want to be bothered with something that's not going to happen for 6 or 8 years. Gradually, as we have worked ourselves through the glut of permits that have to be issued for existing sources, we are beginning to have a much more valid early review process. I feel that the NEPA review is essentially the process that initiated environmental review in which you look at the project as a whole, instead of different parts at various times. We are using NEPA as a qualitative change in our review process. Our enforcement people, for instance, in looking at a water discharge permit, tended to view it from the standpoint of only the water discharge, not of the environmental effects of the nuclear power plant, or whatever the project was as a whole. The environmental review process is having a qualitative, substantive impact on our regulatory programs. In our experience as an environmental regulatory agency, and based in part on my experience with it, we have found relatively few environmental impact statements that involve outright violation of environmental standards. Rather, they raise more subtle environmental issues such as land use and values about community development.

This leads me to believe that the EIS process is vitally needed because environmental standards, at least as they are set and promulgated in this country, and our agency does many, are not going to protect the environment. They come too late and they say too little; they are much too broad (and I think that's about the only way environmental standards can be), so that there's always a role for the case-by-case review.

I agree with Ruth Allen's comments in Chapter 18 that planning programs often give only lip service to analysis. A planning program is often a very political process that winds up being a wish list. The EIS is basically an assessment process that says ok once you've decided what you want to do, integrate into it a good hard analysis of what the alternatives are. In our experience with planning programs, at least in the environmental area, that kind of hard-hitting analysis of alternatives has not traditionally been present; therefore, the EIS process has had a substantive impact on planning as well. I agree also with Laurence Sherman, however, that EIS's do not, cannot, and never will, replace planning. The ultimate goal is to strengthen our environmental planning processes or the environmental parts of our planning processes as well as the analysis or assessment parts of our planning process, and to come up with some fundamental design characteristics that are environmentally sound and which should be built into programs.

Sometimes I think we, as reviewers, are frustrated with the lack of substantive response to our comments on a particular environmental impact statement, especially when they add up to change the project significantly or to abandoning it and trying again. If concerns are that basic, pre-EIS liaison is the only really effective mechanism.

The court cases under NEPA have thrown sand in the gears of some major projects; but I believe that the major value of those cases is not in the individual project that was stopped for the assessment, but in the message that was contained in the stoppage process for all the projects yet to come. Even if we don't get what we want on a particular project, I think there is a reason for optimism, unless it is the only project in town, and that is unfortunate. For those of us who look at a thousand or so projects a year, even if you don't achieve your goal on a particular project because perhaps those concerns were expressed too late in the planning process to affect that project, there *are* concerns that impress the planners in the agencies, that say these kinds of concerns have to be built into our future projects.

Also, the environmental impact statements we see, and we have to remind ourselves of this, are the tip of the iceberg. They are the thousand or so actions each year that are being pushed for their significant economic or social benefits despite their significant environmental impacts. Underlying these are thousands of projects that have undergone environmental review and public participation and have been found to be environmentally innocuous, or have had satisfactory mitigation measures built into them, or were so bad that they are not even being proposed.

Post-project monitoring is badly needed, and I do not believe it is being done. I hope there are some agencies or some individuals who have programs that are working. EPA has talked about this for three or four years, yet continues to assume that once the program is launched, it will run efficiently. In that sense, we are still operating on planning assumptions about what we thought environmental impacts were going to be, based on our experience, and what mitigation measures we thought we were going to achieve. We see a drastic need for some structured, carefully monitored, test cases that will test both the validity of our environmental impact assessment concepts and the effectiveness of built-in mitigation measures.

SECTION V

WHY DID IT FAIL? OR SUCCEED?

Ned J. Cronin and Gerald R. Mylroie

Co-Directors
Environmental and Public Works Staff
Commission on Federal Paperwork
Washington, D.C.

How can one determine whether the National Environmental Policy Act (NEPA) and the Environmental Impact Statement (EIS) process have succeeded? The environmental assessment process can be considered successful if it is incorporated into the project development and approval process and results in better public decisions. This section will focus on some specific cases rather than broad general analyses. It will consider both the EIS and the NEPA processes from four different perspectives:

1. The administrative process: are there ways to carry out compliance with NEPA and prepare EIS's in a manner that does not delay projects and produce volumes of paper?
2. How has NEPA been incorporated into the major decisions which the Department of Transportation has made in the past few years?
3. How well did NEPA work in a project in which the federal agency was unwilling to question the assumptions of the EIS, but the public and various local and state governments were interested in questioning those assumptions?
4. Has NEPA helped Florida Power and Light make better decisions?

It has been said that NEPA has succeeded while the EIS process has failed. Where has it failed? What can we learn from our failures? from our successes?

CHAPTER 23

TOWARD CREATIVE ADMINISTRATION
FOR ENVIRONMENTAL QUALITY

Ned J. Cronin, and Gerald R. Mylroie
Co-Directors
Environmental and Public Works Study
Commission on Federal Paperwork
Washington, D.C.

Most concerns about the National Environmental Policy Act (NEPA) (PL 91-190) have focused on preparation of the environmental impact statement required by Section 102(2)(C). What has been overlooked is the congressional intent that federal agencies consider in decision-making the environment [Section 102 (2)(A & B)] which heretofore may have been unquantifiable. The EIS has become the visible symbol of how a federal agency incorporates environmental considerations into its decision-making.

Some critics say we have been unsuccessful in implementing NEPA; that the EIS process has failed because of excessive paperwork, inefficiency and interminable delays. That criticism is open to question. A study was conducted to analyze the administration of the NEPA process, specifically to identify creative ways both to write EIS's and to make sound environmental decisions.[1] To determine where administrative efficiencies could be achieved, the EIS process was divided into three steps:

1. Information Collection—collecting information on both the natural and man-made environmental elements;
2. Analysis—assessing alternatives, adverse impacts and irreversible impacts, preparing the assessment or EIS; and

3. Decision-making—using the information and analysis (the EIS) to help make a decision. Also included, is extensive review and comment by the public and state and local governments through the A-95 process. Additionally, the decision-making may involve resolving legal challenges.

It was startling to find that the three steps of the EIS process generally are duplicated by other actors besides the agency writing the EIS. If the action is a federal grant, permit, or license, the applicant normally develops an environmental assessment (information collection and analysis) for the state and/or federal agency. The state may be working on its own environmental impact report. After all this work is finished, the federal agency begins preparing its own EIS using much or all of the information. What further compounds the problem is that *the federal agency normally has fewer resources to do an adequate EIS than the non-federal project proponent and it is the latter who should be incorporating environmental considerations into planning.*

The various levels of government sometimes contribute to duplicate analysis and decision-making in the EIS process. The federal agency has to decide on a federal action (which triggered the need for the EIS); the state and localities have to decide about their own actions, which are not formally connected to the EIS process. Meanwhile, the applicant hopes that he can accept delays in construction long enough for the EIS process to be completed.

We believed there had to be a better way to comply with NEPA and prepare EIS's more efficiently. We have discovered that, indeed, in isolated instances, federal, state and local governments have cooperated to efficiently "succeed" in preparing EIS's. In these cases, one or both of two principles were applied:

1. Project planning, environmental evaluation and the EIS preparation were performed at the same time.
2. All levels of government affecting a project were involved in the preparation—not just review.

These concepts are simple, but as previously suggested, have not been incorporated universally. Everyone has heard of the multimillion dollar proposal waiting several years for the EIS process to be completed or a situation where a local government opposes a project which the federal EIS has found acceptable. The administrative efficiencies that have been identified are not a complete list, by any means, but they indicate that under present law and agency regulation or procedures, creative administration is possible.

ENVIRONMENTAL HANDBOOK

The environmental handbook[2] is intended to correlate all environmental statutes and procedures and the environmental impact analysis required by NEPA for federal and federally assisted public works projects. The substantive requirements of each statute and procedure are included, as well as the administering agency, responsible division within the agency, and name and title of the responsible official. The Commission on Federal Paperwork commissioned the model handbook for the San Francisco Bay area.

The purpose of the handbook is to inform managers in federal, state and local governments how they can comply with numerous environmental laws. It indicates, for example, that responsibility for environmental evaluation can be transferred successfully to grant applicants so that any significant environmental problems can be dealt with early in the applicant's planning activities. The responsibility for compliance with these statutes or procedures ultimately resides with the respective agencies. The process does require substantial cooperation among all levels of government. Some specific benefits of the process described in the handbook are:

1. Project managers will be aware of all pertinent legal and regulatory requirements at the start of project planning.
2. Adherence to all regulatory and statutory requirements insures compliance with the law and can reduce later delays resulting from litigation.
3. Techniques outlined in the handbook assure early public participation in the project planning process.
4. Project planning that is guided by the handbook procedures will produce an environmental evaluation which can serve as the draft EIS without unnecessary duplication of analysis when the federal agency has been involved.

ENVIRONMENTAL IMPACT STATEMENTS FROM STATE PLANNING ACTIVITIES

In Utah, the Office of the State Planning Coordinator is responsible for state planning activities and the state's involvement in the federal EIS process. The state acts as a conduit between federal agencies and local communities, and provides its expertise to federal agencies preparing EIS's.

Working with the local governments in areas affected by proposals requiring federal action, Utah has completed the socioeconomic impact analysis section of a Bureau of Land Management EIS on a proposal to mine alunite, a raw material for aluminum. The Office of the State

Planning Coordinator will provide similar services for two regional and
two site-specific coal-leasing EIS's for the U.S. Geological Survey and
will assist the Forest Service with technical services for one of their EIS's.
The state is providing these services on a contractual basis per individual
EIS. The state's goal is to continue to provide these analyses for major
energy or resource development EIS's. In addition, Utah hopes to assist
other federal agencies, such as EPA, DOT and HUD, with their EIS activities for public works projects related to energy or resource development.

Specific kinds of benefits accruing to the state's role include:

1. applicability of the state's predictions for a regional or program EIS
   as background material in future site-specific EIS's. This assures
   consistency of assumptions and avoids duplication; and
2. inclusion of state planning considerations (such as social and economic
   analysis) into what are often narrow technical documents. Implicit
   in the success of this approach is the assurance that local government
   needs and plans can be incorporated into the federal decision-making
   process, which is not always possible.

OPPORTUNITIES FOR IMPROVING INTERGOVERNMENTAL
PLANNING AND DECISION-MAKING

Integration of environmental impact statement considerations into the
planning process can improve intergovernmental planning and decision-
making. Forcing federal agencies to work with state and local governments, creates opportunities to share resources for information collection
and analysis and to share power for decision-making and implementation.
Two case studies illustrate these opportunities and benefits. The first is
the preparation of an areawide EIS by the Department of Housing and
Urban Development's regional office in Denver, Colorado; the second is
the Colorado Review Process adopted by the State of Colorado.

Denver Areawide EIS

On November 4, 1974, HUD adopted regulations which required HUD
staff to prepare an EIS on all HUD-assisted housing projects with 500
or more housing units. Within the HUD Region VIII-Denver office, the
new requirement posed an immediate problem. Hundreds of proposed
housing sites within the Denver metropolitan area, which were applying
for HUD's mortgage insurance guarantees, immediately required an EIS.
HUD had resource limitations and was given no budget increase. HUD
knew that preparing the EIS's meant an immediate increase in workload

and possible delays. For the developers this delay would be costly. Increases in construction costs would be passed on to the home buyer, as would development carrying costs (loans, interest and taxes).

Other federal agencies and citizens criticized the single-purpose, site-specific EIS's that had been prepared because they failed to consider the cumulative environmental impacts of federal actions on the Denver metropolitan area. As a result, the areawide EIS concept was developed. An areawide EIS covers several similar federal actions within a specific geographic area, addresses the cumulative impacts of actions, and can serve as a basis for informed decisions on future actions in the same geographic area.

To initiate the areawide EIS, HUD entered into a "Partnership Agreement" with the Denver Regional Council of Governments (DRCOG), which represents more than 230 local governments and special districts, with a population of about 1.5 million people, over one half the population in Colorado. HUD believed that DRCOG was best suited to collect the large quantity of information needed and to help assess growth implications for the Denver metropolitan area. In November 1976, the agreement was signed. It called for DRCOG to prepare an environmental assessment of the short- (1976-1985) and long-term (1985-2000) impacts of growth in the five-county Denver area.

The results from this areawide EIS will be very beneficial for several reasons. First, the cost of the areawide EIS should pay for itself within one year. HUD estimates that about 10 site-specific EIS's would be required annually without the areawide EIS, and would require maintaining a staff of seven to eight people which would cost the government at least $175,000 per year. With the areawide EIS, HUD estimates that from 8-10 of the EIS's prepared annually for specific mortgage insurance guarantees could be eliminated. This could save about $120,000-150,000 per year or make these limited resources available for more critical tasks.

Second, the use of the areawide EIS as a continuing decision-making tool could be extended indefinitely. HUD plans to amend the statement and keep it current as environmental conditions change or as plans for the metropolitan area are revised.

Third, the application processing time related to environmental assessments could be reduced significantly. HUD plans to use the areawide EIS for conducting lower level clearances in the Denver area which means that an EIS need not be prepared on many applications.

Fourth, HUD's areawide EIS will benefit home buyers by reducing the overall time for developing a new dwelling unit project from about 21 to 12 months.

In addition to these benefits to HUD, the U.S. Environmental Protection Agency's Denver regional office independently decided to prepare a similar areawide EIS and will achieve similar benefits. Currently, EPA must make decisions on whether to approve 12 applications requesting grants for 75% funding to construct wastewater treatment facilities in the Denver metropolitan area. (The grants are authorized under Section 201 of the Federal Water Pollution Control Act Amendments of 1972, PL 92-500.) To make this decision, EPA also is preparing one of the first areawide EIS's, the *Denver Metropolitan Wastewater Facilities Overview EIS*. By contrast to the typical project by project, site-specific EIS, this areawide EIS will assess the cumulative impacts of the 12 facilities. Attention will focus on the facilities' impacts on forecasted growth and development and the growth impacts on air and water quality and agricultural land use and productivity. It should be noted that these studies will be integrated with the HUD EIS to eliminate duplication. HUD and EPA will share the environmental analyses but prepare separate reports.

By using this areawide EIS approach, EPA estimates that between 10 and 12 site-specific EIS's for the treatment plants can be eliminated. This will save several hundred thousand dollars and about 9-12 months on the project decisions.

The areawide EIS approach also has benefits from the state's perspective. In Colorado, the Governor, through the State Planning Council, hopes to use the preparation of an areawide EIS to raise state development issues, frame development assumptions and identify state lead agency responsibility. State personnel believe that this early participation and coordination will save a year in EIS preparation, by contrast to previously uncoordinated federal EIS studies.

Colorado Review Process

The Colorado Review Process (CRP) was initiated in 1975 by Governor Lamm as part of a Winter Resources Management Plan. The CRP and Plan evolved from increasing demands for ski development in the Rocky Mountains and problems resulting from inadequate intergovernmental cooperation. For example, when a developer attempts to build a ski resort, it is required to meet a multitude of federal, state and local regulations. Since the land for the ski lifts usually is located on Forest Service land, the developer must comply with Forest Service regulations as well as federal laws, including the National Environmental Policy Act and its EIS requirement. If the land where the development, including hotels, shops, homes, businesses, parking, etc., will occur, is located within a county or municipal jurisdiction, the developer must comply with these regulations too. Local regulations may cover pollution control, land use, densities, subdivision standards, public facilities and utilities. In addition, the development must comply with state laws and conform to state development policies.

In response to this situation, the CRP was established.

Essentially, the CRP provides for integration by federal, state and local officials prior to a decision to prepare an EIS, rather than having the state or local government use a 30-day period to comment on the EIS after it is prepared. In the CRP, cooperation is achieved when the federal agency, state, areawide, or local government signs a "cooperative agreement," and subsequent "site-specific cooperative agreement." Each agreement specifies minimum cooperative efforts. A schedule for completing tasks is included in the site-specific agreement to prevent delays. The assumption is that if all government jurisdictions and affected parties are involved early in planning, including assessing environmental impacts, and in decision-making, then considerable time, expense and paperwork can be saved.

This sharing of resources for information collection and analysis and sharing of power for decision-making and implementation has several benefits. First, it saves time: issues and solutions can be resolved without unnecessary delays by getting all levels of government involved early in the planning process. Second, it can improve information collection useful for planning and decision-making and eliminate duplicative efforts. Third, it can improve analysis by using the most capable staff and techniques from all levels of government. Fourth, it can improve decision-making by providing better information and analysis to decision-makers at all levels of government. Fifth, and finally, it can improve project implementation by clearly sorting out each level of government's authorities and necessary actions to mitigate environmental impacts.

In addressing environmental issues which know no political boundaries, intergovernmental cooperation is imperative. The EIS requirement is a unique mechanism to promote this cooperation.

In summary, the success or failure of NEPA and its EIS process should be judged in terms of whether it has helped improve public decision-making. From our perspective, it is clear that the potential of making decisions efficiently has not yet been realized fully. However, given the examples discussed here and the additional opportunities for change that exist, the EIS process should continue to improve and succeed in the future.

REFERENCES

1. Commission on Federal Paperwork. *Environmental Impact Statements,* Washington, D.C. (February 25, 1977).
2. Commission on Federal Paperwork, *Evaluating and Addressing Environmental Impacts of Public Works Projects in the San Francisco Bay Area,* Washington, D.C. (March 1977).

CHAPTER 24

CHANGING NEEDS RELATED TO THE
TOCKS ISLAND DAM PROJECT

Thomas M. O'Neill

President, The Center for Analysis of
Public Issues
Princeton, New Jersey

The Tocks Island Lake Project (TILP) is a proposal by the Corps of Engineers and the Delaware River Basin Commission (DRBC) to build a large dam on the Delaware River, about 36 miles south of Port Jervis, New York (Figure 24-1). Despite the production of literally five or six feet of reports, many of them NEPA-related, despite the existence of a regional water management agency, DRBC, which the proposed dam would serve, and despite, or perhaps because of the concentration on this subject by fistfuls of government agencies, and despite 15 years of effort, no real solution has yet been determined.

The question of building a dam on the upper Delaware is still not entirely a closed question. The states affected (*i.e.,* Delaware, Pennsylvania, New Jersey and New York) decided what they want to do, but Congress has not concurred. The reasons why the question to build or not to build remains unresolved are legion. They include changing perceptions of natural resources and environmental policy; competition and disputes among the agencies involved, many of them federal; the complexities and politics of congressional authorization and appropriation; and disputes among the four states in the river basin. Each of these stumbling blocks, and they are important, was made more formidable by inadequacies in the analysis of the project, including failures in the evaluations of the project conducted as a part of the environmental impact statement (EIS) required by NEPA.

Figure 24-1. The Region of the Tocks Island Lake Project along the Delaware River.

These are failures, because in my judgment the EIS and other studies did not lead to an effective decision on the project. The point of any analysis in government, the point of the EIS, is not to make the right or wrong decision, but to present the issue to be decided. But the process requires a decision. If it simply leads to delay and confusion, then the analytical process incorporated into the EIS has failed.

There are also gradations if one agrees with the decision; but one can make a value-free decision on whether the process works simply by seeing whether it leads to a decision. If it does not, it fails. We came quite close to a decision in the Tocks issue, at least within the states involved, because of a special $1.5 million study which was carefully and consciously designed to avoid the pitfalls of previous studies, including the pitfalls in the impact statements.

I want to review this process briefly, looking at some of the highlights. As a participant in and as a student of this project, my views probably are biased. From 1972-1975 I was to look after New Jersey's interest in the Tocks Island debate, including the design and conduct of the special study. To make my view somewhat broader I will present in part the excellent analysis of the Tocks dispute, which is contained in a book edited by my colleagues at the Center for Environmental Studies at Princeton University, and called *Boundaries of Analysis—An Inquiry into the Tocks Island Dam Controversy,* edited by Harold A. Feireson.[1] I shall also deal with a study by the consultants on the project called *Comprehensive Evaluation of the Tocks Island Lake Project and Alternatives.*

The basic question of Tocks Island is simple—should a dam be built on the Delaware River which would provide flood control, increased water supply, a small amount of electric power (about 70 megawatts), and a new recreation facility? The noneconomic costs, the debits of this project, are the impact on local communities, interferences with natural processes and scenic beauty, and possible ecological damage. Now the simple question of whether to build the dam quickly expands into more complex and more abstract issues, that is, preserving versus destroying the natural environment, economic growth versus no growth, recreation for the masses versus the preservation of an elite preserve, sacrificing upstream interests to advance downstream interests.

The idea of a dam on the Delaware, in the vicinity of Tocks, goes back to 1740. It was the disastrous 1955 flood on the Delaware which led to the Corps of Engineers' Basin Study. That comprehensive study, contained in 11 volumes, was completed in 1962, at a cost of $2 million. During the period the Corps was conducting the study, the four basin states—New Jersey, New York, Pennsylvania, and Delaware—were simultaneously engaged in organizing themselves to deal with basin-wide problems. In 1961, the Delaware River Basin Commission (DRBC) was created. It consists of the governors of the four states, plus a federal representative, the Secretary of the Interior.

One of the DRBC's first acts was to adopt the Corps plan as its strategy of river basin development. Congress authorized the Tocks dam, which was the keystone project in that development, in the 1962 Flood Control Act. While flood control was the original impetus for the project, the drought of the early 1960s made water supply the primary justification of the project in two ways: (1) the dam would provide a reservoir out of which New Jersey could draw 300 million gpd of water, and (2) the dam could provide flow augmentation supposedly to hold back the salt line in the Delaware River. The city of Philadelphia draws its water supply from the Delaware River at a point about 12 miles north of Philadelphia called Tooresdale. During the drought of the 1960s, the salt line (the line of 50 parts per million (ppm) salt) moved up the Delaware Bay, as the flows of fresh water down the river diminished, and came quite close to Tooresdale, thereby threatening the Philadelphia water supply.

Those two complex water supply issues, in particular, became the primary focus of analysis, at least from New Jersey's viewpoint. In 1970, during the first years of the new environmental awareness, the Tocks issue was joined. Before 1970, the project enjoyed almost unanimous support, with the exception of some of the landowners displaced by purchases of land for the project and the local environmental groups. It was in 1970 that Congress ordered that construction of the dam should begin, but only after the new impact statement process was completed. Here we have one of these cases in which a project had been designed, justified and had NEPA tacked onto it as an afterthought. The results were predictable. It was around the impact statement that opposition began to crystallize, as was the intent of NEPA. The policymakers began to notice the opposition. The EIS was written by the Philadelphia District Office of the Corps, and issued in 1971. It was criticized on several grounds by environmental groups and by the Council on Environmental Quality.

I want to review in somewhat greater detail New Jersey's reaction to the EIS and also to review the need for a decision by the Governor of New Jersey on the project to illustrate some of the inadequacies of the analysis to this point.

ANALYTIC FAILURES

As Robert Socelow has pointed out in *Boundaries of Analysis,* the failure of technical studies to assist in the resolution of environmental controversies is part of a larger pattern of failures of discourse in problems which put major societal values at stake. Discussions of goals, visions of the future, are enormously inhibited. Technicians writing the impact statements and bosses in the bureaucracies would much rather deal with narrow technical issues than with what people really care about. When we began digging into the EIS and the supporting documents to prepare a decision paper for Governor William T. Cahill in New Jersey, we found that statement to be very true. The discussion dealt with narrow technical issues which excluded a large part of what the decision-makers really cared about: "What's it going to do to my state? What's it going to do to my people? Are we going to be better off? How much is it going to cost us? It this the right thing to do?"

The analysts, especially those in large bureaucracies, tended to follow general guidelines in defining the boundaries and techniques of the analysis, and the scope of alternatives to be considered. Both sides in the debate, it seemed, would rather have discussed technical points than the issues they really cared about. Thus a debate over the future of an entire region, a debate over the methods New Jersey would use to supply water for a growing population, the future of the largest free-flowing river in the East, degenerated into an ill-supported argument over the number of meters or fraction of meters of water through which a Secchi disc* could be seen in a lake to be created behind the proposed dam. Now looking at little plastic discs sink into a hypothetical lake is not what this argument was all about. The analysis became stylized like, in the words of one analyst, "the folk art of an isolated village."

No one wants to make explicit the trade-offs a decision-maker must face. Let me give you an example: suppose it were about 1920 and in the Office of the President. A visionary comes into the office and tells the President that he has solved the problem of transportation for the United States. We need only build up a major automobile industry and a network of highways across the country that will very cheaply and very quickly carry people wherever they want to go, and it will only kill 54,000 people a year." Who would have done it with a trade-off explicit? No one. If all these trade-offs were explicit, nothing would happen.

MAGIC NUMBERS

As another example, the Tocks analysis was riddled with what several of us have called golden numbers: numbers generated by bureaucracy, then cited in support of what it already had decided to do. The numbers take on a life of their own, which is a process called reification.

One of the numbers involved here was maintaining a flow of 3000 cubic feet per second (ft^3/sec) in the Delaware at Trenton to hold back the salt line. Only in the special study in 1974 did we look at the probability of the salt coming up as far as Tooresdale. We found that the probability was about one chance in 500 years. How much money should society spend to prevent this? Should you rather simply use a damage limitation strategy, as opposed to a damage avoidance strategy? That kind of trade-off was not mentioned in the earlier reports. Policy-makers are afraid to record on paper, and their technicians who support them are afraid to tell them, that it might be better to accept a little damage and accept the necessary crisis management activities than to build a totally secure system.

The 1971 Environmental Impact Statement represented all these difficulties. There was a narrow focus on individual environmental problems which ignored the combined effects of these problems. The question of different futures for the region of the dam and for the region which would be served by the dam was ignored. Even those problems that were identified were dismissed as manageable, and their larger implications were ignored; implications

---

*Secchi discs are used to determine the turbidity of water: the greater the depth at which the disc can be seen, the clearer the water.

of how we treat nature and our relationship with it, and should we regard nature as totally changeable? For instance, the flows in the Delaware are governed by a Supreme Court decision. The dictates of that Supreme Court decision were taken as a given—immutable; but the flow of the river, the natural resources of the area were regarded as totally mutable. *It's a strange society that is unwilling to change its laws but is perfectly willing to change the way rivers flow.*

ALTERNATIVE ANALYSIS

Extremely narrow treatment of alternatives was given. The Corps is empowered to handle interstate, multipurpose projects; therefore, single-purpose projects within a single state were ignored as alternatives. What the Corps of Engineers could not do was also ignored. One of the alternatives to this water supply function of the dam, for instance, was for the state to supply its own water. That was not considered as an alternative.

The cost/benefit analysis was presented, but not the distribution of the costs and benefits. We knew the cost and the benefits, but not who were the winners and losers in the cost/benefit analysis. The regional distribution of the cost and benefits was nowhere described, even though the people who had to make decisions on this issue were four governors primarily interested in the effect of the project on their own states. There was no concept of different goals. The study simply asumed that everyone wanted to maximize economic growth. There was no concept of taking a lesser path of economic growth and substituting environmental quality for some of that economic growth. There was no concept of different levels of supply. Alternatives were designed which could meet those levels established by Tocks. In other words, the amount to be supplied by Tocks became the need level that had to be met by the alternatives rather than having a fresh examination of needs and a range of different alternatives and a range of different needs generated to match those.

So the needs define the alternatives and were defined by the project. Finally, the needs were treated as needs. There is no price attached to the word need. It implies that the need is absolute, that we will pay anything for it, just as we need air to breathe. But these are not requirements; there is a probability attached to every level of need and that went unrecognized.

THE ISSUE OF EUTROPHICATION

The project was slowed down, not because of issues people cared about, but because the CEQ seized upon the issue of possible eutrophication of the lake behind the dam. Upstream of this lake, in upper New York State, are the chicken farms that supply the chickens and eggs to New York City. This became a very hot issue for the New York governor, not because the population in the chicken farm area had such a large vote, but in one of those odd twists of politics it was this area that provided the kosher chickens for most of Manhatten and Manhatten represented many votes.

I think the most interesting fact I learned from the entire Tocks debate is that a five-pound chicken produces three pounds of chicken manure every day. It was suggested that manure would be washed by the rains into the Delaware River and into the Tocks Island lake, which would turn into a mass of algae. The Corps responded to this technical criticism by doing technical studies. It hired a good consultant to find out if eutrophication would occur. During the entire debate on eutrophication, not a single series of data was collected on the quality and flow, over time, of water in the Delaware River. Everything was done entirely theoretically with models that bore a questionable relationship to the truth, but no one was willing to take a year or two to perform the baseline studies and collect the data necessary to obtain a complete picture. As everyone was in a hurry, the scientists were always able to criticize the studies because there were no data. Therefore, they called for more studies, which were also executed quickly, again leaving no time for data collection.

CAHILL'S OBJECTIONS

During this period, New Jersey was conducting its own studies, which resulted in objections by Governor Cahill which finally began to grapple, although in sometimes hidden terms, with actual concerns of the governors. Governor Cahill stated, in what I thought was a clever way, "I cannot approve this project until these seven conditions are met." The conditions were designed consciously as to be hard to meet, so there would be enough time to take a hard look at this project. He had to phrase his objections in that way because he had no alternative to provide. None of the studies done so far provided concrete sets of alternatives. He wanted "breathing space" for generation of those alternatives. He stated objections in the fields of land use, floodplain management, limitations on the number of people who would be coming to the recreational area, assurances of the water quality in the lake, and provision of money for the highways necessary to take the visitors to the recreation area which would surround the lake. Cost of the highways necessary to take visitors to this project exceeded the cost of the project and would have to be borne by the states rather than the federal agencies building the dam.

ANOTHER STUDY

Cahill's objections slowed things; after his decision satisfied nobody, the Corps and the DRBC began to respond to his conditions. New Jersey elected a new governor in 1974 who followed the Cahill strategy for a time. However, the Congress wanted the Tocks Island project to move ahead. The idea was proposed of conducting a special study to evaluate the project in its entirety. As the Princeton analysis of the project stated: did anyone ever really expect that a study, no matter how thorough and imaginative, would change attitudes toward the project, would goad reluctant politicians to a decision? Yet the study did promise some benefits: it might make it easier for the skeptics in Congress and the states to find a basis for finally opposing the project outright. Anyhow, it would forestall the start of construction for still another year. To project supporters in Congress, the significance of the study promised to be its insignificance. With its completion, stallers would lose their last excuse for delay. There was also a small hope, held by some on both sides of the controversy, that perhaps the study would in fact finally resolve the outstanding issues and persuade the other side that it was in error.

The study was designed to overcome the very failures of the previous studies. The birth struggle of this special study, and the argument over designing the study itself, was characterized by a debate between those who wanted a broad-ranging independent policy analysis and those who wanted a narrower, technical review of feasibility—the same kind of narrow review that had failed. In Congress, those who supported Tocks, or at least supported the Corps of Engineers, wanted the study conducted by the Corps itself. Those who initiated the idea of the study, and who had doubts about Tocks or who opposed it, wanted an independent agency, able to undertake a broad analysis not limited to the methods, techniques, or boundaries that strictured the Corps.

Senator Clifford Case of New Jersey finally came up with the idea of a broad, factual study which would inquire particularly into alternatives to Tocks and answer questions of comparative environmental impact. The original idea was to have the study performed by the National Academy of Sciences under contract to CEQ, but for a number of reasons, that was not done.

Congress did dictate, however, when it finally decided who should do the project, that the study was to be cooperative between the Corps, the Delaware River Basin Commission, and the four states involved. It then became necessary for the Corps and the states to define cooperation. The many interested parties were brought together by Congressman Howard Robinson of New York. It was made clear to the Corps that the basin states were to play a real role in the study. They were not to be treated as mere advisory appendages.

Due to Congressional support for the role of the states, the Corps finally did what it said it would do, and also selected a contractor able to conduct the study. The Corps officials charged with the conduct of the study prepared a preliminary plan of study which broadly outlined the material to be studied and the procedures under which the study would proceed.

STUDY SCOPE DEVELOPMENT

The actual plan of study in draft form was sent to interested parties so there could first be a public hearing on what was to be studied. The draft went through several tortuous public hearings and drafts before being finalized. The original plan described a very narrow study. It proposed, for instance, only to examine alternatives to Tocks which satisfied the needs of the region to the same level as Tocks. The plan provided only a limited role for the agencies with which the Corps was to cooperate. The draft created much concern among the states and among the anti-dam public. These groups saw the document as confirming their worst fears about the Corps: that it would conduct a narrow review of the project and that the study would be dominated by Corps interests. The document provoked a storm of criticism; New Jersey, in its official comments, said that rather than the narrow review described in the draft, the study should contain the policy analysis necessary for a final decision. New Jersey also demanded that the DRBC states be given a full role in revising the plan of study and in overseeing its conduct. This was a key element of the study's success.

We also pressed for the reexamination of the numerical constraints on river performance, such as the 3000 cubic feet per second flow requirement. In other words, we wanted to tarnish the golden numbers. That request was to lead to a real breakthrough in this project, which developed the lack of probability that the salt water would actually travel up the Delaware. The draft eventually adopted provided for a full review of all alternatives and replaced the Corps of Engineers control group with a study management team to oversee the study, which involved representatives of all the interested parties, including private groups.

The clearest issue in the study was whether the dam was needed—whether there were ways to achieve the project benefits of water supply, flood prevention, power and recreation without building Tocks Island. That question can be both narrowly and broadly interpreted. In the narrow view, the issue was whether the benefit defined by the Tocks project could be met if the dam were not built. Could other ways be found to reduce flood damage on the main stem, provide mass recreation, implement large-scale storage of energy, provide water for power plant cooling, and above all export water to northern New Jersey. The search for alternatives was also given a broader interpretation; it was the one that we followed and it was the one that led to the success of the study because it more nearly touched the kinds of argument that protagonists in the controversy actually cared about deeply. The analyst need not restrict himself to the specific purposes defined by the Tocks project but could instead inquire more generally into the ways to achieve a balance of water supply and demand in the basin service region: flood reduction not only in the main stem; flood insurance instead of building dams; flood-plain management instead of building dams. Thus, for example, instead of investigating a natural systems alternative for the recreation area, one could instead consider ways to maximize recreation opportunities throughout the entire region, building swimming pools in urban areas, for example. Such an investigation was especially appropriate as a response to the oft-stated concern of some of the dam's supporters, that recreation should be given a high priority.

STUDY RESULTS

In January 1975, the contractors were chosen. They completed their work by late summer. In August, the Delaware River Basin Commission met, casting its vote not to request the construction of the Tocks Island dam. The two most striking findings of the study were: (1) it was very unlikely the salt water was going to come running up the Delaware River, and (2) even though the Corps of Engineers was building this dam at no local cost, it would be cheaper for New Jersey to meet its water supply needs in the northeast region by building itself a combination of small, in-state water supply facilities. We had not known this because we assumed that the federal government was going to give us a dam and we were going to get water. However, in adding up the cost of pipelines to get it there, highways and the other facilities necessary, we found that just by building a number of small reservoirs and some high-flow skimming pumps on some of the rivers we could meet all the foreseeable water demands, up to about 2020, cheaper than by getting a free dam from the federal government.

SUCCESS FACTORS

The study still has not convinced Congress to deauthorize Tocks. It worked to the extent it did because the public and interested parties at all levels were involved in the preparation and management of the study, not just in finally reviewing a draft put out by some other agency, probably the one that wanted to build it in the first place. The study was extremely broad. It dealt with every conceivable alternative to this multipurpose project and with single-purpose projects which, if added up, would do the same kind of job. It was an objective study because the study management team was drawn from all interested parties. A wide scope of alternatives was presented to the policy-makers involved. Choice of a particular set of alternatives would result in certain impacts; to maximize growth in an area, one might follow a particular set of alternatives; to balance economic growth and environmental protection, here is another set, and here are the consequences. By choosing a project now, it can shape the future of a region. It did not present one set of needs to be met regardless of the cost.

Can every study do this? Yes, if from the very beginning, there is a broad approach to evaluation of alternatives, evaluation of different means of accomplishing ends, and evaluation of the ends themselves. It is very difficult to take these on at the end, after a number of people have committed their careers to a particular project. If it is done again, we probably will need, at least for most of the federal agencies involved, some kind of special authority for it. It is very difficult for a federal agency to look at alternatives beyond what it is allowed by statute.

Each agency really has a broader authority under NEPA, and that is to consider the environment in each of the decisions it makes. Perhaps we need not put a special bill through Congress every time we want to do this kind of study. Perhaps we just have to re-read NEPA.

REFERENCES

1.   Feivreson, H. A., *et al.*, Ed. *Boundaries of Analysis: An Inquiry into the Tocks Island Dam Controversy* (Ballinger Publications, 1976).

CHAPTER 25

POWER PLANT SITING UNDER THE NEPA PROCESS:
SUCCESS OR FAILURE?

W. Samuel Tucker, Jr.

Manager of Environmental Affairs
Florida Power & Light Company
Miami, Florida

NEPA AND POWER PLANTS

Has the realization of the intent and spirit of the National Environmental Policy Act as applied to the power plant siting process been a success or a failure? I would not be so discouraging as to say that power plant siting under the NEPA process has "succeeded in failing," but I *would* have to say that it has "failed to succeed" for a number of reasons.

Reasons for NEPA Failure

First, like too many good ideas caught up in the maze of government bureaucracy, the NEPA process has become synonymous with paperwork. Secondly, through NEPA's "comprehensiveness" requirements, federal agencies have been forced to make decisions in areas in which they have had no historical involvement, no technical expertise and, at least until NEPA, no authority. Finally, what the process has created (by this I mean the reports, the agencies, the hearings, the legal actions, the delays, and so forth), can be, and actually has been, counterproductive to the whole purpose of NEPA.

Without quoting largely from the Act or subsequent court decisions, I would say I understand NEPA to express the desire of Congress to give due consideration to the total human environment in federal decision-making, with documentation of that consideration for major actions taken by federal agencies. I do not know, and it probably does not even matter, whether those who framed the Act foresaw the vast repercussions or "chain reaction of spheres of influence," which so totally involved the private sector in the NEPA process. The fact is, and ironically enough it may have taken NEPA to show it so dramatically, hardly any project of significance in the private sector does not involve federal money, federal approvals, or some type of federal action.

In our particular industry, nuclear power plants came under NEPA in a major way, as we shall see in the Calvert Cliffs decision against the old Atomic Energy Commission (now the Nuclear Regulatory Commission). Hydroelectric power plants were included under NEPA via the Federal Power Commission or Bureau of Reclamation, and now new oil or coal power plants will be added by way of the Environmental Protection Agency's responsibilities under the 1972 Water Act Amendments.

Duplication of Review

NEPA has also spawned many "mini-NEPA's," or state acts which closely resemble the federal act in language and/or intent. While it would seem that such state acts are only indirectly related to the topic at hand, this is not the case. Power plants in Florida, for example, fall under both state and federal (*i.e.,* NEPA) comprehensive environmental review processes. Typical "States Rights" attitudes combine with court-interpreted limitations on the delegation of federal agency NEPA responsibilities to create two almost simultaneous and identical, but completely separate,* review processes. Thus, in a sense, duplication of NEPA is also a result of NEPA. The only usual outcome of such duplication is an incredible strain on human and financial resources with, of course, the inevitable delays and paperwork.

The bottom line, considering both NEPA and all related laws and ordinances, is that the desire to give due consideration to the total human environment has also permeated the private sector, whether or not the private sector so desired.

Positive NEPA Effects

What has the NEPA process done for, or to, Florida Power & Light Company? It has lead to the creation of a large Department of Licensing and Environmental Planning. To some degree, a new dimension has been added to Company planning. I would not hesitate to say as an aside,

---

*Some states, such as California, have provisions for consolidation of state and federal environmental review.

however, that the Company did its share of sound environmental planning before the Act. It might have then been termed "most cost-effective" or "practical." The environmental way is not always the most expensive.

Further, it has opened to public scrutiny at virtually every step our plans and decisions concerning power plant siting, construction and operation. This has resulted in much more thought, time and effort being put into the front end or initial planning stages of a project. The risk, financially and time-wise, of making plans which, for some environmental reason, are later found unacceptable, is simply tremendous.

A few years ago, a power plant site we had chosen on the west coast of Florida was determined environmentally unacceptable. This site was selected before the NEPA process applied. We had to find another site after spending quite a significant amount of money. Had that decision been made under NEPA, we would have avoided the original location. The new siting procedures we now follow under NEPA can take years, with site selection studies involving expert outside consultants and costing hundreds of thousands of dollars. In several cases, we have actually written a book on some environmental site aspects. In addition, interested members of the public are consulted and involved in the earliest stages of a project.

While the effort required is intense, I believe that results of NEPA have generally been positive. The chances of ultimate public acceptance are greatly enhanced with our more open siting program. We have been able to develop extensive information at an early date, identify potential problem areas related to site environmental features, provide input to expedite later engineering design and construction efforts and, I believe, save money in the long run. These efforts can be the beginnings of general support for the project on the part of the scientific community, interested citizens and reasonable environmentalists. I use the word "reasonable" here because I have come across individuals calling themselves environmentalists whom you could not convince that the sky was blue once they discovered you work for the power company. On the other hand, we have had representatives of organizations like the Audubon Society, Wildlife Federation, and others speak in support of a power plant project.

Negative NEPA Effects

I will now consider the proverbial dark cloud that hides these silver linings. I mentioned paperwork. One can follow the bureaucratization of NEPA simply by observing the tremendous physical changes in the Environmental Reports for nuclear power plants over the past few years. An Environmental Report (ER) is the document that an electric utility prepares for the Nuclear Regulatory Commission (NRC) in response to

NEPA. The NRC uses the company's ER on a nuclear power plant project, together with hearings and its own analyses, to prepare the required Environmental Impact Statement (EIS).

The Proliferation of Paper

Our first Environmental Report, filed in 1970, contained 33 pages, with about 200 pages of reference material. Following the Calvert Cliffs decision in 1971, we submitted a supplemental report on the same project containing an additional 300 pages of information. At about the same time, we submitted an ER for another nuclear site comprised of one volume in a three-inch binder. Two years later, the ER for a second unit at this new site was double the size of the first. Now, seven short years after NEPA, we are in the final stages of preparing an ER for a new nuclear power plant project, which in its glorious splendor will contain eight three-inch-thick volumes of environmental impact analysis. I should point out that this report is preliminary; we are currently modifying it to meet the requirement of a newly revised regulatory guide (it will probably be an additional volume larger). Cost-wise, we have gone from about $100,000 per ER to over $6 million for this latest effort.

Looking at the latest report in the cold light of its intended use, instead of as a work of art, one can only be horrified. I doubt that there will be a single person who will really read, know, or care about what is in all eight volumes. As an intellectual or academic exercise, EIS's as a class probably have no equal. But as a decision-maker's tool or public document, one wonders.

I have mentioned that in the process of preparing such a document, the company must consider all aspects of a project and can identify and avoid potential problem areas. However I question, whether we all could not glean just as much essential information from the expenditure of $1 million, and save the remaining millions for a more tangible social benefit. I personally feel that the earlier reports were much more understandable and useful to those really concerned.

Because of their enormous scope, current ER's are reviewed piecemeal by highly specialized individuals. Unfortunately, it is difficult to find two experts who agree; also, reviewers tend to feel they are not demonstrating their expertise unless they can make a few critical comments. The result often is a "can't see the forest for the trees"-type situation, in which a few negative comments by highly specialized experts in a very specific subject area (which may even be academic in nature) can have an impact on the overall evaluation of the project, and on the total cost/benefit ratio, far beyond their relative importance.

THE NEPA PROCESS

I have been speaking of the Environmental Report or Environmental Impact Statement which is a part of the process, but not the actual process itself. The NEPA siting process can only be termed a lawyer's delight. It takes years to process. Public hearings often seem to be for the lawyers rather than for the public. The presence of such lawyers, while for good purpose, almost guarantees an adversary-type proceeding.

Furthermore, there are those who readily admit that they intend to use the NEPA process to delay or increase the cost of projects they deem unacceptable. The process, which was established to ensure rational environmental decision-making and minimization of environmental impact, apparently is not able to cope with this manner of attack. The only recourse is the court system, which in and of itself means further delays. Delays on our power plant projects are measured in terms of millions of dollars per month. We have been on the verge of cancelling an entire project, not because of any substantive issues or problems, but simply because of the delays being encountered. The end result, time and again, after months of procedural nightmares, is an outcome little or no different from what was obvious in the first place.

PROPOSED SOLUTIONS

What can be done to improve the NEPA process in the siting and construction of power plants? First, agencies must again do what they were originally intended to do. NEPA has really confused the picture in this area. The lead agency concept and the various memoranda of understanding, such as between EPA and NRC, between the Corps of Engineers and the NRC, represent a step in the right direction. There should be more of this delineation of responsibilities.

Second, issues included under NEPA comprehensiveness must be dealt with on the right level and in the right forum. Land use and many types of environmental issues are the concerns of local government or of state government and that is where they belong—not in federal hearings. All levels of government are going to review what they feel is important to them. Either we differentiate what ought to be covered where, or this unbelievable redundancy will continue, especially in states with siting acts and in localities with their own mini-NEPA reviews.

We need to find a way to redefine the scope of environmental documentation so that useful and understandable information returns to decision-makers and the interested public. There is a place for experts and lawyers, but few understand or trust their opinions anyway when "push comes to shove." I feel that guidelines for preparing NEPA statements should be re-evaluated to sort out the type and level of detail that is really essential.

To some extent, the type of action necessary to realize the amibitions of NEPA may require changes to NEPA itself. While the thought horrifies some, I feel no law is sacred. Actually, although much careful thought went into the Act, it *was* a first step in a new direction. After seven years, some hard scrutiny is justified. I do believe that allowances for delegation for some NEPA responsibilities should exist. In the area of power plant siting, some delegation to states with siting acts is entirely justifiable. I also feel that there ought to be a way for agencies to distribute some of their NEPA responsibilities to other agencies more qualified in specific areas.   In other words, I do not believe that the NRC, which is and has been responsible for nuclear health and safety, should be counting frogs and turtles.

In conclusion, I believe that NEPA was a truly landmark legislation and has been of benefit to the nation. But we need to cure the excesses and waste of the NEPA process before they cancel the benefits and progress achieved.

CHAPTER 26

THE ENVIRONMENTAL IMPACT STATEMENT AS A TOOL FOR TRANSPORTATION DECISION-MAKING

Martin Convisser

Director
Office of Environmental Affairs
U.S. Department of Transportation*
Washington, D.C.

This subject warrants discussion for two reasons: (1) its significance and (2) the Department of Transportation's extensive experience with the EIS process.

First, I believe the value of the EIS as a tool to improve decision-making has been largely overlooked in all the arguments about both substantive environmental issues and the procedural questions of so-called red tape, project delays and litigation.

Second, the Department of Transportation (DOT) is one of the major developers of EIS's in the government, and I believe we have probably done as much as any agency in integrating the EIS into the decision-making process.

I would first like to summarize some particular features of the EIS process in DOT; and then discuss specifically how I think the EIS has improved transportation decision-making.

THE EIS PROCESS IN DOT

Implementation of NEPA is established by a departmental order prepared by our Office of Environmental Affairs. This order sets forth the

---

*Prepared with the assistance of Ms. Leslie Baldwin, Office of Environmental Affairs.

overall guidance and procedures for implementation of NEPA in the DOT, and requires each of its operating administrations, such as the Federal Highway Administration, the Federal Aviation Administration, and the Urban Mass Transportation Administration, to develop more detailed implementation instructions to carry out the general instructions in our departmental order. These implementation instructions, in turn, have to be approved by the Assistant Secretary for Environment, Safety and Consumer Affairs, who is the top departmental environmental officer. Some key points of the DOT environmental order are

1. EIS's should be prepared early enough in the decision-making process to make a meaningful contribution to that process.
2. Where public hearings are required as part of the decision-making process, the draft EIS should be available before the public hearing and be a subject for comment at the public hearing.
3. Grant applicants, such as state highway departments, airport operators and mass transit agencies, can be called upon to undertake environmental analysis and prepare appropriate documents, in the form of a proposed draft EIS, for consideration by the Department. Whoever prepares the initial draft material, whether an applicant or an outside consultant, the Department of Transportation must provide guidelines for and be involved in its preparation, review it, revise it as appropriate, and take full responsibility for its scope and content.
4. The Assistant Secretary for Environment, Safety and Consumer Affairs must concur with all major environmental impact statements; the review by the staff of the Office of Environmental Affairs and the action of the Assistant Secretary relate not only to the adequacy of the EIS itself as a document, but also to the substantive content of the action which is proposed.

IMPROVED DECISION-MAKING

Let me now broaden the discussion of our process by focusing on the EIS as a tool for transportation decision-making. In doing this, I will highlight under five basic headings what I believe to be the major improvements in the decision-making process brought about by NEPA: (1) the EIS as a "full disclosure" document; (2) how it has improved consideration of alternatives; (3) how it has increased attention paid to secondary and long-term effects of immediate decisions; (4) how it has increased public input into governmental decision-making; and (5) how it has improved interagency coordination.

Full Disclosure

The EIS is, in a sense, a "full disclosure" document, as it requires detailed information to be set down in writing regarding a proposal: what it is and what its effects will be. This is a rather simple-minded concept; nevertheless, before NEPA, major decisions were often made without the proposal being documented in detail, and its impacts analyzed and set down in writing. Moreover, if such analysis were accomplished and written up, rarely was it put forth for public scrutiny.

The very fact that a document is going to be available for review, analysis and comment by other parties, including the public, the press, the Legislative Branch, and possibly the Judicial Branch, tends to have a remarkable effect on what is written in such a document. Wild, self-serving statements tend to be muted somewhat, data tends to be collected to support arguments, and unsubstantiated assertions decrease in number. Grudgingly perhaps, points of view other than those of the project proponent are noted, and other values considered. In short, public disclosure has an elevating effect on the quality of the discussion and on the analysis that underlies it, and a broadening effect on the values that go into the ultimate decision.

For example, during the early days of NEPA, I recall noting in many EIS's for highway projects, that those who wanted highways to speed them from home to business were in some way public-spirited and progress-oriented, while people who opposed highways in their backyards were somehow selfish and narrow-minded. This viewpoint in numerous EIS's and the reaction to it have tended to alter the perceptions of many highway project planners. Highway agencies now seem to understand better that those who oppose highways may sometimes reflect reasonable values and valid perceptions regarding transportation, urban development and the environment. In short, the EIS as a full disclosure document has tended over the years to raise the level of discourse with respect to highway projects.

Another, more concrete example relates to the considerable effort now going into the design and construction of noise abatement features in connection with new highway projects. Noise analysis must be a part of any major highway impact statement: it identifies noise-impacted areas, and disclosure of these impacts tends to create considerable pressure for dealing with them. In the absence of this kind of analysis and disclosure, the noise problem would probably be receiving considerably less attention than it does now.

A further broadening of this "full disclosure" approach to public decision-making was undertaken during the past two years by former

Secretary of Transportation, William Coleman. On several major decisions he set down in writing his own rather detailed analysis of the key issues and his reasons for arriving at his decision. These decision documents, while far more succinct than the typical EIS, were far more detailed than the customary announcement of a government decision. Several of these decision documents will be dealt with later in this chapter.

Consideration of Alternatives

A basic element of the EIS, of course, is the requirement that it propose alternatives to the proposed action. Again, this is a rather simple concept, but one that frequently was neglected. There is often a tendency to identify a problem and propose a solution, without presenting to the decision-maker any meaningful alternatives. In transportation impact statements, we require consideration of a wide range of alternatives, including, where relevant, other modes of transportation. By presenting all *feasible* alternatives to an action, the public benefits by knowing what options are available and, after the process is completed, what factors contributed to the final selection. Decision-makers benefit by having the factual information they need to identify the problems and advantages of each alternative, and to make informed decisions.

One recent example of extensive consideration of alternatives involves a decision by the Department to provide funds for a new airport to serve the expanding aviation needs of the St. Louis metropolitan area. An analysis was undertaken of the alternative of continuing in operation and improving the existing airport. Although the decision was finally made to approve the grant for the new airport, in my view the degree of genuine consideration of the alternative was an excellent example of how to make public policy decisions. That case is one in which former Secretary Coleman published a *Decision Document* summarizing his view of the major considerations that led to his decision, including his evaluation of the major alternatives.

Long-Term and Secondary Effects

The NEPA process has increased our attention to secondary and long-term effects in making major decisions. Section 102 (2) (C) of NEPA explicitly states that the EIS should include consideration of the relationship between short-term use of the environment and "the maintenance and enhancement of long-term productivity" of the environment. This requirement reflects the popular view that many of the environmental problems we face today are long-run consequences of actions and decisions made many years ago, made with consideration of their immediate effects only. The air quality problems of many major urban areas, for example, result from past failures to consider the cumulative and long-term impact of numerous individual decisions.

As the EIS requires us to address long-term, cumulative and secondary impacts, it can only result in better long-term decisions. It goes without saying that transportation facilities have the potential not only to significantly impact the environment directly, but also indirectly as a result of their effects on land use. Highways and airports can have drastic consequences on population trends and economic activity in an area, and these longer term, secondary effects must be considered in transportation decisions.

An example of this point is the decision made by the Department not to permit development of a major new air carrier airport just north of the Everglades National Park. Various public groups had expressed concerns about the impact of the proposed airport. Contrary to the popular understanding of the situation, it is unlikely that the airport itself would have had any serious detrimental effect on the Everglades. However, the secondary effects of the airport, that is, the development around the airport which would have occurred as a normal result of the development of such a major transportation hub, would have had serious effects on the quantity and quality of water flowing into the Everglades National Park. Thus, it was the long-term, secondary effects of the jetport which necessitated the Department's actions to forestall its completion.

Land use considerations have become a much more important part of transportation decision-making as a result of this greater attention to long-term effects. Our office, in reviewing transportation EIS's, pays particular attention to assuring that the important effects of transportation projects on future land use are adequately considered.

Public Input

Two other elements of the NEPA process have resulted in improved decision-making.

One extraordinarily important part of the NEPA process is the availability of a draft EIS to the public for comment, prior to completion of the government decision-making process. This opportunity for public input through NEPA has created a major change in government decision-making. While there have been opportunities for public hearings on many government actions in the past, I believe that having available to the public for comment, at a public hearing or in writing, a document which sets forth a proposal, alternatives and impacts, creates an opportunity for public involvement more extensive in nature, and of a higher quality than previously; and this public involvement has had its effects.

A good example of the effect of public involvement in the EIS process is I-66 in the Virginia suburbs of Washington. One may disagree with the decision made by former Secretary Coleman, which was recently reaffirmed by Secretary Adams, to approve the most recent proposal by Virginia for construction of that highway. However, I do not believe that one could legitimately dispute that the highway as approved is different and better in many fundamental ways from the highway originally proposed in the first Draft EIS.

What was originally proposed as an eight-lane facility, double-decked in some locations, has—as a result of public reaction and public input into the decision-making process—turned into a four-lane highway, below grade at some sensitive locations, with extensive land buffers. What was proposed as a general-purpose highway has turned into a parkway-type facility, excluding heavy trucks, and limited to buses and carpools in the peak hours in the peak direction. Noise will be reduced by the extensive use of noise barriers. Public parkland will actually be increased by the conversion of excess rights-of-way into public park uses.

In short, the public brought about enormous changes in the final decision. While many did not gain what they wanted completely, which was no project at all, they did gain a substantial improvement and certainly a far better decision than would have occurred in the absence of public input.

I might add that I-66 provides an example of a new dimension in public input, in the sense that former Secretary Coleman personally conducted two public hearings on the subject.

Interagency Coordination

The final point I would like to deal with relates to how the NEPA process has improved interagency coordination leading to decisions.

Clearly, the opportunity which federal, state and local agencies have to comment on draft EIS's helps them to provide input into decisions that may affect their interests. Less obviously, the fact that a government agency will be commenting on a transportation EIS tends to lead to early coordination, to avoid adverse comments on the public record. Thus, the NEPA process has had a subtle influence in requiring agencies to cooperate on matters of common interest. We find, for example, that field staffs of the Department of Transportation and the Environmental Protection Agency deal with each other more extensively than they did some years ago, improving communication and coordination. Moreover, we utilize the NEPA process to meet the relevant statutory requirements of other agencies. For example, we address in our EIS's, where relevant, Interior's requirements with respect to rare and endangered species, Commerce's requirements with respect to the coastal zone, the concerns of the Advisory Council on Historic Preservation with respect to historic sites, EPA's requirements with respect to water quality and air quality, and numerous other matters of interest to other agencies.

A NEPA-BROADENED PERSPECTIVE

By its very nature, the NEPA process introduces a much broader perspective into our decisions than would otherwise be possible. It enables us to look simultaneously at ways to further our transportation goals, and at the total environmental effect of our decisions. We know that this is more important today than ever before for substantive reasons and, not incidentally, when citizens demand greater control over government decisions affecting their lives, and more frequently challenge our decisions in the courts. Consequently, we are making a major effort to ensure that our programs and policies are consistent with environmental objectives, and that specific projects are studied and modified before problems erupt. The NEPA process has enabled us to do this better and to arrive at better decisions by requiring us to document and disclose a detailed analysis of our proposals and their impacts, to explicitly consider a wide range of alternatives, to consider long-term and secondary impacts, and to increase public input and interagency coordination as part of government decision-making.

Thus, NEPA has not only had a major effect on how we treat the environment, but it has had a major beneficial effect on how the government makes decisions.

APPENDIX
TESTIMONY BEFORE THE COUNCIL
ON ENVIRONMENTAL QUALITY

In May 1977, President Jimmy Carter issued an order directing the Council on Environmental Quality to streamline the NEPA process. In June 1977, CEQ held three days of hearings to receive public suggestions on how to improve the process. Mr. Charles Warren, Chairman of CEQ, selected NAEP as the appropriate professional society to provide testimony and invited Charles Zirzow, the Association's President, to do so. Since the testimony, as developed and presented, was in great part based on the findings of the NAEP Seminar, and summarizes many of the problem/solution recommendations, the testimony has been incorporated into this book.

TESTIMONY OF CHARLES F. ZIRZOW, EP, PE, PRESIDENT, NATIONAL ASSOCIATION OF ENVIRONMENTAL PROFESSIONALS BEFORE THE COUNCIL ON ENVIRONMENTAL QUALITY IN WASHINGTON, D.C.–10:00 A.M. TO 12:00 NOON, JUNE 8, 1977

Mr. Chairman, Members of the Council: on behalf of the National Association of Environmental Professionals, I thank you for inviting me here today to present our views on possible actions to improve the NEPA process. Indeed, Mr. Chairman, our Association was founded to provide a forum for addressing the exact kinds of problems inherent in your fourteen questions. Briefly, by way of background, we are a young organization, incorporated in July 1975 as a professional society for those engaged in interdisciplinary environmental planning, management or assessment; or research or education in support thereof. Our "Code of Ethical Practice" unifies our multifaceted membership which works toward improving communications and advancing the state-of-the-art of the environmental planning process. More than two-thirds of our members are senior-level professionals with many years experience in the environmental field and are fairly evenly divided between government, industry and academia.

The theme of our last annual seminar held in Washington, D.C. in February of this year dealt with probing questions that have surfaced in the environmental professional community after six years of experience with the National Environmental Policy Act of 1969. Our five technical sessions addressed the following questions:

- How much information is sufficient to assess an environmental impact adequately and to make a decision? Do environmental documents "overkill?"
- Are federal and state requirements complementary or competing? To what extent can both be met by a single environmental study?
- What is the public's role and responsibility in the environmental assessment process? What are the ethical problems for the public and for the assessment preparer?
- How can agency and public review be better organized to provide early, continuing and pertinent comment?
- How successfully does the current assessment process improve the quality of environmental decision-making?

Margot Hornblower of the *Washington Post* covered the Seminar and her article appeared on the front page of the Sunday issue, February 13, under the headline: "The Cumbersome Ways of Bureaucracy/Impact Data: What's Wrong?" In the article, the author concluded: "The impact statement originally forced the nation to pay more attention to the environment, but today it has lost its force," that "environmentalists have found that the National Environmental Policy Act provision has largely outworn its usefulness," and "not that the result (of the EIS) helps the environment much." These are her conclusions, not ours. However, the basic information she presented was fairly accurate, for our seminar clearly focused, as did the *Post* article, on the many problems that have accompanied the past six years development of the Environmental Impact Statement Process. The process is often inefficient; much of the content is irrelevant to the decision at hand; often the focus is stolen away from the real issues underlying a controversy; there could be significant economies from one "generic" or "areawide" EIS (*e.g.*, for all power plant development in the state of Washington) rather than many "project" EIS's; there is often little follow-up monitoring after a project is approved.

The author fairly described the bureaucratic quagmire created by NEPA; however, she is wrong in her conclusions that the impact statement process has "lost its force," outworn its usefulness" or fails to "help the environment much." The fact is that significant environmental benefits have been and continue to be derived from the EIS process.

Take the first major public works project to which the NEPA process applied. This was a site to replace the controversial "Everglades Jetport" project in the Big Cypress Swamp in Florida. As a result of the environmental impact study, a new and environmentally compatible site was selected. Though the study cost of approximately a million and a half appears high, the inevitable loss of estuarine and Gulf of Mexico fisheries production that would have been brought about by a fully developed airport in the Big Cypress did not occur. More important though than examples of specific projects that have received public attention because of controversy, are those that have been planned and designed from the beginning to incorporate environmental consideration, thus avoiding the pitfalls of the NEPA process. Project sponsors are learning more and more that it is plain smart business to avoid rather than try to correct environmental mistakes. Perhaps when all have learned to do this, the EIS process will have outlived its usefulness. . . but not before.

Now to address the purpose of these hearings—"how to reform the implementation of the National Environmental Policy Act."

Sometimes complex problems such as streamlining the EIS process, are better handled by finding solutions for smaller component problems, each of which contributes to the overall solution. We offer the following series of such problems along with comment and or possible solutions.

PROBLEM: EIS's covering controversial projects contain excessive detail on insignificant points in order to avoid court challenge on the grounds of procedural noncompliance with Section 102 (2) (C).

POSSIBLE SOLUTION: Over the past six years the courts have provided, through their decisions, the definition of "detailed statement" required by Section 102 (2) (C) since the law did not define it. Consequently, consideration should be given to changing the law to include a definition which would limit the detailed statement to significant and substantive issues.

PROBLEM: Many actions are well into the planning stage before entering the EIS process and the actions are therefore subject to delay by the process itself. This is often a symptom of the disease that regards the EIS process as another hurdle, after an alternative has been selected.

POSSIBLE SOLUTION: Executive order could make it mandatory that the final document demonstrate the simultaneous consideration of environmental, economic and engineering factors in conceptual definition of alternatives.

PROBLEM: Many who prepare and review EIS's are highly qualified professionals, but with training and experience in only a single discipline. There is a natural tendency to assess or comment in detail on matters involving their discipline without being able to put them in perspective to the interdisciplinary whole. At best, many data are added to the statement that is not usable to the decision-maker in addressing the substantive issues. At worst, project sponsors are asked to carry mitigation actions well beyond reasonable and prudent limits.

POSSIBLE SOLUTION: Many of the agencies are attempting to solve this problem through training programs and improved guidance. However, there are currently no uniform standards for an interdisciplinary, trained professional who can relate the significant aspects of all disciplines to the substantive issues of a major action. We suggest that perhaps CEQ could sponsor or coordinate a study to determine training and performance requirements for such positions. NAEP is in the process of providing inputs to EPA, which is currently working with the Department of Labor to update the Dictionary of Occupational Titles to include such environmental positions. Our Association is also in the process of establishing an education committee to look into what university curricular changes would better prepare a student in a given discipline for work in the environmental field upon graduation. I feel certain that CEQ would have the cooperation of all who are involved in such an endeavor.

PROBLEM: There is much duplication of effort in developing background and baseline data for individual EIS's.

POSSIBLE SOLUTION: Consideration should be given to establishing a central data bank for such information. Each EIS preparer would have access and would be obligated to enter all new data developed during the EIS into the data bank.

PROBLEM: Reviewing federal agencies frequently comment on the inadequacies of an EIS and request additional information when they themselves have the expertise and are the best source for the answers.

POSSIBLE SOLUTION: Consideration should be given to requiring an agency to provide its expertise and data in the form of proposed text. We do not feel, in general, that the EIS process should be forced to advance the state of knowledge.

PROBLEM: My interpretation of NEPA is that it requires a systematic interdisciplinary approach to presenting the facts of alternative actions, including recommendations for mitigating adverse effects and for enhancing the environment, so that the decision-maker is fully aware of the environmental consequences before the final decision is made. In simpler terms, the requirement is to tell it all and tell it the way it is. This demands total impartiality; however, there are some who still use the process to justify a given action or project.

POSSIBLE SOLUTION: Our Association has a code of ethical practice to which each member is required to subscribe. It does require impartiality and objectivity in the preparation of EIS's. Though we are exploring certification and/or registration programs for the environmental professional and hope ultimately to provide the standards for the profession, this does not appear possible in the near future. In the interim, however, an Executive Order could require the preparer of an EIS to legally certify that the document was prepared impartially and objectively, and require that contributors be listed, by discipline as applicable.

Mr. Chairman, I would like to conclude my formal presentation by pledging the support of the National Association of Environmental Professionals to assist the Council in whatever way it can to improve the NEPA process. I would be pleased to answer any questions the Council might have.

BIOGRAPHICAL INFORMATION FOR PARTICIPANTS IN SECOND NAEP SEMINAR

Allen, Dr. Ruth Hamilton: Senior Environmental Planner with the Department of Water Resources of the Metropolitan Washington Council of Governments; past Assistant Director of the Institute of Ecology Environmental Impact Assessment Project. Educational background: biology, anthropology, forest science, Yale, Ph.D. in Environmental Studies. Author of Chapter 18, member NAEP.

Ames, George F.: Head of the Environmental Matters Section of the Washington Suburban Sanitary Commission, which provides water and wastewater services to Montgomery and Prince George's Counties, Maryland. Educational background: forestry, Yale, M.F. in natural resources management. Author of Chapter 3, member NAEP.

Arnold, Norman W.: Chief of the Environmental Planning Branch, Office of Airport Programs, Federal Aviation Administration. Participated in writing EISs for several FAA projects. Listed in Who's Who in the East. Educational background: State University of New York, Albany, B.A. in Physics, Math. NAEP Seminar General Chairperson, member NAEP Board of Directors.

Barske, Dr. Phillip: Wildlife Management Institute Field Representative for Northeastern United States and Canadian Maritime Provinces; private consultant; member Connecticut State Commission on Environmental Protection and Economic Development. Educational background: forestry, conservation and wildlife, Union of Graduate Colleges, Antioch, Yellow Springs, Ohio, Ph.D. in Applied Ecology. Author of Chapter 16.

Bendix, Dr. Selina: Environmental Review Officer, City and County of San Francisco; head of Office of Environmental Review in Department of City Planning which handles review under state law and delegated NEPA review. Educational background: chemistry; University of California at

Berkeley, Ph.D. in Zoology. Co-editor of this volume, author of Chapter 12, member NAEP Board of Directors.

Benson, Carol Ford: Private consultant specializing in socio-ecology, environmental and business management, analysis of environmental aspects of transportation systems and system safety. Founder of the Association of Environmental Professionals and the National Association of Environmental Professionals. Educational background: sociology, University of California at Berkeley, B.A. in Sociology. Chairperson, Session III, author of Chapter 13, member NAEP Board of Directors, past Executive Secretary NAEP.

Blomquist, Dr. Arnold W.: President, National Biocentric, Inc., Minneapolis, Minnesota, specializing in environmental analyses and preparation of environmental impact analyses, market analyses and industrial development planning. Educational background: University of Minnesota, Ph.D. in Biological Science. Co-author of Chapter 9, Co-Chairperson of Session II, president of Minnesota Association of Environmental Professionals; member NAEP Board of Directors.

Bogdan, Edward: Senior Environmental Planner with Raymond, Parish & Pine, Inc., Tarrytown, New York, involved in environmental document preparation and in studies of land use management, solid waste recovery and flood control. Educational background: chemical engineering, chemistry, University of California at Berkeley, M.S. in sanitary engineering. Author of Chapter 14.

Burger, James M., Esq.: Attorney, Shaw, Pittman, Potts and Trowbridge, specializing in economic and environmental support of transatlantic route proceedings. Educational background: Attorney and political science; New York University, J.D. Author of Chapter 17.

Canny, Joseph: Chief, Analysis Division, Office of Environmental Affairs, United States Department of Transportation. Presented Chapter 26 for Martin Convisser.

Convisser, Martin: Director, Office of Environmental Affairs, U. S. Department of Transportation. Involved in policy and program development, review and coordination in broad fields of urban transportation and the environmental impacts of transportation. Educational background: Government and public administration, Cornell University, B.A. in government.

Cronin, Ned J.: Co-Director of the Environmental and Public Works Study of the Commission on Federal Paperwork, Washington, D.C.; past Environmental Protection Agency NEPA compliance manager for water pollution source permit program. Educational background: Syracuse University, Masters of Public Administration. Co-Chairperson of Session V, co-author of Chapter 23.

De Santo, Dr. Robert S.: Chief Ecologist, DeLeuw-Cather, New Haven, Connecticut, ecological evaluation, planning and research. Educational background: physiology, cytogenetics, Columbia, Ph.D. in environmental physiology. Author of Chapter 4.

Evans, Ernest P.: Assistant Director for Advocacy of the Commission on Federal Paperwork; past Chief Investigator for the United States Senate, Select Committee on Small Business. Educational background: University of Maryland, B.S. in public administration and political science. Chairperson of Session I.

Franz, Gerald Jay: Partner in McKeown & Franz, a multidisciplinary environmental planning and policy firm. Formerly Director of Environmental Planning, Department of City Planning, New York City. Educational background: biology, ecology and environmental management, Hunter College of the City University of New York, M.S. in Environmental Management. Author of Chapter 2, member of NAEP.

Gallop, Earl G., Esq.: Worked on Development of Regional Impact and Area of Critical State Concern Programs for Florida Division of State Planning, Bureau of Land and Water Management; member Florida bar. Educational background: Florida State University law degree. Co-author of Chapter 7.

Graham, Herbert R.: Task Manager, TRW Energy Systems, specializing in environmental evaluation of advanced power plants, air, transit, rail and highway transportation modes. Educational background: California Institute of Technology, M.S. in aeronautics. NAEP Seminar Program Chairperson, co-editor of this volume, member NAEP Board of Directors.

Grear, Michael J.: Environmental Analyst, Washington Suburban Sanitary Commission. Presented Chapter 3 for George S. Ames.

Hanmer, Rebecca: Assistant Director, Resource Development Liaison, United States Environmental Protection Agency Office of Federal

Activities; coordinates liaison with federal land and resource development agencies. Educational background: American University, Washington, D.C., M.A. in political science. Co-chairperson of Session IV.

Harrison, Penny L.: President, Harrison Associates specializing in association management, conferences, meetings, fund raising. Accredited member of Public Relations Society of America. Educational background: Santa Monica College, B.A. in Journalism. Executive Director, NAEP, NAEP Seminar General Arrangements.

Heiser, David W.: Responsible for all environmental analysis and environmental permits for Washington State Parks and Recreation Commission, which manages some 82,000 acres of land with 169 separate park sites, Olympia, Wahington; past fisheries manager. Educational background: Masters Degree in Fisheries Management. Author of Chapter 11.

Henningson, John C.: Senior environmental analyst with Malcolm Pirnie, Inc., Consulting Environmental Engineers; responsible for coordination of firm's environmental services. Educational background: biology, Rensselaer Polytechnic Institute, M.S. in environmental engineering. Author of Chapter 15, member NAEP.

Herner, Saul: Senior resident consultant and President of Herner and Company specializing in environmental information, information systems, storage and retrieval, youth surveys, documentation research and library planning and design. Educational background: University of Wisconsin, B.S. in biochemistry and library science.

Kanerva, Roger A.: Deputy Director for Operations, Maryland Water Resources Administration, Annapolis, Maryland; A-95 Project Review Officer for the Agency; past Chief of the Agency's Enforcement and Permits Divisions. Educational background: University of Arizona, M.S. in watershed management. Author of Chapter 20.

Kauders, Andrew E.: Director, Environmental Affairs, General Services Administration, responsible for antipollution, environmental improvement and historic preservation programs. Educational background: Boston University, B.S. in Public Relations. NAEP Seminar Local Arrangements, member NAEP Board of Directors.

Milledge, Allan: Senior partner, law firm of Milledge & Hermlee, Miami, Florida; specializing in land use law and federal litigation; member Florida bar, admitted to practice in the United States Supreme Court; past chairperson Environmental Land Management Study Committee of Florida. Educational background: Harvard law degree. Co-author of Chapter 7, member NAEP Board of Directors.

Mylroie, Gerald R.: Co-Director of the Environmental and Public Works study at the Commission on Federal Paperwork, Washington, D.C.; past Director of Professional Development at the American Institute of Planners. Educational background: landscape architecture, University of Southern California, Master of Planning. Co-chairperson of Session V, co-author of Chapter 23.

O'Brien, Frank: Director of Regulatory Services, Fluor Pioneer, specializing in sound energy system planning, policy and execution. Educational background: St. Peter's College, B.S. in Physics. Member NAEP Board of Directors.

O'Neill, Thomas M.: President of the Center for Analysis of Public Issues, Princeton, New Jersey, a public interest research group which engages in policy research on investigative journalism; editor of Center's monthly magazine; member, New Jersey Water Policy and Supply Council. Educational background: Wesleyan University, Middletown, Connecticut, bachelor's degree in political science. Author of Chapter 24.

Pennington, W. Herbert: Director, Office of NEPA Coordination, United States Energy Research and Development Administration, Washington, D.C.; member, New England River Basin Commission. Listed in Who's Who in America. Educational background: Chemistry and nuclear energy, Franklin & Marshall College, B.S. in chemistry. Past President NAEP, member NAEP Board of Directors.

Printz, Albert C., Jr.: Environmental Coordinator, Agency for International Development; chairperson of the AID Committee on Environment and Development; involved in analysis of environmental impacts of AID programs and assistance to developing countries in management of their environmental problems. Educational background: University of Florida, M.S. in sanitary engineering. Author of Chapter 5.

Robertson, John (Jock) L.: Vice President for Planning, National Biocentric, Inc.; past Assistant Director for Environmental Planning, Minnesota State Planning Agency. Educational background: architecture, University of Washington, M.A. in Urban Planning. Author of Chapter 9; member Board of Directors, Minnesota Association of Environmental Professionals.

Schiff, Dr. Stefan O.: Chairperson, Graduate Genetics Program and Department of Biological Sciences, George Washington University, Washington, D.C.; research on effects of microwave radiation on mammalian sensory structures. Educational background: University of Tennessee Ph.D. in radiation biology. Presented paper not included in this book.

Sherman, Laurence: Director, IBI Group; past partner in charge of Urban Design and Facilities Development, Peat, Marwick and Partners. Educational background: architectural engineering, city planning, University of Pennsylvania, Master of Architecture; Registered Architect, Pennsylvania. Author of Chapter 21.

Sizer, Joseph E.: Director of Environmental Planning, Minnesota State Planning Agency; responsible for technical assistance review and coordination of natural resource planning. Educational background: University of Minnesota, M.S. in agriculture and agricultural economics. Co-author of Chapter 9.

Sparks, Lynne: Environmental Specialist, Environmental Planning Branch, Office of Airport Programs, Federal Aviation Administration specializing in ecology and endangered species, archeologic and historic sites, public recreation areas. Educational background: political science, international relations, environmental studies, Georgetown University, M.A. in International Relations. Member NAEP, NAEP Seminar Co-chairperson.

Thompson, James K.: Private consultant on environment- and energy-related matters, specializing in analysis of methods for energy conservation without adverse effect on the quality of life; past Chief of Environmental Planning for the National Airport Development Air Program supervised by the Federal Aviation Administration. Educational background: meteorology, mathematics, music, aeronautics, physics and management. Author of Chapter 1, member NAEP.

Thurber, Robert P.: Senior Environmental Analyst with the United States Department of Transportation's Office of Environmental Affairs; oversight of DOT's NEPA procedures; DOT liaison with the American Institute of Planners' Environmental Planning Department. Educational background: University of California at Berkeley, Master of City Planning. Co-chairperson of Session IV; member NAEP.

Tipton, Lindsay M.: Environmental Task Manager, TRW Energy Systems, specializing in environmental planning, energy assessment, environmental impact statement requirements and analysis. Educational background: University of New Mexico, B.S. in Biochemistry. NAEP Seminar Program Co-chairperson.

Tucker, W. Samuel, Jr.: Manager of Environmental Affairs for Florida Power and Light Company, where his responsibilities include site selection, environmental impact assessment, construction and operation permits; past Florida Secretary of Administration. Educational background: graduate of Tulane University. Author of Chapter 25.

Watkins, Susan C.: National Program Manager for NEPA compliance in nonregulatory activities, U.S. Environmental Protection Agency. Served as liaison with Council on Environmental Quality and other federal agencies. Listed in World Who's Who of Women. Educational background: journalism and communications, University of North Carolina, M.A. in Communications. Member NAEP, NAEP Seminar Publicity Chairman.

Wilburn, Susan T.: Acting Administrator, Council on the Environment, Commonwealth of Virginia. Formerly, Environmental Impact Statement Coordinator. Educational background: psychology, urban affairs and management, Mary Baldwin College, B.A. in psychology. Author of Chapter 10.

Winder, John S., Jr., Esq.: Member, Committee on Citizen Participation in Transportation Planning of the Transportation Research Board, National Academy of Sciences, Vice-Chairperson Environmental Quality Committee, American Bar Association; member District of Columbia Bar. Educational background: political science, George Washington University, J.D. Co-author of Chapter 18; member NAEP.

Wood, William M.: Social Scientist with the Federal Highway Administrator's Office of Environmental Policy; responsible for review, analysis and evaluation of state highway agencies' public involvement programs and for EIS review. Educational background: University of Virginia, bachelor's degree in sociology and anthropology. Author of Chapter 20.

Yonker, Terry L.: Environmental Specialist, Division of State-Federal Program Coordination, Michigan Department of Management and Budget; Executive Secretary, Michigan Environmental Review Board; Chairperson, Interdepartmental Environmental Review Committee. Educational background: University of Wisconsin, Madison, B.S. in sociology and meteorology.   Author of Chapter 8; member NAEP.

Zigman, Paul: President of Environmental Science Associates, involved in basic and applied-research programs and environmental document preparation.   Educational background: University of California at Los Angeles, B.S. in chemistry.   Co-chairperson, Session II, author of Chapter 6, vice-president of NAEP, president of California Association of Environmental Professionals.

Zirzow, Charles F.:   Director, Department of Environmental Quality and Conservation, Howard, Needles, Tammen and Bergendoff.   Involved in over 100 environmental impact statements.   Educational background: biology and civil engineering, University of Illinois, B.S. in Civil Engineering.

AUTHOR INDEX